# CHARACTER MATTERS

ALSO BY JEAN BECKER

*The Man I Knew*

# CHARACTER MATTERS

## AND OTHER LIFE LESSONS FROM GEORGE H. W. BUSH

## JEAN BECKER

TWELVE

*New York   Boston*

Twelve
Hachette Book Group
1290 Avenue of the Americas, New York, NY 10104
twelvebooks.com
twitter.com/twelvebooks

First Edition: April 2024

Twelve is an imprint of Grand Central Publishing. The Twelve name and logo are trademarks of Hachette Book Group, Inc.

The publisher is not responsible for websites (or their content) that are not owned by the publisher.

Twelve books may be purchased in bulk for business, educational, or promotional use. For information, please contact your local bookseller or the Hachette Book Group Special Markets Department at special.markets@hbgusa.com.

Library of Congress Cataloging-in-Publication Data
Names: Becker, Jean, approximately 1956- author. | Baker, James Addison, 1930- writer of foreword. | Quayle, Dan, 1947- writer of epilogue.
Title: Character matters : and other life lessons from George Herbert Walker Bush / Jean Becker.
Other titles: Life lessons from George Herbert Walker Bush
Description: First edition. | New York : Twelve, 2024.
Identifiers: LCCN 2023036567 | ISBN 9781538758571 (hardcover) | ISBN 9781538758595 (ebook)
Subjects: LCSH: Bush, George, 1924-2018—Anecdotes. | Character. | Leadership—United States. | United States—Politics and government—1989—Anecdotes. | Bush, George, 1924-2018—Friends and associates. | Presidents—United States—Biography. | Conduct of life.
Classification: LCC E882.2 .B437 2024 |
DDC 973.928092 [B]—dc23/eng/20230810
LC record available at https://lccn.loc.gov/2023036567

ISBNs: 9781538758571 (hardcover), 9781538758595 (ebook)

Printed in the United States of America

LSC-C

Printing 1, 2024

*To George Herbert Walker Bush, who taught me almost every single day that character really does matter.*

# CONTENTS

# GEORGE H. W. BUSH
## TIME LINE

**June 12, 1924:** Born in Milton, Massachusetts, to Prescott and Dorothy Walker Bush; family moved to Greenwich, Connecticut, six months later.

**June 1942:** Graduates from Phillips Academy, Andover, Massachusetts.

**June 12, 1942:** Enlists in the United States Navy on eighteenth birthday.

**June 9, 1943:** Receives gold wings, becoming youngest naval aviator.

**September 2, 1944:** Shot down near the island of Chichijima while flying combat missions off the aircraft carrier USS *San Jacinto*; after parachuting out of the plane, rescued a few hours later by the submarine USS *Finback*.

**January 6, 1945:** Marries Barbara Pierce in Rye, New York.

**September 18, 1945:** Released from active duty.

**July 6, 1946:** Son George Walker Bush born in New Haven, Connecticut.

**June 1948:** Graduates Phi Beta Kappa from Yale University with bachelor's degree in economics.

**June 1948:**      Moves to Odessa, Texas, to take job as equipment clerk for Dresser Industries/ IDECO.

**1948–1951:**      As part of training program, holds variety of jobs for IDECO, including oilfield supply salesman and factory worker, moving from Odessa to California in 1949, then back to Midland, Texas, in 1950.

**December 20, 1949:**      Daughter Pauline Robinson Bush (Robin) born in Compton, California.

**1951–1953:**      Cofounder, with John Overbey, of Bush-Overbey Oil Development Corporation, in Midland.

**February 11, 1953:**      Son John Ellis Bush (Jeb) born in Midland.

**October 12, 1953:**      Robin dies of leukemia.

**1953–1959:**      Cofounder, with Hugh and Bill Liedtke, of Zapata Petroleum in Midland.

**January 22, 1955:**      Son Neil Mallon Bush born in Midland.

**October 22, 1956:**      Son Marvin Pierce Bush born in Midland.

**August 1959:**      Moves to Houston, Texas, to run spin-off company, Zapata Offshore, a pioneering offshore drilling contractor.

**August 18, 1959:**      Daughter Dorothy Walker Bush (Doro) born in Houston.

**February 1963:**      Elected chairman of Harris County Republican Party.

**November 3, 1964:**      Loses Texas Senate race to Democratic incumbent Ralph Yarborough.

**November 5, 1966:**    Elected congressman from Texas Seventh District; serves on House Ways and Means Committee.

**November 3, 1970:**    Loses Texas Senate race to Lloyd Bentsen.

**February 1971:**    Sworn in as US ambassador to the United Nations.

**January 1973:**    Becomes chairman of the Republican National Committee.

**October 1974:**    Moves to Beijing as chief of the US Liaison Office in the People's Republic of China.

**January 1976:**    Sworn in as director of Central Intelligence Agency.

**January 1977:**    Returns to private life in Houston.

**May 1, 1979:**    Announces candidacy for President of the United States.

**July 16, 1980:**    Becomes the running mate of former California governor Ronald Reagan.

**November 4, 1980:**    Elected Vice President of the United States, Reagan-Bush defeating Carter-Mondale.

**March 30, 1981:**    Assassination attempt made on President Reagan, who was seriously wounded.

**November 6, 1984:**    Reelected Vice President of the United States, Reagan-Bush defeating Mondale-Ferraro.

**March 1985:**    Meets Mikhail Gorbachev for the first time while attending funeral of Gorbachev's predecessor, Konstantin Chernenko.

| | |
|---|---|
| **November 8, 1988:** | Elected forty-first President of the United States, Bush-Quayle defeating Dukakis-Bentsen. |
| **May 28, 1989:** | Attends NATO Summit in Brussels. |
| **July 9, 1989:** | Visits Poland and Hungary. |
| **November 9, 1989:** | Berlin Wall falls. |
| **December 2, 1989:** | Meets with Gorbachev off Malta. |
| **December 20, 1989:** | Launches military operation in Panama to restore democracy and to capture renegade dictator and international drug trafficker Manuel Noriega. |
| **May 31, 1990:** | Bush-Gorbachev first official summit meeting in Washington. |
| **July 26, 1990:** | Signs Americans with Disabilities Act. |
| **August 2, 1990:** | Iraq invades Kuwait. |
| **August 5, 1990:** | Announces, "This will not stand, this aggression against Kuwait." |
| **September 30, 1990:** | Announces a bipartisan federal budget agreement that breaks a budget deadlock and is a first move toward reducing the federal deficit. |
| **October 3, 1990:** | West and East Germany are united. |
| **November 15, 1990:** | Signs the Clean Air Act. |
| **November 22, 1990:** | Spends Thanksgiving Day with the troops in Saudi Arabia. |
| **January 16, 1991:** | Orders the beginning of Operation Desert Storm to drive Iraqi forces out of Kuwait. |
| **February 27, 1991:** | Suspends combat operations in the Persian Gulf after Kuwait is liberated. |

**December 25, 1991:** Gorbachev resigns and the Soviet Union dissolves.

**November 3, 1992:** Loses reelection bid for a second term, Clinton-Gore defeating Bush-Quayle.

**January 20, 1993:** Returns to private life in Houston.

**November 8, 1994:** Son George W. Bush elected governor of Texas.

**March 25, 1997:** Fulfills a lifelong dream by making a second parachute jump.

**November 6, 1997:** Dedication of the George Bush Presidential Library at Texas A&M University.

**November 3, 1998:** Son Jeb Bush elected governor of Florida; George W. Bush elected to second term as governor of Texas.

**May 14, 1999:** Commencement ceremony for first master's degree graduates from the Bush School of Government and Public Service at Texas A&M.

**January 20, 2001:** George W. Bush sworn in as the forty-third President of the United States.

**September 11, 2001:** The worst terrorist attack in the history of the United States.

**June 2002:** For the first time since being shot down on September 2, 1944, returns to Chichijima.

**June 12, 2004:** Celebrates eightieth birthday by jumping out of another perfectly good airplane. Birthday party raises $56 million for MD Anderson Cancer Center, the George Bush Presidential Library Foundation, and Points of Light.

**December 26, 2004:** A tsunami in the Indian Ocean devastates South Asia. At the request of President George W. Bush, teams up with Bill Clinton to raise money in the private sector for disaster relief.

**January 20, 2005:** George W. Bush sworn in for a second term.

**August 29, 2005:** Katrina comes ashore near New Orleans as a category 3 hurricane, and becomes the costliest natural disaster in American history. Teams up again with President Clinton to form the Bush-Clinton Katrina Fund, raising more than $135 million.

**January 10, 2009:** The USS *George H. W. Bush* aircraft carrier commissioned in Norfolk, Virginia.

**June 12, 2009:** Another parachute jump with the Army's Golden Knights parachute team, to celebrate eighty-fifth birthday.

**February 15, 2011:** Receives Medal of Freedom from President Obama in a White House ceremony.

**March 21, 2011:** Honored by Points of Light at a star-studded event at the Kennedy Center—including Presidents Carter, Clinton, and George W. Bush—for inspiring the volunteer movement.

**May 4, 2014:** Receives the John F. Kennedy Profile in Courage Award from the Kennedy Library Foundation, which cited his courage in negotiating and signing the 1990 budget deal.

**April 17, 2018:**    Barbara Bush dies at home, with her husband of seventy-three years holding her hand.

**November 30, 2018:**    President Bush dies at home, surrounded by friends and family.

# AUTHOR'S NOTE

While I was having lunch with my editor in October of 2022, he surprised me by asking me to write another book where George Herbert Walker Bush was the star.

"The world is not done with him," were Sean Desmond's exact words.

I confess I looked at him across the table and said, "You do know he died at the end of the last book?" (That would be *The Man I Knew*, which came out in 2021.)

But after we talked it through, I realized what a brilliant idea it was.

Let's be honest: Our beloved country is not in a good place. Our partisan divide gets worse almost every day. We get angry at even the hint of a slight. Too many of us have forgotten the art of agreeing to disagree—and then maybe go get a beer and talk about sports or the weather.

Instead, we use social media or other avenues to attack and defame and humiliate those who don't see the world as we do.

There are days when I think Merriam-Webster should remove the word "compromise" from its dictionary. It's not used much anymore.

It wasn't always this way.

It doesn't have to be this way now.

I know someone who can help.

Our forty-first President left us a blueprint on how to get back to a more civil society that respects the rule of law; that respects and even likes one another; that looks to the future with optimism and hope.

I am not trying to claim that the forty-first President is the only leader, past or present, to whom we can turn now for inspiration and some valuable life lessons. But he is the man I knew. He is the man who taught me so many things: how to think through an issue but then be decisive; how to lead with integrity; how to give back; how to make a difference.

How to be a better person.

Whether you agreed with his politics or not, everyone who knew him remembers the same thing: He was one of the kindest, most decent, and most honorable men they knew. And if you disagree with that, then my guess is you never met him.

So, you might ask, if he was so kind and decent and honorable, how did he manage to become the most powerful person in the world? Sadly, most people assume, rightly or wrongly, that politicians don't have such qualities.

Well, hopefully this book will help answer that question.

It's not intended to be a historical account of either President Bush's life or his years in office. Those subjects have been covered, and then covered again.

Instead, this is a book about his leadership skills and style, about his big heart, his humility, his courage, his character.

This book is about what we can learn from him that maybe can help our nation's leaders get to a better place.

Actually, help all of us get to a better place.

But before we go on, I'd like to make one important point:

He was not perfect.

His oldest son acknowledged his imperfections when he eulogized his father at his state funeral at the National Cathedral in Washington, DC: "To us, he was close to perfect. But, not totally perfect," said President George W. Bush. "His short game was lousy. He wasn't exactly Fred Astaire on the dance floor. The man couldn't stomach vegetables, especially broccoli. And by the way, he passed these genetic defects along to us."

Just from my twenty-five years as his chief of staff, I would admit President Bush could be stubborn, single-minded, and sometimes exhausting. I once left the office, slammed the door behind me, and went home for the day because he had so irritated me.

And yes, he could be tough.

Although he was not considered a gifted politician, he was still a politician. When he had to, he knew how to play political hardball. If Bob Dole were here, he would attest to the rough and tumble of their 1988 Republican primary disagreements; as would Geraldine Ferraro, his vice presidential sparring partner in 1984. Certainly both Michael Dukakis, his opponent in the 1988 general election; and William Jefferson Clinton, the man who defeated him in 1992, could tell a story or two about how cunning George Bush could be in the political arena.

Yet, at the end of the day, he and his opponents shook hands and moved on.

Although he never became close with Governor Dukakis, they became friends, beginning with a lunch Vice President Bush hosted soon after the 1988 election was over.

He called Geraldine Ferraro shortly before she died to tell her that he loved her. Yes, they had become close friends.

A very frail Senator Dole painfully hoisted himself out of his wheelchair to pay his respects to his old political opponent when 41★ lay in state in the Capitol Rotunda. When I asked him why he had done that, his answer was simple: "I had to stand for the President. It didn't feel right to be sitting down when I saluted that amazing man."

And if she were here, Barbara Bush would tell you her husband became the father that President Clinton never knew.

Jon Meacham, while writing his biography of George H. W. Bush, *Destiny and Power*, observed:

"What is critical to understand about Bush is that winning was not the end of his endeavors, but the means—the way by which he could bring a sense of decency and of dignity to a public arena often bereft of both. As he observed as his mind turned to his 1988 White House run: **If you want to be President—and I do—there are certain things that I have to do, certain speculation that I have to put up with, and certain ugliness that will crop into a campaign or into the pre-campaign.** His impulses to do good and to do in his opponent were intertwined."

He, of course, won in 1988, but then lost his reelection bid in 1992. Some of you might argue that makes him a loser. President Bush himself described his loss as the equivalent of being fired by the American people.

So just what can we learn from someone who suffered such a public—and what he considered a humiliating—defeat?

You could say he lost the battle but won the war. When he died twenty-six years later, he was one of the most revered men in the world.

To help explain the person who was George Herbert Walker

---

★ I will not always call the forty-first President "41" in the book, but I reserve the right to do so often for two reasons: (1) He loved the nickname; and (2) it will help me on the word count.

Bush, I reached out to a wide variety of his friends, former staff, colleagues, former heads of state, members of the media, and even a celebrity or two and asked them to write about one of these topics: (1) What did you learn from George H. W. Bush?; or (2) tell a story that illustrates something about his character.

Their answers included everything from how he ended the Cold War without a shot being fired to how he taught them to drink a martini.

You definitely will notice a common theme and a repetition of his virtues, yet each story is unique; each one an important building block that helps tell the story of George H. W. Bush.

(I admit I was amused by how many of them started their stories by saying that 41 said to them: "I have an idea." I have stated before that those were the scariest words he said to me while I was his chief of staff.)

So what can we learn from all these stories that might help make our country—and us—kinder and gentler?

That at the end of the day, a true leader is courageous, decisive, humble, kind, and wise.

And character really does matter.

*Jean Becker*

To help you follow all the voices in the book:

- **Everything President Bush said or wrote is in bold.**
- The contributors speak in regular font. (They will be identi-fied as we go—especially how they fit into 41's world—but if you wish to know more about them, please see the glossary at the end of the book.)
- *The narrator (that would be me) speaks in italics.*

- When I or any of the contributors talk about President Bush, we are talking about the forty-first president. If we are referring to the forty-third president, we will specify that it's President George W. Bush. Likewise, when we write about Mrs. Bush, that would be Barbara and not Laura.

- A few years ago Mary Kate Cary, one of President Bush's White House speechwriters, put together a documentary about President Bush, *41ON41*, which featured forty-one people talking about . . . well, 41. She very generously gave me the transcripts of all her interviews, which allowed me to include in this book some of the people who knew President Bush best but who for various reasons were unable to contribute to this book. (Barbara Bush and General Brent Scowcroft immediately come to mind.) When I use quotes from *41ON41* it will be noted in parentheses. Note: The documentary came out in 2014, four years before President Bush passed away, so most of their quotes are in present tense.

# FOREWORD

*By James A. Baker, III*

Knowing yourself is the beginning of all wisdom.

—*Aristotle*

I never met a man who had a better understanding of himself, or of his role on the world stage, than President George H. W. Bush. He was simply comfortable in his own skin. The President knew who he was, both his strengths and his weaknesses, a trait that gave him wisdom to make the right and often courageous decisions.

Such a moment occurred on November 9, 1989, the day East Germans took sledgehammers to the Berlin Wall that had divided them from the West for twenty-eight years. As the end of the Cold War appeared closer than ever, the time for jubilation seemed appropriate. Why not celebrate? After all, military expenditures had cost the United States an estimated $8 trillion since the end of World War II, and almost one hundred thousand Americans died during the Korean and Vietnam Wars.

But the President refused to dance on the ruins of that wall, even when goaded.

"You don't seem elated," one reporter commented hours after the wall had started to fall.

**I'm elated**, the President deadpanned, never smiling during a ten-minute press availability that day in the Oval Office. **I'm just not an emotional kind of guy.**

In truth, President Bush was elated, as were all of us in the White House. It was a thrilling moment. Upon learning of the history-shaking development in Berlin, I quickly concluded a meeting at the State Department with a toast to this historic moment and then dashed over to the Oval Office to meet with the President and National Security Adviser Brent Scowcroft before the press was invited in.

Though upbeat, the President was wary. He wanted to avoid a boastful act that hard-liners in the Soviet Union might misconstrue as arrogant triumphalism. Chest-thumping, he worried, could hinder future negotiations with our longtime rivals in Moscow. Worse, it might spark a violent response like the one that had occurred earlier that year at Tiananmen Square in China.

Instead, the President's self-awareness allowed him to demonstrate heroic restraint. Although criticized by some at home for refusing to take a victory lap, he was able to move forward with even more dramatic victories, including the reunification of Germany as a member of the North Atlantic Treaty Organization; the first reduction of nuclear arms by the United States and the Soviet Union; and the eventual peaceful conclusion to the Cold War.

The summer after the Berlin Wall fell, another critical moment arose. On August 2, 1990, Iraqi strongman Saddam Hussein sent his troops into neighboring Kuwait. Three days later, the President resolutely responded: **This will not stand, this aggression against Kuwait.**

By then, he had already started to mount international opposition. Within hours after the invasion, President Bush had convinced the United Nations Security Council to unanimously condemn the heinous act. Four days later, the Security Council imposed sanctions. The President also ordered US military forces to the region.

In November, however, Iraq's troops still remained in Kuwait, and it was evident that the sanctions alone would not get the job done. A more forceful response would be needed to end this stalemate and liberate Kuwait.

Across the Atlantic Ocean, British prime minister Margaret Thatcher was encouraging an end of talks and the start of military action. She opposed seeking another United Nations Security Council resolution, one that would allow for military action if Saddam did not pull his troops out of Kuwait. Thatcher didn't believe that such permission was needed, and she feared seeking it risked rejection. "Oh, George!" she told him. "Let's just go do it!"

The President was willing to go it alone had the situation warranted it. But he understood the serious implications of attacking a member state of the United Nations to settle what then was a regional dispute.

His was the right way forward. With support of the Soviet Union, which had formerly been a strong ally of Iraq, the Security Council set a January 15 deadline for Iraq to withdraw from Kuwait and empowered other nations to use "all necessary means" to force Iraq out of Kuwait after the deadline. When congressional approval soon followed, the President had both domestic and foreign support.

The rest is history. The United States led the largest international coalition since the end of World War II to liberate Kuwait in forty-two days. Once again, the President's wise decision to forgo hubris had paid off.

George H. W. Bush got a healthy dose of self-awareness from his mother, Dorothy Walker Bush, who constantly reminded him about the consequences of his actions. She lectured him not to gloat. She was more concerned about how his baseball team at Yale University did than his individual performance. Don't act like you know an answer to a problem, she advised, go out and find a solution. With her voice always in his mind, he led a life focused on job performance rather than self-aggrandizement. It is one of the many character traits that made him a fine human being as well as a great leader.

Sadly today, modesty and mindfulness have become vanishing virtues as braggadocio and pomposity too often rule the day. And so I am glad that Jean Becker has collected stories from those who knew President Bush and weaved them together in her book *Character Matters: And Other Life Lessons from George Herbert Walker Bush.* Her wonderful book is a reminder that the Boy Scout qualities of loyalty, kindness, truthfulness, and bravery are not antiquated vestiges of the past. They remain critical components of a successful human being.

After reading this book, people will understand why I am confident that history will remember George H. W. Bush as the best one-term President in American history, and one of the very best Presidents of all time.

I bless the day, all those many years ago, when I met this wise and honorable gentleman. And I bless the day the American people elected him President to safely guide us through one of the most dramatic and dangerous periods to ever confront our great nation.

*James A. Baker, III*
*Secretary of State*
*1989–1992*

# CHARACTER
# MATTERS

# CHAPTER ONE

# WHAT MAKES A LEADER?
## *Character*

How much better our world would be if more politicians followed the Masterclass in Statesmanship as epitomized by George H. W. Bush.

—*Sir John Major*

*W*hat *was it about* George Herbert Walker Bush *that made him such an effective leader?*

*For that matter, what is the definition of "leadership"?*

*Former White House staffer Roman Popadiuk tried to answer that question in his book* The Leadership of George Bush.* *He began by making this observation:*

"It is debatable whether or not leadership can be taught. Many believe it is an innate quality or somehow a combination of natural ability and conscious development. Irrespective of that debate, one can learn much from observing the qualities and characteristics of successful leaders in whatever field they occupy. This is particularly

---

* Published in 2009 by Texas A&M University Press.

true of George Bush, whose style and personal demeanor serve to underscore that leadership is a fusion of character and experience, with character being at the forefront."

*Lucky for us, some of the people who worked with President Bush closely over the years—especially when he was President—gave us their insights.*

*We'll start with some of his peers on the world stage:*

### John Major, former prime minister of the United Kingdom:

The older I get, and the more politics I see, the more I miss President George H. W. Bush.

In many ways, George was the antithesis of the stereotypical politician. He could be shy; diffident; was a good listener; and spoke only when he had views worth sharing. He was also decent, wise, incorruptible, and had a gift for seeing the best—or, at least, finding some good—even in the worst of people.

George found his personal relationships of great strength, and none more so than the force of nature that was Barbara Bush. Forever watching George's back and poised to protect him from all comers, Barbara had an acute antenna for political danger well before it materialized.

In government, George gathered real talent around him. His foreign policy team of Jim Baker as secretary of state and Brent Scowcroft as national security adviser was the most formidably impressive I have ever known, and the friendship of the three remained close and lifelong.

But what of George Bush the man? He was a patrician with the common touch. It is inconceivable that he would ever be unkind—most especially to those who served him, or who were in no position to answer back. His God, to him, was real—and he strove to maintain the Christian standards that were the framework of his life.

He had more friends—*real* friends, not merely acquaintances—than anyone I knew. In good times he was the first to praise; in bad, the first to console; and at *all* times he kept in touch. He was, without doubt, a world-class user of the telephone.

Nonetheless, George was no paragon. Few of us are, especially those who get to be President of the United States. But he did not possess the "black arts" that are so commonly assumed to be in the armory of every politician and, even had he done so, his character and conscience would have always dissuaded him from deploying them.

He loved gossip—and had a great sense of the absurd. Immensely competitive in all things, he would drive his cigarette boat at great speed around the waters of Kennebunkport, with the Secret Service trailing in his wake. "What if they lose you?" I asked, as yet another wave bounced me out of my seat.

**Don't worry. It'll be reported and they'll get a faster boat. Then we can have even more fun!**

We once met up in the Middle East—long after we had both left office—and were invited into the desert for a tented lunch with a member of the ruling family who had a passion for the game of boules.★

Before the game began, our respective ambassadors whispered in our ears that our host was "expected" to win. **The heck with that**, proclaimed George.

Our host came in third.

There was an audible intake of breath from those around us. "Aha!" our host exclaimed. "You never told me you were both star players. That's the *best* game I've ever had." George beamed. I

---

★ Boules is the French version of boccie ball, and the American version is bowling.

beamed. Our host beamed, before leading us both arm in arm for some more refreshments.

There are so many other memories of our time together, all of which I will cherish for the rest of my days.

What are the "life lessons" I learned from George H. W. Bush?

I learned that it was possible to be the most powerful politician on the planet, without ever once abusing that power to impress or influence others. I learned that—through his modesty, wisdom, empathy, infectious sense of mischief, and deep-down decency—I had found a friend for life.

How much better our world would be if more politicians followed the Masterclass in Statesmanship as epitomized by George H. W. Bush.

Brian Mulroney, former prime minister of Canada:

George Bush was truly a great international leader. The day after the Iraqi invasion of Kuwait, he invited me to Washington, DC, to join him for dinner in the family quarters of the White House. Present were Barbara; National Security Adviser General Brent Scowcroft; Deputy Secretary of State Larry Eagleburger; my chief of staff, Stanley Hartt; the Canadian ambassador to Washington, Derek Burney; and me, to whom President Bush handed the raw CIA intelligence report just received from Baghdad.

This was a very alarming situation, but the President discussed options in a thoughtful and careful manner. Questions raised and resolved included: Immediate response? Should we seek a UN Security Council resolution to ensure the creation of a strong coalition? Size of military force to be raised? And when to counterattack?

In a discussion of the role of our allies, I urged that he call President Mitterrand first. As head of America's oldest ally in Europe, it would be vital for him to feel he was a trusted and important player in what was to become a vast military and diplomatic operation. I further indicated that he should reach Mitterrand in Paris at the start of business the next day because Mitterrand would know—and greatly appreciate—that President Bush had gotten up at 3:00 a.m. Washington time to call.

The President thought for a moment, then picked up the phone that was anchored just under the dining room table to his right. **Please awaken me at 3:00 a.m. and put me through to President Mitterrand at Élysée Palace at 9:00 a.m. Paris time**, he told the White House operator.

He did precisely that and Mitterrand, deeply appreciative of the fact that he was the first European leader approached, turned out to be one of our most supportive allies from beginning to end.

I mention this only to indicate the Bush approach to important matters: careful planning, consideration of allies, respect for international institutions, and a sensitive understanding of human relations. To him, no detail was unimportant in the successful prosecution of a historic military operation.

Which, under his leadership, the first Gulf War turned out to be.

*And now a few stories from some of his staff who witnessed the President at key decision-making moments—moments that truly defined his character.*

*In late 1989, the relationship between the United States and Panama was deteriorating at a rapid pace. The Panamanian de facto leader, General Manuel Noriega, was wanted in the United States for racketeering and drug trafficking; he had overturned by brute force a democratic election to stay in power; and he was threatening Americans who lived in Panama, including our military serving in the Panama Canal Zone.*

*The "last straw" for President George Bush was the death of a Marine and the harassment of several other Americans. As the President wrote in his diary on December 17:*

**Last night a young Marine was killed in Panama. Hectored by blockade guards, the Marine and his three companions tried to get away from a roadblock, but they had gotten lost, and they were shot at. The Panamanians claim that the Marines fired on them, which was bull because none of them had any ammunition or guns.**

**Shortly after that a Navy lieutenant and his wife were taken in by the same check point people and harassed for 30 minutes. He was kicked and brutalized, kicked in the groin. A day or so before that, the Panamanians declared war on the United States, and they installed Manuel Noriega as the maximum leader...**

*We'll turn the story over to Andy Card, who was then deputy White House chief of staff:*

On December 17 there was an Oval Office meeting with Secretary of State James Baker; Secretary of Defense Dick Cheney; National Security Adviser Brent Scowcroft and his deputy, Bob Gates; and the director of operations for the Joint Chiefs, Lieutenant General Thomas Kelly.

And me. As deputy chief of staff, my job was putting up the easel and displaying the photos and charts provided by the CIA and the military.

At issue: Should we go to war with Panama?

After much discussion, Jim Baker stood up and said to the President that he had all the information available, and it was his decision to make. Baker then walked out of the room. It was an awkward moment as everyone else then walked out too.

I was the only one in the room with the President as I was picking up documents and photos from the floor. The President got up and went to sit at the desk and closed his eyes with his hands folded. I am fairly sure he was praying.

He opened his eyes, looking at me but really right through me, and then said:

**I am making a decision that will cost young men their lives.**

He then got up and walked out the door to the Rose Garden.

As I continued cleaning up the Oval Office, I thought to myself: "I just watched the President make a presidential decision."

The moment left a lasting impression on me. He was decisive and sure, but with tremendous empathy for those who would have to implement that decision and with concern for the unintended consequences.

The war ended fairly quickly, with Noriega surrendering to American forces on January 3 (after hiding out in the Vatican embassy for about ten days), but not until twenty-three of our soldiers died.

In January the President was making a trip to Cincinnati to highlight an education program for disadvantaged youth at Taft High School. Prior to any trip, I would always ask for a summary of letters that had been sent to the President from zip codes in which the President was to travel. The idea was to determine if there were any issues of which we should be aware and what was on people's minds in that area of the country.

I noticed one letter in the Cincinnati zip code sent by a woman, Sandra Rouse, who wanted to meet with the President to call him a murderer to his face because he killed her son. Her son was Private First Class James Markwell, killed in Panama.

When I followed up, I discovered that a letter had been sent from the President to Mrs. Rouse, as he wrote the families of any soldiers who died.

Just moments after I found this letter, my pager went off. The President needed me in the Oval Office.

As he was giving me instructions for a new task, he noticed I was troubled. He stopped the conversation and asked what was bothering me. I told him about the letter.

He immediately said he would like to meet with her.

Brent Scowcroft was not happy when he found out I had mentioned the letter to the President. He insisted the President should not meet with a woman who wanted to call him a murderer to his face.

Nevertheless, the meeting was arranged.

In Cincinnati, while the President was giving his speech at Taft High School, Marlin Fitzwater and I went to the classroom where Mrs. Rouse; her husband, William Rouse, who was James's stepfather; and James's brother Brandon and sister Dawn were waiting.

When we walked into the room, Mrs. Rouse verbally ripped me apart and was very angry. Shortly thereafter, the Secret Service told me the President was on his way. I stepped out of the room to warn him this was not going to be easy.

When the President entered the room, Mrs. Rouse was visibly upset and stepped up to only about six inches from him before saying: "You murdered my son." The President just stood there and let her speak. When she was done, he said:

**Your son was a hero. I could not do my job if not for people like your son. I want to hear all about him.**

The President then talked to the stepfather, the brother and the sister, and then the mother again and listened to their stories.

Everybody was crying.

The mother then took an envelope out of her purse, which she gave the President. He put it in the inside pocket of his jacket, hugged everyone, and left.

Once in the limousine, he pulled out the envelope from his suit pocket. There was an essay and a letter. The essay was written when James was fifteen: "When I grow up, I want to be a soldier and fight for my country."

The letter was written to his family shortly before he died, as he tried to prepare them for the worst: "Remember I joined the army to serve my country and to ensure that you are free to do what you want and live your lives freely. But most of all don't forget that the Army was my choice, something that I wanted to do."

There were tears in the President's eyes.

It took incredible courage for the President of the United States to walk into that classroom to face a family who swore they hated him. But he knew what they were feeling. And he knew they needed their son's commander in chief to let them cry on his shoulder.

What makes a leader? Empathy. And the courage to show it.

*As a footnote to Andy's story, I found a letter that President Bush wrote his mother, his five children, his five siblings, and several uncles about this meeting with the mother of a fallen solider. Here are parts of his letter:*

**At our meeting Mrs. Rouse was courageous and strong; her faith in God sustaining her. She cried. I put my arm around her shoulder.**

**I thought—I sent her son into this battle and here she is telling me with love about her son and what he stood for. She said, "You did the right thing."**

**PFC Markwell died, I'm told, as he attended to a wounded man. Yes, he was taught to kill and to save . . .**

**I just wanted to share this with the family . . . When I mourn our dead and wounded, when I think of their families and loved ones, I also think of the courage of our troops.**

**I expect I'll remember PFC James W. Markwell as long as I live. I'll remember a loving mother's grief but also her pride in one young, courageous, and patriotic soldier.**

Marlin Fitzwater, White House press secretary:

The history of President George H. W. Bush is replete with stories of courage and character—in war as a Navy pilot in the Pacific; as an oil executive who spent hours in the air looking for a lost oil rig; as a father who lost his daughter to leukemia; and as an envoy to China when he could have gone to Paris or London.

Less understood was as President, how he guided the United States and the Soviet Union to the end of the Cold War.

As the White House press secretary, I was lucky to have a front-row seat as the drama unfolded. I was not a decision-maker, but President Bush was great about keeping me in the loop so I could do my job of keeping the press—and therefore the American people—informed the best I could.

My story is really about one key effort, and one very special relationship, in changing the direction of those years. In December 1989, President Bush opened the door at the Malta Summit between himself and Mikhail Gorbachev when two men of courage, compassion, and strength agreed to a new direction for their countries.

President Bush had met the new leader of the Soviet Union a few times during the Reagan administration, though not often enough to establish a personal relationship. But he wanted to because that's how George Bush does business. So as the new occupant of the Oval Office in 1989, he started calling Gorbachev to talk about issues between our countries, and especially about scheduling their first meeting as leaders.

Meanwhile, the media did not think the President was doing his job when it came to Gorbachev. Gorbachev was making headlines as he toured Europe while our President stayed quiet. The American press corps was clamoring for a summit meeting.

Finally, after several months of dealing with the demands from the reporters, the President called me to the Oval. He wanted to give me some advice on how to handle the situation from the White House press room podium.

**Only Baker and Scowcroft know this, but I want to tell you that Gorbachev and I have agreed to a summit meeting in December. No one else knows. And I have told President Gorbachev that we will not leak this meeting to the press. I just wanted you to know so you could say the right thing.**

This was typical George Bush. He had taken charge of arranging for a summit, deciding the agenda, and working directly with President Gorbachev. This said a lot about the courage and independence of the President, and it sent a message to staff that George Bush was running the show, knew what he wanted, and put a high value on loyalty. These qualities became part of the Bush presidency, known to everyone.

It soon became clear to President Bush that Gorbachev was very loyal to his country. But Gorbachev also knew his country needed economic help. As the months passed, and the two men had further discussions about their economic and political needs, President Bush—with Baker and Scowcroft—started to develop ideas about how the US should relate to the Soviet Union, and how the two countries could work together while still respecting their political differences.

After many internal discussions, President Bush asked Secretary Baker and the State Department team to put together a list of items that could form the basis for the President's opening statement at the Malta Summit. They did, and it looked very good, outlining the steps that America could consider in helping the Soviet Union's economy. But that would be a big step, and a big risk, in helping Russia after seventy years of cold war.

Nevertheless, the President wanted to do it. High risk always requires courage. He wanted to consider his words carefully.

As the President and his staff boarded Air Force One for Malta, there was still an ache in his mind that something wasn't quite what he wanted. So about halfway across the ocean, he asked General Scowcroft, Chief of Staff Sununu, myself, and about a half dozen others regardless of rank or position to join him in the plane's conference room.

The State Department contingent was meeting elsewhere on the plane, and the President decided not to interrupt them. I actually think he wanted to hear reactions to his remarks by people not directly involved.

He started by asking this question: Do you all believe in President Gorbachev? The President called on Brent for a first opinion, which put the staff at ease. The general said yes. Then the President went around the room asking for opinions. In one way or another, everyone there said yes.

He said that if we believe in Gorbachev, why are these talking points so conditional? Why don't we just say we're going to do it?

Then the President started reading, speaking as if talking to Gorbachev.

**What's wrong with saying I'm going to waive Jackson-Vanik.\* Let's not be negative. I want to be positive. I want**

---

\* According to the Wilson Center: The "Jackson-Vanik Amendment, enacted as part of Title IV of the Trade Act of 1974, prohibits any nation with a non-market economy that restricts the emigration of its people from achieving most-favored nation status with the United States."

to do it, so let's say it. I propose we start NOW to negotiate a trade agreement.

I want you to be an observer at GATT.*

I want to be very frank in our talks. No hidden agenda.

The more you can intersect with the OECD the better—the better to see how free market economies work.† After you get some of these things, then you can get Most Favored Nation status.

Here's a list of 20 refuseniks,‡ 96 divided families. Let's have a goal of getting all these contentious cases cleared up by the 1990 Summit. And let's set a date for our next summit.

On almost every one of these points, the President took his pen and crossed out the "conditional" words. His main purpose was clear: To help bring Mr. Gorbachev into the world economy. And to help the people of the Soviet Union. And to do it NOW.

When we arrived in Malta, the President met with Secretary Baker and his team. He presented the exact same words to this group. These were our foreign policy experts, and I think they were surprised by the directness of the ideas. But they approved.

The next morning, at the opening of the summit, Gorbachev said he wanted to first voice a concern about the term "Western values," a term that some people and press used in discussing their differences

---

\* Per Wikipedia: "The General Agreement on Tariffs and Trade is a legal agreement between many countries, whose overall purpose was to promote international trade by reducing or eliminating trade barriers such as tariffs or quotas."

† Quoting Wikipedia: "The Organization for Economic Co-operation and Development is an international organization with 38 member countries founded in 1961 to stimulate economic progress and world trade. Member countries describe themselves as committed to democracy and the market economy,"

‡ Soviet citizens who had been denied the right to emigrate.

with Eastern Bloc countries.* Gorbachev said this term was offensive to his people. Secretary Baker asked if "democratic values" would be a better term. Gorbachev considered it, and said he thought it would. The first bump in the road had been resolved.

Then President Bush asked if he could go first in opening remarks. Gorbachev agreed. The President gave his presentation for the third time in two days.

When he finished, there was silence in the room as everyone waited for Gorbachev's reaction. Gorbachev said nothing at first. Then he pushed his chair back from the table and looked at the floor. Then he looked forward, put his hands on the table, and said, "That is exactly what I wanted to hear."

Everyone relaxed. And the summit began in earnest.

The next morning, Gorbachev began with this sentence: "The Soviet Union no longer regards the United States as an adversary."

It was the beginning of the end of the Cold War, as orchestrated by George H. W. Bush.

Robert Gates, former secretary of defense and head of the CIA:

It was my great good fortune to serve as deputy national security adviser to President Bush during the historically momentous years 1989–1991. I spent time with him almost every day during those years. I also saw him often in his post-presidential years, especially when I was dean of the Bush School† and president of Texas A&M

---

* Countries aligned with the Soviet Union.

† The Bush School of Government and Public Service: Part of the library center, the school opened in 1997 and is part of Texas A&M University. The Bush School offers undergraduate degrees in international affairs and political science; master's degrees in international affairs, international policy, national security and intelligence, and public service and administration; an online executive master's degree in public

University, the site of his presidential library and museum.* Every day I was around him was a learning experience, and I am happy to recount a few of those many lessons.

I learned from him the importance of loyalty, both up and down. Just as I watched him be deeply loyal to Ronald Reagan for eight years, I saw him be just as loyal to those working for him. Everyone who worked closely with him experienced it. In 1991, when my confirmation hearing to become director of Central Intelligence ran into rough water, I learned that several senior White House advisers were urging President Bush to pull the plug on my nomination. But the President stood by me and, in ways small and large, public and private, made his firm support known to all who mattered—and especially to me. At one point, Senate Minority Leader Bob Dole told the President I might not have the votes to get confirmed. Bush replied that that would be the country's loss but his gain because then he could keep me by his side at the White House. Ultimately, I was confirmed by a comfortable margin thanks to the President's steadfast support—his loyalty to me.

He showed everyone that you could have the weight of the world on your shoulders and still have a great sense of humor. The President was fun to work for. He loved jokes, including practical jokes—even when played on him—and could give as well as he got. Garry Trudeau's *Doonesbury* comic strip often starred the President's

---

service and administration; and a PhD program in political science. The school also has a teaching site in Washington, DC. When I talk about the Bush School, I mean this school.

* The George H. W. Bush Library and Museum, opened in 1997 on the campus of Texas A&M in College Station, Texas, are part of the National Archives. All of President Bush's presidential papers, and most of his personal ones, are housed in the library. The Bushes are buried on the library grounds. In this book, when I talk about the library, I mean this library.

invisible other self—"President Skippy"—represented in the strip simply with an asterisk. One morning, when the President stepped out of the Oval Office during a meeting with John Sununu, Brent Scowcroft, and me, we had a photographer come in and take a picture of the three of us gesturing vigorously at an empty presidential chair. We later presented a framed copy of the photo (which we all had signed) to him inscribed, "To President Skippy, from the gang that knows you best." He smiled, and then turned the tables on us. He faked a look of horror and, framed photo in hand, suddenly got up, then strode out of the Oval Office and down to the press room to show them the photo, declaring there was a plot against him in the White House. I should add his unannounced appearance nearly provoked a press riot.

He then blamed the entire thing on a completely innocent Marlin Fitzwater, his press secretary. Our prank became his joke on us.

There were many other things I learned from President Bush, but three major ones will have to do:

The first is the importance of a leader having vision—the ability to see a better, different future and the equally important ability to bring that vision to reality.

President Bush was often accused of not having "the vision thing." Far from it. Just ask any disabled person who has benefited from his 1990 Americans with Disabilities Act or consider the impact on the environment of the 1990 Clean Air Act. But my favorite example of his vision was the peaceful reunification of Germany. The Bush administration rightfully gets credit for bringing about reunification, but it was Bush personally—not his advisers—who was the moving force.

On September 18, 1989, I flew with him to Helena, Montana, where he celebrated the state's centenary. He later gave a press conference at the statehouse, where he was asked whether he thought a reunified Germany would be a stabilizing or destabilizing force in Europe. He responded:

**If that was worked out between the Germanys, I do not think we should view that as bad for Western interests. I think there's been a dramatic change in post–World War II Germany. And so, I don't fear it . . . I think there is in some quarters a feeling—well, a reunified Germany would be detrimental to the peace of Europe, of Western Europe, some way, and I don't accept that at all. Simply don't.**

After his statement, I immediately called Brent and asked him if the administration had a position on German reunification. He said no, the bureaucracy was tied up in knots over the issue. He then wondered why I asked, and I replied, "Well, if we didn't have a policy on reunification before, we have one now—the President just announced he's all for it." That was nearly two months before the Berlin Wall came down, and I learned a powerful lesson about both vision and bold leadership.

A second big lesson I learned from President Bush came through observing how he treated people.

In personal relationships, he was oblivious to rank. He was as interested in the lives, families, and well-being of the White House groundskeepers as he was in those of his cabinet members and other world leaders.

He especially was most interested and solicitous if someone had an ill family member. I saw this firsthand when Brent's wife, Jackie, who had long been in ill health, periodically would be taken to the hospital. Brent worked outrageous hours, often in the office until nine or ten o'clock in the evening. Even when Jackie was in the hospital, Brent wouldn't leave the office to visit her until the President had left the Oval Office and gone to the residence for the evening. So he and I conspired against Brent. When Jackie was in the hospital, I would surreptitiously let the President know. He then would call Brent about five o'clock and tell him he was headed home for the evening. Brent would make a beeline for the hospital and, once he had gone, I'd sound the all clear, and the President would return to work. Such presidential empathy and caring were familiar experiences for many in the President's orbit.

I had another, exceptionally moving experience with those qualities of the President. On April 19, 1989, a gun turret on the battleship USS *Iowa* exploded, killing forty-seven sailors. I accompanied President Bush in the Marine One helicopter to the memorial service in Norfolk on April 24. On the way, as he was going over his speech, he kept tearing up as he reviewed passages about the lost sailors. At one point, he paused his reading and told me he had once asked President Reagan how he got through emotional passages in speeches. Reagan had said that he just kept practicing the passages over and over. With tears in his eyes, Bush told me, **That doesn't work for me**. He was later criticized for rushing through his remarks at the ceremony; I knew from the helicopter ride that that was the only way he could get through the remarks without breaking up.

He cared deeply about people, but especially men and women in uniform. Years later, as secretary of defense in wartime, I very often thought of him and how much he cared when I likewise would weep for the fallen.

There is one more big lesson I learned from George H. W. Bush. In a short biography of Winston Churchill, Paul Johnson wrote that "Churchill wasted an extraordinarily small amount of his time and emotional energy on the meannesses of life: recrimination, shifting blame onto others, malice, revenge seeking, dirty tricks, spreading rumors, harboring grudges, waging vendettas...[T]he absence of hatred left plenty of room for joy in Churchill's life."

I saw repeatedly the absence of meanness and hatred in President Bush. And so the biggest lesson he taught me, by his example, was the importance of living a life of service and a life with plenty of room for joy.

Condoleezza Rice, former secretary of state:

As one of Brent Scowcroft's deputies, I was the young Soviet specialist for President Bush when the extraordinary events of 1989– 1991 took place. I was well known in academic circles but not in government ones. I was thirty-four years old.

Imagine my surprise at the Malta Summit when the President called me over to introduce me to Gorbachev. He put his hand on my shoulder, turned to Gorbachev, and said:

**This is my Soviet adviser, Condoleezza Rice. She is a professor at Stanford University. She tells me everything I know about the Soviet Union.**

Gorbachev mumbled something in Russian like, "I hope she knows a lot."

But of course the President's comment wasn't really meant for Gorbachev. It was meant for all of those people standing around— including US and Soviet government officials who were twice my age. I was a young, Black woman in whom the President was investing great trust and confidence at a critically important time in his presidency. I was grateful that I never had to worry that I might somehow be discounted by others.

There are often questions about how people who look different are treated. We talk about inclusion and empowerment. The very best empowerment that you can give to a young person is to let it be known that you trust them and that everyone else had better do so too.

This was a great act of mentorship for which I will always be grateful. And it allowed me to do an even better job for the President, fully empowered by him. And it was pure George H. W. Bush—understated, elegant, and yet a powerful signal.

### John Sununu, White House chief of staff:

As chief of staff to President George H. W. Bush during the collapse of the Soviet Union, I had the privilege of witnessing the power of earned trust in the hands of a strong leader. President Bush demonstrated that personal relationships and credibility, built over a lifetime of fair treatment, integrity, and humility, can be invaluable in achieving success in even the most monumental negotiations.

President Reagan had set the foundation for the demise of the Soviet Union with his strategy of "peace through strength." When President Bush succeeded Reagan, he recognized that the task of achieving global consensus and ending nuclear confrontation required the committed support and assistance of strong and independent world leaders, including British prime minister Margaret Thatcher; French president François Mitterrand; German chancellor Helmut Kohl; Canadian prime minister Brian Mulroney; and Soviet president Mikhail Gorbachev.

Through decades of public service, President Bush already had earned their respect. They trusted him. And it was that trust that made possible the cooperation that led to the demise of the Soviet Union, the end of the Cold War, and the reunification of Germany.

As President of the United States, it was his responsibility to define and implement a strategy to lead them all to real consensus and, in partnership with them, bring closure to a half century of

East-West conflict. George Bush knew that each of these political leaders, and the countries they led, had very different perspectives on how to move forward, with different ideas on what steps should be taken, and even different visions of what the results should be.

It was not going to be easy.

I watched how, over a period of around a year and a half, the President was able to convince them all—individually and collectively and through frequent phone calls, face-to-face meetings, and international conferences—to embark on a strategy that would change the world. He listened to their concerns, answered their questions, found compromises to their conflicts, and patiently moved the process forward.

He convinced Mikhail Gorbachev that it would be better for the Soviet Union and its people to be part of a mutually beneficial world economy.

He convinced Margaret Thatcher and François Mitterrand, leaders of two nations that only a generation before had been devastated in war by Germany, to support the reunification of Germany to create what would become the most powerful nation in Europe.

He convinced Helmut Kohl to accept East Germany as a partner and provide significant economic aid to the former Soviet puppet state to rebuild a unified Germany.

President Bush's decades of integrity and credibility allowed him to move these powerful leaders in unison toward a common goal. They trusted his tactics and strategy, and most importantly they trusted that he would ensure that they shared the credit for the success of this world-changing effort.

The collapse of the Soviet Union demonstrated the power of earned trust in the hands of a strong leader. George H. W. Bush's personal relationships and credibility—cultivated over a lifetime of fair treatment, integrity, and humility—were invaluable in achieving monumental negotiations and bringing closure to a half century of nuclear confrontation.

*To illustrate the great diversity of George H. W. Bush's life, we'll end this chapter with thoughts from two close friends: the first, a story from Senator Alan Simpson; the last, from President Bill Clinton.*

<u>Alan Simpson, Republican senator from Wyoming:</u>

I first met my dear friend in 1962. My father, Milward Simpson, was elected to the US Senate, and I accompanied him to Washington, where he was assigned a new office being vacated by one Senator Prescott Bush—George's father! A life-changer for me.

Before I tell my story, you need to know I have a rather checkered past from my tenure in Washington—I tumbled down from the A social list to the Z list, and never came back up! Most of my wounds were self-inflicted. Some thought I was "thin skinned." I responded, "You couldn't find my skin with an electronic microscope!"

Once, in the midst of my miasma, George called early one morning (always early), with country music blaring in the background, and said, **I see the media is shooting you pretty full of holes!** Actually he said it with more pungency! He chuckled and then said, **Why don't we go to Camp David and have a weekend together?**

His popularity rating was then 93 percent; mine was .93 percent.

The media were gathered around as we four—George of course invited my wife, Ann, as well—headed to Marine One.

**Now, Al, wave to all your pals over there in the media!**

They didn't wave back.

The next morning, going through all the newspapers and also looking at network television, he said, **Ah-ha! This is what I'm**

**looking for!** A picture of Barbara, Ann, and George—with his arm and hand on my back.

After a vigorous day of competitive sports, we were having a sauna, and I said, "George, I'm well aware of what you are doing here—you're salving my recent wounds and here you are at the top of your game, and you reach out to me while I'm tangled up in rich controversy taking my lumps from the Fourth Estate."*

**Yup. There are staff members who told me not to do this. But Al, it's about friendship and loyalty.**

Sound familiar?

We always had a great deal of fun too. One night we four went to see Michael Crawford, singing the songs of Andrew Lloyd Webber. We were singing as we went back to the White House, "Don't Cry for Me Argentina" and songs from *The Phantom* and other magic of Webber. A few days later he's getting hammered by the press for some petty bit of trivia, and suddenly he blurts out, **Don't cry for me Argentina!** The press then reported he was surely losing his marbles! I found them to be a rather humorless bunch.

We often shared a fact our mothers taught us that "humor is the universal solvent against the abrasive elements of life." And so it is! We also compared our beautiful mothers as loving "velvet hammers."

Any President knows well of "the slings and arrows of outrageous fortune." It goes with those who hold that office. He was a class act—from birth to death.

The history books will—and are—treating him most fairly while noting his most powerful traits: his great competitiveness, character, raw courage, kindness, loyalty, humility, and self-discipline. He was a living vessel of those traits.

---

* A nickname for the media.

Recall that those who travel the high road of humility in Washington, DC, are not bothered by heavy traffic!

When those really tough choices came to his desk, he would say:

**It's the country, it's not me, or the Democrats, or the Republicans, this is for our country that I fought for.**

He had one serious flaw known to all close to him. He loved a good joke—the richer the better—and he'd throw his head back and give that great laugh—but he never could remember a punch line! Ever!

He never hated anyone, and knew well what his mother and my mother both knew: "Hatred corrodes the container it's carried in."

His words and presence are always in my mind: **What would we do without family and friends?!** He lived that.

He also would say, **If you have integrity, nothing else matters—and if you don't have integrity, nothing else matters.** Not a day goes by where I don't think of my old chum. A most comforting thought for me in the remaining time I have on this Old Apple! My life is richer for having shared a portion of it with him.

Bill Clinton, forty-second President of the United States:

My friendship with President George H. W. Bush was one of the great privileges of my life.

His inherent decency and the firm strength of his personal character have become part of his enduring public legacy, but from the first moment I met him, I was also struck by his devotion to his family and how he saw his public life as inextricably connected to the families of others, particularly children and young people.

Maya Angelou famously said, "When people show you who they are, believe them." George showed me from the start that families and children mattered to him. In the summer of 1983, when I was a young governor, we held the National Governors Association annual meeting in Portland, Maine, and we were all invited to a cookout at then Vice President Bush's house in the beautiful oceanside town of Kennebunkport. George and Barbara were gracious hosts, but George took it to the next level when Chelsea, who was three years old then, marched up and said she needed to go to the bathroom. The Vice President of the United States took her by the hand and led her there himself.

Nobody who knew George would have been surprised by that. As a young congressman concerned about American families being able to have a decent home, he supported the Fair Housing Act and defended his vote superbly in a speech before members of his conservative—and deeply skeptical—Houston district, in the end getting a standing ovation from the crowd.

As President he championed and signed the Americans with Disabilities Act and specifically mentioned Lisa Carl, a teen with cerebral palsy who had been kept out of her local movie theater due to her wheelchair; and a group of Little Leaguers who teamed up with disabled players to make sure they weren't missing out on all the fun.

When George and I worked together to raise funds and awareness in the aftermath of the terrible South Asia tsunami in 2004, we traveled all over the devasted region, including a trip to Sri Lanka, where we visited a coastal city that had been hard hit, with tremendous damage and heartbreaking loss of life. Grief counselors there had been working with local children who had lost loved ones by encouraging them to make drawings to express their feelings, many of which portrayed their personal traumatic images of destruction, but some eventually showing tentative rays of hope in the form of playing children and a bright sun.

Before we left, a few of the drawings were gifted to George and me. I'll never forget the compassionate way George responded to those kids who had lost so much, or how he treasured their drawings, holding them as if they were priceless masterpieces. For him, they were.

A few years before he died, the internet celebrated the gracious note George left for me in the Resolute Desk when he departed the White House. I won't include the whole thing here, but just mention that after several lines of encouragement and wisdom about the challenges of the office, he said:

**I wish you well. I wish your family well.**

That was vintage George, taking a moment to include Chelsea and Hillary in that note from one President to another, reminding me that we're all people in the end, with families, children, and the hopes and dreams we all carry for them.

In countless moments small and large, fleeting and historic, there was an essential part of George's character that embraced our common humanity as surely as he held Chelsea's hand so many decades before. I think George saw in young people the same limitless possibilities that he saw in himself as a young man, his life of tremendous achievement still ahead of him, already determined to take chances and do well in a life devoted to public service.

He did just that, showing us all, time and again, who he truly was.

# CHAPTER TWO

# WHEN THE TOUGH GET GOING...
## *Courage*

As always, he did the right thing for the country he had
served in so many ways, so faithfully.

—*Senator Rob Portman*

*L*ooking for a fight?

*Mention to a George H. W. Bush family member or friend the 1987*
Newsweek *cover that suggested the former World War II pilot was a wimp.
Specifically, the headline read: "Fighting the 'Wimp Factor.'"*

*Yeah, that will get you a fight.*

Newsweek *ran the now infamous cover story shortly after then Vice
President Bush announced he was running for President. You could say it got
the campaign off to a rather bumpy start and enraged his supporters.*

*When President Bush died in 2018,* Newsweek *editor Evan Thomas
wrote a column that could be called his mea culpa:*

"The clear implication of the cover story (which I edited, pencil-
ing in the word 'wimp' over the objection of the story's reporter,
Margaret Warner) was that Bush somehow lacked the inner fortitude
to lead the free world.

"How wrong we were."

*This chapter will help Mr. Thomas count the ways in which he was wrong.*

*When I asked President Bush's White House staff to write about what they learned from him, the answers were variations of the same theme: He had the courage to do what he felt was right—right for the country; and sometimes right for the world.*

*Long before he took the oath of office, George H. W. Bush showed us he was not afraid to do the unexpected; to take a path less traveled; to make the tough and sometimes bold decision.*

*To show courage.*

*At age twenty, when his plane was hit during a bombing run, he first finished his mission—dumping his payload over a key Japanese radio tower— before parachuting out.*

*At age twenty-four, after graduating Phi Beta Kappa from Yale, he turned down the safe career choice of following his father to Wall Street and instead struck out on his own, driving his Studebaker to Texas to take a job as an oil equipment clerk. (However, the real hero of this part of the story might be Barbara Bush, who of course made the move with her husband and their two-year-old son, George W., sharing for a while a duplex with a mother-daughter prostitute team.)*

*Fast-forwarding nearly fifty years, President Bush shocked a lot of his friends and fellow Republicans when he very publicly resigned from the National Rifle Association in 1995, after he received what he considered a deeply offensive fund-raising letter.*

*These are examples of some of the very personal decisions he made as a private citizen, but he was no less bold when leading from a public platform.*

*The first best example came in 1968, when Congressman George Bush voted for the Fair Housing Act, designed to end housing discrimination. The vote came in the same month when Martin Luther King Jr. was killed, and civil rights riots were raging in our cities. Congressman Bush's conservative constituents were not happy with his vote. Most of them thought it was just fine for Blacks and whites to live across the railroad tracks from each other.*

**I am being fitted for my lead underwear**, *he wrote to his friend Chase Untermeyer after he had received five hundred letters against his vote; two letters in favor. Nevertheless, he went back to Houston to face his constituents in a town hall meeting. Here are excerpts from his speech:*

**And now I'd like to frankly discuss my recent vote for the civil rights bill, a vote which has brought some approval and much concern...**

**Much of the other mail was persuasive and well done— some of it was filled with hatred...**

**The unsigned letter.**

**The threat.**

**The "sell-out" approach.**

**The phone call.**

**The "nigger-lover"—this in 1968 with our country ripped apart at the seams.**

**The base and mean emotionalism that makes me bow my head in sadness.**

**There is an irony here—much of the mail comes from people who have written me in favor of the Dirksen amendment for prayer in schools...**

**Here is my position—I liked some of the provisions—I didn't like others...**

**What this Bill does do in this area is to remove an obstacle— what it does do is try to offer a promise or a hope—a realization of The American Dream.**

**In Vietnam I chatted with many Negro soldiers. They were fighting, and some were dying, for the ideals of this Country;**

some talked about coming back to get married and to start their lives over.

Somehow it seems fundamental that this guy should have hope. A hope that if he saves some money, and if he wants to break out of a ghetto, and if he is a good character and if he meets every requirement of purchaser—the door will not be slammed solely because he is a Negro, or because he speaks with a Mexican accent.

In these troubled times, fair play is basic. The right to hope is basic. And so I suggest that there are things wrong with this Bill and there are things right with it.

I have been accused of killing the Republican Party. With one of the more conservative voting records in the House, I am now accused by some of killing the Republican Party by this one vote . . .

But I don't believe it. All Republican Senators voting except 3 voted for this Bill—

100 out of 184 Republicans in the House voted for it.

Richard Nixon and about every national Republican leader advocated its passage . . .

But I voted from conviction.

And so I voted . . . not out of intimidation or fear, not stampeded by riots—but because of a feeling deep down in my heart that this was the right thing for me to do. That this was the right thing for America.

*All these years later, Mary Matthews Raether, then Congressman Bush's legislative assistant, still remembers vividly how difficult the days after the Fair Housing Act vote were:*

Although the Bush experience of the activities around the Fair

Housing Act of 1968 has been written about often, I don't remember reading about its effect on his congressional staff. The number of telephone calls overwhelmed us. Most of them were not nice.

Mr. Bush was in Houston soon after the vote and overheard the vehemence of these calls firsthand. He calmly walked out of his office, took the receiver from the hand of his office manager, and told the caller that they should not treat his people like that, and slammed down the telephone. (By way of background, the congressman from his first day in office established rules: Staff should see that all constituent mail was responded to within forty-eight hours, preferably less. Telephone calls were to be handled politely by the appropriate staffer in the office. I guess he thought this was an exception.)

We were all proud that Congressman Bush needed to vote for the welfare of the country at large rather than cater to the prejudices and biases of some of his constituents.

*A few years later, as chairman of the Republican National Committee, George Bush would again disappoint some of his Republican colleagues and friends when after months of trying to defend President Nixon against the charges of Watergate, he advised the President of the United States he should resign. Here are excerpts from a letter he wrote to his four sons in the midst of the tumult. I took out the specifics of the scandal and skipped ahead to the lessons he wanted his sons\* to learn from Watergate:*

*July 23, 1974*

**Dear Lads,**

**We are living in "the best of times and the worst of times."**

---

\* In *All the Best*, President Bush's book of letters published in 1998, he footnoted that at the time he wrote this letter, he must have thought Doro was not old enough to deal with Watergate. She was fourteen.

You can sort out our blessings as a family. We have a close family; we have a lot of love around. You guys come home (and this sure is a blessing for Mum and me). We've got enough things. If we get sick, we can get well, probably, or at least we can afford to pay the doctor and the schools.

More blessings—you guys know no prejudice. You judge people on their worth. You give your grandmother and your parents a lot of happiness. You will do well in a world full of opportunity. Our country gives us a whale of a lot, and so we are privileged people in a privileged country. We are in the best of times.

My Dad felt strongly the firm obligation to put something into the system. He felt compelled to give, to be involved and to lead—and that brings me to the worst of times. I mean the part about Watergate and the abysmal amorality it connotes. You must know my inner feelings on this. Because of my job and because of my past associations with the President, it might well be that you don't know how I feel.

. . . It's important because as Dad helped inculcate into us a sense of public service, I'd like you boys to save some time in your lives for cranking something back in. It occurred to me your own idealism might be diminished if you felt your Dad condoned the excesses of men you knew to have been his friends or associates.

Where to begin—The President first. He is enormously complicated. He is capable of great kindness. When Dad was dying of cancer, I was leaving the Oval Office one day, having conferred on some UN matter, and I lagged behind to mention this to the President. His response was full of kindness and caring. He tried then to phone and wish Dad well . . .

You should know that I continue to respect the President for his enormous accomplishments and for some personal things too.

But you must know that I have been disappointed and disillusioned by much that has been revealed about the man from Watergate tapes and other sources . . .

I shall stop with this gratuitous advice. Listen to your conscience. Don't be afraid not to join the mob— if you feel inside it's wrong.

Don't confuse being 'soft' with seeing the other guy's point of view.

In judging your President, give him the enormous credit he's due for substantive achievements. Try to understand the 'why' of the National Security concern; but understand too that the power accompanied by arrogance is very dangerous. It's particularly dangerous when men with no real experience have it— for they can abuse our great institutions.

Avoid self-righteously turning on a friend, but have your friendship mean enough that you would be willing to share with your friend your judgment.

Don't assign away your judgment to achieve power.

These have been a tough 18 months. I feel battered and disillusioned. I feel betrayed in a sense by those who did wrong and tracked corruption and institutional subversion into that beautiful White

House. In trying to build Party, I feel like the guy in charge of the Titanic boiler room—one damn shock after another . . .

Civility will return to Washington eventually. The excesses condoned by the press will give way to reason and fair play. Personalities will change and our system will have proved that it works—more slowly than some would want—less efficiently than some would decree—but it works and gives us—even in adversity—great stability.

I expect it has not been easy for you to have your Dad be head of the RNC at this time. I know your peers must put you in funny positions at times by little words in jest that don't seem funny or by saying things that hurt you because of your family loyalty.

I can't wait to see you all in August. I'm still family champ in backgammon.

Devotedly,

Dad

*Which brings us to his presidency.*

*One of President Bush's most consequential—and courageous—decisions was the 1990 budget deal. Consequential for two reasons: (1) It later was credited for setting the stage for the economic boom of the 1990s; and (2) it probably cost George H. W. Bush the presidency.*

*Then, like now, the federal budget was seriously out of whack. Spending levels were 22 percent of the gross domestic product; revenues were only 19 percent. The President was determined to do something about it, but he had a rather large problem: He had famously promised in 1988, in his acceptance speech at the Republican Convention, he would not raise taxes. His exact words: "Read my lips—no new taxes." But the Democrats, in control of Congress, announced they would not agree to spending cuts unless the President compromised on raising revenue.*

*And there it was, THAT word: "compromise."*

*President Bush knew from Day One that the budget would be one of his bigger and more difficult challenges. He said in his inauguration speech:*

**To my friends—and yes, I do mean friends—in the loyal opposition—and yes, I mean loyal: I put out my hand. I am putting out my hand to you, Mr. Speaker. I am putting out my hand to you Mr. Majority Leader.\* For this is the thing: This is the age of the offered hand. We can't turn back clocks, and I don't want to. But when our fathers were young, Mr. Speaker, our differences ended at the water's edge. And we don't wish to turn back time, but when our mothers were young, Mr. Majority Leader, the Congress and the Executive were capable of working together to produce a budget on which this nation could live. Let us negotiate soon and hard. But in the end, let us produce. The American people await action. They didn't send us here to bicker. They ask us to rise above the merely partisan. "In crucial things, unity"—and this, my friends, is crucial.**

*We will turn the story over to former senator Rob Portman, who in 1990 was deputy assistant for Legislative Affairs on the White House staff:*

While doing advance work for Vice President Bush and then serving in his White House, I had the chance to learn from GHWB simply by watching how he conducted himself. He led by example, not by preaching.

---

\* The Speaker of the House was Jim Wright; the Senate majority leader was George Mitchell. Tom Foley would be the Speaker by June and would remain so throughout the rest of 41's presidency.

I remember a bunch of instances where 41 demonstrated his character but one stands out because the consequences were so significant.

It involves the controversial decision that many believe was the primary reason he lost his 1992 reelection campaign. Two years into his first term, in 1990, with Democrats in control of both chambers of Congress, the deficit was rising and the economy faltering. Against the advice of his political advisers, 41 decided what was best for the country was to set aside his "no new taxes" pledge, and work with Congress to achieve a budget agreement to reduce the deficit and help the economy from falling into a recession by cutting spending and raising taxes.

As a member of the Legislative Affairs team, I sat behind the President in the cabinet room for his meetings with senators, members of Congress, and his cabinet.

The advice he got from his economic team was that without action, the growing deficit and weakening economy were headed in a dangerous direction. I heard the President being told that if Congress did not act, foreign investors would pull back from US Treasuries, raising interest rates and adding to our woes. The President firmly believed that the fragile economy was going to get worse without a deficit reduction plan.

He was also told in every meeting with Democrats that with Democratic majorities in both the House and the Senate, cuts to spending—especially mandatory spending*—were possible only if there was also new revenue. It was clear that was the price to get an agreement.

The 1990 agreement, which was negotiated at Andrews Air

---

* Mandatory spending is the part of the federal budget spent on programs required by law, such as Social Security and Medicare.

Force Base, did raise income taxes but only slightly—from 28 percent to 31 percent—but relied more on other revenue raisers.* It also cut mandatory (entitlement) spending by over $100 billion, put caps on domestic discretionary spending, and provided more funding for national defense.

Despite the political fallout, 41 demonstrated political courage and character by doing what he knew was right for the country. He also showed character through his willingness to take the heat. He told members of the Republican Party that they should blame him.

**Tell them you really held your nose and that you hate that bastard in the White House,** he suggested in a closed-door meeting with Republican members of Congress. He also said he would ask Republican voters to **forgive them as they supported this wayward President**.

Although President Bush went on to lose the election in 1992, the economy did improve in the fourth quarter of the year—just not in time to convince the voters. And the deficit reduction was real, forming the basis for a balanced budget by 1998.

As always, he did the right thing for the country he had served in so many ways, so faithfully.

*We now know that President Bush was well aware of the consequences of the budget deal. As early as 1989, after meeting with a group of economists about how to fix the problem, he wrote in his diary:* **I think some of these [proposals] could mean a one-term Presidency, but it's that important for the country.**

*In 2014, a few years after this diary entry became public, he received the*

---

* For example, consumption taxes were raised, such as the gas tax. Consumption taxes are defined as taxes on what people spend and not what they earn.

*John F. Kennedy Profile in Courage Award. The citation said in part: "In order to reach the deal, Bush agreed to a tax increase as part of the compromise, and he was pilloried by conservatives for doing so. Although he recognized the 1990 budget deal might doom his prospects for reelection, he did what he thought was best for the country and has since been credited with helping to lay the foundation of the economic growth of the 1990s that followed."*

*It seems fair to give President Bush the last word on this topic. In* All the Best, *he called it the biggest challenge of his life "by far." (Maybe he forgot being shot down?) Here is what he wrote nine years after "the deal":*

**We eventually did get a budget deal, and although it was not as good as our original one, it was a major step in the direction of getting our deficit under control. Through a combination of tax increases and spending cuts, it slashed the accumulated deficit by $500 billion over five years. We also set strict limits on discretionary spending. I will confess to feeling a little vindicated in 1998 when the federal budget deficit was finally erased and a number of economists, journalists, and government officials cited "Bush's 1990 budget compromise" as the beginning of the end of our deficit problem.**★

---

★ Sadly, we know it was not the end of the "deficit problem." It has come roaring back.

# CHAPTER THREE

# JUST DO IT
## *Decisiveness*

He left a legacy of public service and character that will stand down the ages.

—*Vice President Dick Cheney*

*P*resident Bush never was much for sitting around and waiting for things to happen. Our first hint of that trait might have been when he joined the Navy in 1942 on his eighteenth birthday.

A clear example was his quick and decisive response to Saddam Hussein's invasion of Kuwait, which surprised even some of his own team members— and most likely, Saddam Hussein.

Years after the war, President Bush told his friend British journalist David Frost:

**Saddam never believed I would use force . . . maybe he read the Wimp cover in *Newsweek*; maybe he was listening to the post-Vietnam syndrome in the US as it surfaced through the lips of some senators. Whatever the reason, he miscalculated.**

Secretary Baker, Sir John Major, and former prime minister Brian Mulroney have already shared their thoughts about President Bush's leadership *through what became known as Desert Storm. Now it's time to hear from one of the men who helped execute that war, President Bush's secretary of defense, Dick Cheney.*

President George H. W. Bush held many titles in a lifetime of service, and he reflected honor on every one of them. His sense of duty was uncompromising, yet he carried himself with gentle ease and without pretense or self-regard. I count it as a great privilege of my life to have known President Bush and to have served in his cabinet as secretary of defense.

During his time in the White House, he was tested repeatedly. No one could have predicted the magnitude of historic events that would occur on his watch—the liberation of Panama, the disintegration of the Soviet Empire, the collapse of the Berlin Wall, the defense of Saudi Arabia, and the liberation of Kuwait in Desert Shield and Desert Storm. President Bush was more than equal to the challenges, managing these unprecedented global events with calmness and clear thinking, and emerging as one of the most respected statesmen of his era.

The nation was fortunate that George H. W. Bush was our President when we faced our first major crisis of the post–Cold War era— the invasion of Kuwait. From the earliest days of the crisis, he refused to ignore or pander to aggression. His clarity of purpose focused the world on the need for action. He was a tremendous leader. His wisdom had seen us through changes more significant than any of us could have imagined.

If you were to go out and design a president to be commander in chief in a crisis like Desert Storm, you would have designed someone like George H. W. Bush. His ability to match that historic moment was developed from his years of experience as a bomber pilot in World War II, a member of Congress, ambassador to the

United Nations, US liaison to China, director of the CIA, and as vice president. His knowledge and judgment gave him the foresight to know early on that facing this challenge was going to be a combined political, diplomatic, and military operation.

The team he put together upon assuming the presidency enabled him to undertake this effort with individuals around him who brought their own expertise to the table, while standing firmly behind his unequivocal leadership. I had the honor of serving him at the Pentagon, while Secretary of State James Baker, National Security Adviser Brent Scowcroft, Deputy National Security Adviser Robert Gates, and Chairman of the Joint Chiefs of Staff Colin Powell were all trusted voices. But there was never any question about who was in charge or where the buck stopped. President Bush's leadership style during this time had a rare combination of military and diplomatic experience and it proved to be an unmatched resource for the country at a pivotal moment.

During the first weekend of the Gulf crisis, he sent me out to get permission from Saudi Arabia and Egypt for the deployment of US forces on their territory. When I asked King Fahd for approval to deploy US forces to Saudi Arabia after a two-hour briefing, his response was, "Okay, we'll do it. We'll do it because I trust George Bush."

After my stops in Saudi Arabia and Egypt, I was on a flight back to the US when President Bush called me and said: **You've got to stop in Morocco.** He had just gotten hold of the king of Morocco and wanted me to stop in and brief him and get the Moroccans on board as well. Over the next several months, I visited many countries at the direction of the President to enlist other nations to join our effort. By the time US troops ultimately deployed to Iraq and Kuwait, the President had built a coalition of forty countries united in our mission to free Kuwait and defend Saudi Arabia.

Saddam Hussein had multiple opportunities over many months to comply with United Nations Security Council resolutions requiring him to withdraw from Kuwait. President Bush was determined to exhaust all possible diplomatic options, but he knew the invasion could not stand.

On January 16, 1991, President Bush announced that allied air forces had begun an attack on military targets in Iraq and Kuwait. Because of the tremendous work of our US servicemen and servicewomen, Desert Storm only lasted forty-three days. Kuwait was liberated after a six-week campaign of airstrikes and a hundred-hour ground operation that centered around the deployment of half a million US troops as part of the operation.

Another hallmark of President Bush's leadership was his love of the men and women in our armed services, and he never forgot the young soldiers under his command. At the conclusion of Desert Storm, our servicemen and servicewomen returned home with the celebration they deserved. There were many moments of high emotion and celebrations across the country. On June 8, 1991, we honored our troops in Washington. The day began with a prayer service at Arlington National Cemetery to honor the 219 souls who had not returned and to express our gratitude to the families of those who made the ultimate sacrifice. President Bush spoke about the dream of **a commonwealth of freedom** that is at the foundation of who we are as a people:

**America endures because it dares to defend that dream. That dream links the fields of Flanders and the cliffs of Normandy, Korea's snow-covered uplands, and the rice paddies of the Mekong. It's lived in the last year on barren desert flats, on sea-tossed ships, in jets streaking miles above hostile terrain. It lives because we dared to risk our most precious asset—our**

**sons and daughters, our brothers and sisters, our husbands and wives—the finest troops any country has ever had.**

When I first met President Bush in 1969, little did I know he would later play such a large role in my life and in the life of our country. He was a president who welcomed responsibility, kept his nerve, stood behind his team, and brought out the best in all of us. He left a legacy of public service and character that will stand down the ages. It was easy to feel loyalty and affection for him because he was such a thoroughly admirable and decent man. He had no illusions about politics or life, but there wasn't a trace of cynicism in him and he embodied the traits and characteristics that all Americans should aspire to.

*Colin Powell was chairman of the Joint Chiefs of Staff during Desert Storm. He talked about his commander in chief to Mary Kate Cary while she was filming 41ON41:*

He was uniquely capable and qualified for the position of the presidency...during his time as Vice President and at the CIA, he had been exposed to military operations and knew the challenges he would face and the decisions he would have to make. He also knew it from the perspective of having...fought in World War II, having been shot down. That gives anybody in the position of commander in chief a unique perspective of the sacrifices made by our young men and women as they fight the nation's battle.

...I was home watching on television that Sunday evening when he landed on the South Lawn of the White House and the reporters started shouting at him. And his simple answer: **This will not stand, this aggression against Kuwait.**

And that was my order, whether I knew it or not.

...He is very decisive. But he was only decisive after he had thought about it, and after he had been briefed by his staff. And after we had pointed out the upsides and downsides of it all. And the rest is known to history.

...He understood the military chain of command. He knew the importance of giving authority to people and empowering people. He knew he was the boss, but he wanted to empower the rest of us so that we had a structured way of dealing with this conflict. That meant a lot to me.

*Before we leave Desert Storm, I think it would be appropriate to share the letter President Bush wrote to his five children on New Year's Eve, 1990. He knew war was coming.*

**Dear George, Jeb, Neil, Marvin, Doro,**

**I am writing this letter on the last day of 1990.**

**First, I can't begin to tell you how great it was to have you here at Camp David. I loved the games (the Marines are still smarting over their 1 and 2 record), I loved Christmas Day, marred only by the absence of Sam and Ellie.\* I loved the movies—some of 'em—I loved the laughs. Most of all, I loved seeing you together. We are a family blessed; and this Christmas simply reinforced all that.**

**I hope I didn't seem moody. I tried not to.**

**When I came into this job, I vowed that I would never ring† my hands and talk about "the loneliest job in the world" or ring my hands about the "pressures or the trials."**

---

\* They had spent Christmas with their father. Doro and Billy LeBlond had divorced earlier in the year.

† Yes, the President meant "wring." He self-typed this letter on a typewriter on New Year's Eve, worried about the gathering storm clouds. My guess is there was no Wite-Out nearby.

Having said that I have been concerned about what lies ahead. There is no 'loneliness' though because I am backed by a first-rate team of knowledgeable and committed people. No President has been more blessed in this regard.

I have thought long and hard about what might have to be done. As I write this letter at Year's end, there is still some hope that Iraq's dictator will pull out of Kuwait. I vary on this. Sometimes I think he might, at others I think he simply is too unrealistic—too ignorant of what he might face. I have the peace of mind that comes from knowing that we have tried hard for peace. We have gone to the UN; we have formed an historic coalition; there have been diplomatic initiatives from country after country.

And so here we are a scant 16 days from a very important date—the date set by the UN for his total compliance with all UN resolutions including getting out of Kuwait—totally.

I guess what I want you to know as a father is this: Every Human life is precious. When the question is asked "How many lives are you willing to sacrifice"—it tears at my heart. The answer, of course, is none—none at all.

We have waited to give sanctions a chance, we have moved a tremendous force so as to reduce the risk to every American soldier if force has to be used; but the question of loss of life still lingers and plagues the heart.

My mind goes back to history:

How many lives might have been saved if appeasement had given way to force earlier on in the late '30's or earliest '40's? How many Jews might have been spared the gas chambers, or how many Polish patriots might be alive today? I look at today's crisis as "good" vs. "evil"—Yes, it is that clear.

I know my stance must cause you a little grief from time to time and this hurts me; but here at 'years-end' I just wanted you to know that I feel:

—every human life is precious—the little Iraqi kids' too.

—Principle must be adhered to—Saddam cannot profit in any way at all from his aggression and from his brutalizing the people of Kuwait.

—and sometimes in life you have to act as you think best—you can't compromise, you can't give in—even if your critics are loud and numerous.

So, dear kids—batten down the hatches.

Senator Inouye of Hawaii told me "Mr. President, do what you have to do. If it is quick and successful everyone can take the credit. If it is drawn out, then be prepared for some in Congress to file impeachment papers against you"—that's what he said, and he's 100% correct.

And so I shall say a few more prayers, mainly for our kids in the Gulf. And I shall do what must be done, and I shall be strengthened every day by our family love which lifts me up every single day of my life.

I am the luckiest Dad in the whole wide world.

I love you, Happy New Year and May God Bless every one of you and all those in your family.

Devotedly,
Dad

*As his post-presidency chief of staff, I witnessed nothing quite as dramatic as going to war. But throughout our twenty-five years together, I never ceased to be in awe of how decisive he was. If he saw something that he felt needed fixing, he immediately tried to help: visiting a synagogue to show his dismay with the rise of anti–Semitism; hosting a meeting between Houston police officers and Black pastors; inviting himself to a Muslim dinner shortly after 9/11, to assure them we did not think they were the enemy.*

*Speaking of 9/11 . . .*

*After the horrific events of September 11, 2001, President Bush was frustrated as he watched his fellow former presidents give interviews about the terrorist attacks. Wanting to stay out of the way of his son the President of the United States, he declined to do so. But what he really wanted was to DO something; not just SAY something.*

*Then he had an idea.*

*About a week after 9/11, he was supposed to fly by private plane from Kennebunkport to Houston. Commercial flights were back up and running, but no one was flying. People were terrified. So President Bush decided to set an example. He canceled his private ride to Houston; the staff booked a Continental Airlines\* flight from Boston to Houston; and he told me to ask NBC anchor Tom Brokaw if he would meet President Bush at Logan Airport in Boston.*

*Brokaw told Mary Kate Cary for her 41ON41 documentary: "He wanted to make the point it was safe to fly again . . . that was so typical of him. But this is a guy who at age eighteen was flying fighter planes off carrier decks. So he knew something about risk and bravery."*

*I asked Ned Walker, then Continental Airlines' senior vice president of Corporate Communications, to tell the rest of the story:*

The fear about what might happen next in the days following the terrorist attacks of September 11, 2001, was palpable. It was also personal for the tens of thousands of employees of the airline industry who had seen their workplaces used as weapons of mass destruction. Their fear wasn't just for their personal safety, but also for their industry's future.

---

\* Continental Airlines merged with United Airlines in 2010.

The Federal Aviation Administration had immediately halted air travel nationwide as a result of the attacks. The industry struggled to return to service after the ground stop was lifted, facing a staggering drop in customer bookings. Gordon Bethune, the CEO of Continental Airlines, was the first to act. Four days after the attack, he announced the layoff of twelve thousand employees, more than 20 percent of the company's workforce, saying the company was losing $30 million a day, as its massive fixed costs continued. He predicted that layoffs industry wide would total one hundred thousand in the coming days. Meanwhile, the government was implementing drastic security measures for commercial flights.

Flying would never be the same.

President George H. W. Bush knew all this, and also knew that the airline industry would have to revive if the nation's economy was going to do so. He wanted to demonstrate that he was not afraid to fly and show others that they could fly with confidence.

So, on September 27, 2001, he boarded a Continental flight in Boston, first giving an interview to NBC's Tom Brokaw, demonstrating confidence in flying. He spoke from Continental's lounge, aptly named the Presidents Club. Oh, and he made sure the viewers could see one of our planes outside the lounge window.

After an uneventful flight, Mr. Bethune and a crowd of grateful Continental employees and news reporters greeted him on arrival. President Bush spoke to as many as he could, accepting no help with his bag, which he threw over his shoulder.

**I think people are ready to start living again. People are going to have some inconvenience, but this is America. We are strong...**

Maybe it was easy for the man who was shot down over the Pacific in World War II and who served as commander in chief to show such resilience and calm in the wake of the 9/11 terrorist attacks. But President Bush didn't have to do what he did that day—he had a ride on a private plane! But he knew that it was the right thing to do, and he made it happen.

Typically, when President Bush flew commercially, the Secret Service picked him up planeside. Not on this day. He accompanied Mr. Bethune for a long, strong walk down the airport concourse, which was beyond a welcome sight to employees, customers, and the American public. "President Bush's magnificent gesture was a significant, early step in rebuilding public confidence in commercial air travel," Mr. Bethune remembers.

It seemed at that moment that things were going to be okay.

*One of my favorite illustrations of President Bush's quick thinking and decisiveness is his "dead or alive" phone call to Prince Bandar. I told the story in* The Man I Knew, *but I get asked a lot to "tell it again." So I think it's worth repeating, and it's a fun way to end this chapter about "just do it."*

*From* The Man I Knew:

*One night in 2012, Margaret Tutwiler—a former ambassador and top aide to former secretary of state James Baker—called me at home to ask if I knew anything about President Bush's longtime friend, Prince Bandar of Saudi Arabia, being assassinated by the Syrians. There were rumors everywhere, but she could not confirm. She asked if I could "check my sources."*

*What she wanted was for me to call the CIA, which maintained a special relationship with President Bush. After all, he once was the top boss there, and CIA headquarters in McLean, Virginia, is named "The George Bush Center for Intelligence."*

*So I called, and my point of contact told me they were aware of the rumors; they were trying to confirm; they had "boots on the ground," checking sources.*

*By noon the next day we had heard nothing. Then Margaret called to*

*update me that the French press was reporting that Prince Bandar had indeed
been assassinated.*

*This was tough news to break to President Bush. Prince Bandar had been
the Saudi ambassador to the United States from 1985 until 2003. They were
very close, and I knew President Bush would take this news hard.*

*We were sitting outside President Bush's office in Kennebunkport, enjoy-
ing the weather and going over some work when I told him. I explained that
the CIA had not yet confirmed that Bandar was dead but feared it was true
since no one had seen or heard from Bandar in months.*

*Then of course he had an idea.*

**Did you think about calling him?** *he asked me.*

*The answer would be NO. It never occurred to me to call and ask Bandar
if he were dead or alive.*

**Well, let's get him on the phone.**

*I hollered through an open window to his aide Jim Appleby and asked him
to get Bandar on the phone. Jim leaned out the window and mouthed to me,
"Haven't you told him?!"*

*"Yes, I told him," I assured Jim. "Ring his cell phone."*

*A few minutes later an incredulous Jim leaned out the window, saying
"Prince Bandar on Line 1."*

*President Bush picked up the phone and literally asked his friend,* **Hey,
Bandar, dead or alive? Everyone here thinks you are dead.**

*At some point, he covered the phone's mouthpiece and whispered to me,*
**He's alive!**

*Yes, I got that.*

*As it turns out, Bandar knew the Syrians were trying to kill him, so he
was in hiding but safe.*

*When the call was over, President Bush rang his friends James Baker and
Brent Scowcroft and assured them Bandar was alive. Then he turned to me
and said:*

*See, Jean, that's the best way to figure these things out, if you aren't sure if someone is dead or alive, call them. And if they answer, they are alive.*

And with that he triumphantly drove off on his golf cart, on his way to the house for lunch. His work here was done.

A few hours later, the very apologetic CIA officer called to tell me they still had been unable to confirm the rumor, but they feared it was true. I took a deep breath and told her Bandar was indeed alive.

"How would you know that?" she asked.

"Because President Bush called him," I replied. "Bandar confirmed he was alive."

There was a long pause, and she said, "We have to put that man back on payroll."

# CHAPTER FOUR

# THE BOSS
*Loyalty*

Living lives with honor, honesty, loyalty, and integrity were paramount to Barbara and President Bush. How to instill this back into our American discussion and life should be what drives each of us daily.

—*William Webster, former director of the FBI and CIA*

*W*hen President Bush's presidential library was close to completion, he did a final walk-through before it became too late to make changes. He was very pleased—even overwhelmed—with it all, but as soon as we got in the car for the drive back to Houston, he confided in me that one thing in particular bothered him:

**My name and photo are everywhere. It's too much about me.**

*Slightly exasperated, I pointed out that it was, after all, the George H. W. Bush Presidential Library. It was meant to be about him.*

*He said there needed to be more about the team; without the team, there would be no George H. W. Bush.*

*Without a doubt, President Bush would love that this chapter is devoted to that team.*

*And speaking of the team—I couldn't decide what the chapter's subtitle should be; that one word that best described what kind of boss George Bush was. So I did a callout and asked for help. Some of their answers: caring, inspiring, loving, forgiving, humble, benevolent.*

*And then came the word "loyalty." That was it!*

*Next problem: How to organize this chapter. I thought about trying to arrange them in the order of each person's rank—a member of President Bush's cabinet, for example, should appear before a campaign volunteer. But then I realized just how inappropriate that would be. One of the great lessons we all learned from George H. W. Bush is we are all created equal.*

*So alphabetical order it is for these stories about George Bush, the Boss. (A reminder: If you want to know a little more about everyone's life and career, it's all in the Glossary of Contributors at the end of the book.)*

Theresa "Tee" Elmore Behrendt, longtime fund-raiser and supporter:

Half a century ago a life was changed with a brief but lasting encounter.

The familiar voice was heard introducing his current guest to the assembled officials. Upon departure he happened to see a busy file clerk. Making a slight detour, RNC Chairman George Herbert Walker Bush introduced Ambassador Shirley Temple Black to the young girl.

**I want you to meet Tee Elmore, our Georgetown University intern and a rising star.**

Yes, that young girl was me. Three warm smiles were exchanged with an expression of gratitude. The moment was over, but the memory and inspiration lasted a lifetime.

George H. W. Bush, in that moment and many others, taught us all that it is what you say and do to those you meet every day that defines your character.

★ ★ ★

<u>Susan Biddle, White House photographer:</u>

A few months after we left the White House in 1993, my phone rang and much to my surprise it was President Bush calling to see how I was. After I spilled my news, he said something like this:

**Well you won't believe what I was doing this morning. I spent the morning with a closet designer who wanted to know how long my pants were, how I liked to hang them, did I have many pairs? Can you believe I'm the former leader of the Free World and today I spent my morning with a closet designer?**

He taught all of us not to take ourselves too seriously. If he didn't, nobody should.

<u>Taylor Blanton, longtime volunteer:</u>

Grace in adversity would describe the future President in 1965 when Hurricane Betsy sank a Zapata Offshore rig, one of several drilling off the coast of Louisiana. President Bush chartered a plane to take him and some of his executives to search for the rig.

I was at their house visiting Barbara when he returned that evening. He was in shock that the rig had just disappeared into the Gulf. As he related it to us, they had flown repeatedly over the area and had found no trace of what was supposed to be an unsinkable rig. Fortunately, the crew had been evacuated before the storm struck.

It was a serious financial blow to the company, which he planned to sell when he filed to run for a congressional seat in early 1966. Even though he was stunned by the loss, there was no anger, cursing, or any other reaction a less-balanced person might have exhibited. He was crestfallen but went to work the next day determined to recover from this disaster.

★  ★  ★

Phil Brady, White House staff:

I think you would call this story throwing yourself under a bus—or in this case, the boat.

Dave Demarest and I were traveling with the President when he went to Greece and Turkey to thank their leaders for their support during Desert Storm. One of our jobs was to provide the President with his remarks at a harbor event in Greece to highlight the cooperation between the two countries' navies. Our opening sentence was about how the "bow to bow almost touching of the US and Greek warships moored on the dock very well symbolized the great cooperation between the two countries during the conflict."

Unfortunately for our reputation and dangerously for our leader, the boats were stern to stern. Happily, the former Navy pilot caught the error and made the change before he delivered his remarks. International crisis averted.

Back on Air Force One, Dave and I received a handwritten note that began with:

**Dave and Phil, my resident geniuses, the bow is the pointy end of the boat . . .** But typical of the President, he gave us a hard time and then moved on, oddly, his trust in us still intact. The note highlighted his ever-present sense of humor and attention to detail.

Christopher Buckley, Vice President's staff:

I learned early on, as a speechwriter for Mr. Bush, that he was a complete marshmallow. Bear with me as I explain.

He was giving a talk at the CIA, out in Langley, where he'd served as director of Central Intelligence. We were going over the draft of his remarks. With his ever-present Sharpie, he scribbled at the top a line about how of all the flags arrayed behind his desk in the

White House, the CIA flag was the one of which he was especially proud.

To my rookie ears, this sounded like the sort of thing a politician would reflexively say. Then I watched as he said it to the hundreds of spooks* gathered in the CIA auditorium. He got so choked up he couldn't go on. I thought: "He actually meant it."

This was the first in a series of Bush blubber moments that I would observe over the years. Whenever the band struck up "The Navy Hymn"—tears, floods, cataracts. That wasn't the only song that dissolved him. The national anthem, which he probably heard hundreds if not thousands of times, would routinely cause the dam to burst.

After his mother, Dorothy, died, I asked him if he was going to speak at the private memorial at Camp David.

**No. I couldn't. If I did, I would be permanently ensconced in the Bawl Brigade.**

This was the Bush family term for those of its members prone to crying at emotional occasions. For a blue-blood, New England Yankee, Mr. Bush had the tear ducts of a Sicilian grandmother.

I was at the National Cathedral in 2004 for the memorial service for President Reagan. Mr. Bush was one of the eulogists. When he took the podium, I muttered a nervous prayer—for him—wondering how on earth he would get through it without dissolving into a puddle. He made it, though there were a few moments when I held my breath.

Sitting in those same pews fourteen years later at his funeral, I was among many who didn't make it through the tributes without drenching our handkerchiefs.

---

* A nickname for spies, or at least a nickname 41 often used.

★ ★ ★

Mary Kate Cary, speechwriter:

In his biography of President Bush, *Destiny and Power*, Jon Meacham includes this account:

"The trip from the White House to the J.W. Marriott Hotel at Thirteenth Street and Pennsylvania Avenue NW was brief. The president used the few minutes in the car to go over the speech he was about to deliver to the American Society of Association Executives at 11 a.m. on Wednesday February 27, 1991, the day the [First Persian Gulf] war ended. The subject was domestic policy, and Bush read the text with a sinking feeling. It was, he thought, a rather poor effort, full of platitudes about the American Dream and forced language about his vision for the nation at home. Looking up at Dave Demarest, the White House director of communications, Bush said, **You don't expect me to read this shit, do you?**

"Demarest tried to laugh it off, but the president was serious. Pushing his way through the speech at the hotel, Bush was horrified at the silence in the room. **It fell flat**, he dictated [to his diary]. **Not one clap of applause.** Returning to the White House, Bush told [Chief of Staff] John Sununu that the entire episode was **frankly quite embarrassing**." (End of Meacham excerpt.)

It's very difficult for me to read that passage because I was the author of that speech.

I had gone to the speech that day, riding over to the J. W. Marriott in the back of the presidential motorcade and standing in the rear of the room. As the event started, the President received a warm welcome from the audience. This was his first big domestic policy speech since the start of the war, which had ended that very day. Everyone in the domestic policy side of the administration, the cabinet, and on Capitol Hill seemed to want to get their two cents into it. There were more meetings about what they hoped would be "the domestic Desert Storm" speech than any other one I had written, and the stakes were high. As he started speaking, I was nervous.

As the speech unfolded, the applause stopped. For the rest of the speech, not one person clapped. It was horrible, and the twenty-minute speech felt like it lasted for days.

When the President finished, those of us on the White House staff headed with the President to a freight elevator offstage, which would take us to an underground parking garage where the motorcade was waiting. Several dozen of us crammed in, and as the giant elevator doors closed, there was an uncomfortable silence.

The President broke the silence: **Mary Kate! What the hell just happened in there?** I shrank behind a towering Secret Service agent and, choking back tears, said simply, "I don't know, sir. I'm so sorry."

Most speechwriters would have been fired after a debacle like that. When we got back to the White House, I got word that Dave Demarest, my boss, wanted to see me in his West Wing office.

"Here it comes," I thought.

Instead, Dave suggested I write a memo to the President titled, "Silence Is Golden," listing all the great quotes over the centuries about the value of silence. I crowdsourced it with all the researchers, who found gems such as the Taoist Lao-tzu's "Silence is a source of great strength," and Mother Teresa's "God is the friend of silence." It was funny. We sent it in.

Nothing happened, and I got assigned more speeches. I was astonished. I had been given a rare second chance. I didn't know why.

The next time I was reviewing a speech with him, President Bush asked me, **So are people going to clap this time?** I told him from now on I'd sit up front and lead the applause for every speech of his.

He laughed. I was serious.

To this day, I continue to believe the members of that audience were heavily medicated, comatose to the point of paralysis, and physically unable to applaud. And President Bush continued to tease me about it for decades.

In the silence of that ballroom so long ago, I learned a lot from George Bush: humility, humor, and grace. Some guys would have let the speechwriter go, but he didn't. He stuck with me. That taught me to give people a second chance.

I learned other things from him about a life well lived—not just about trusting people, but about not bragging, about making and keeping good friends, about laughing at yourself, and about treating everyone with the same dignity and respect, whether they are the Queen of England or the cook in the kitchen. Or a young female speechwriter just starting out.

And so the lesson stuck with me: that out of cringe-inducing, humiliating failure can come years of laughter, a wonderful speech-writing career, and a lifelong friendship. Now I know why I was given that second chance so long ago. For the rest of my life, I'll be grateful to George Bush.

Jim Cicconi, White House staff:

So many people wonder why George Bush never said publicly that "the Cold War is over," even though it definitely ended on his watch.

I was one of a few on the White House staff who argued that he should do this. After the fall of the Berlin Wall, GB famously said (in private) that he wasn't going to go "dance on the wall," largely because of how it would embarrass and pressure Gorbachev.

But by spring of 1990 it was very clear that the danger from

Soviet Russia was receding fast. Yeltsin was rising, and Gorbachev had far more pressures than he could handle.

My job was to process all incoming info for the President, including national security information. The latest assessments seemed to underscore the point, and I was about to take them upstairs to the President.

This is where personal feelings impact policy, I suppose. I felt strongly that George Bush had a huge role in bringing about this historic moment. Plus, unabashedly, I'd grown up in politics as a Jim Baker protégé, and I knew 41's reelection was not a sure thing. But a video clip of him declaring, "The Cold War is over," with the strong implication that he had won the war, would be an electoral home run.

I'd been having a genial debate on this with Brent Scowcroft for months, one of the most wonderful men I worked with in government. But Brent was cautious; I was in my thirties and full of myself. He was reluctant; I pushed. Then we both found ourselves in the Oval as I came in with the latest intel dispatches.

President Bush read them as I stood there, waiting to be dismissed. But it didn't happen. President Bush kind of shook his head at the gravity of the news, and I saw my moment. I said, "Mr. President, this might be a proper time to declare that the Cold War is over. I know some folks will say 'politics,' but I do think there's a duty to history here."

The President looked at me, then at the intel, then looked at Brent.

**Y'know, Brent, I think Jim might have a point here. What do you think?**

Brent hunched his shoulders, a modest kind of gesture that was always endearing to his listeners, then said, "If you want to, Mr.

President, we can do that. I just wonder what the Chinese will think..."

**That we might be ganging up on them...**

"Yes, sir."

**Thanks, Jimmy,** he said, handing me back the folder.

So close. As we left the Oval Office I looked at Brent and said, "Awww, c'mon, Brent," at which he smiled and said, "All's fair."

I can still see his little grin. But he was right. I was cloaking a political argument in a duty to history. Brent saw that and brought the President back to thinking about his duty. Not that he ever needed much reminding.

George Bush always put duty and country above politics. Brent knew that, and I learned it in those few minutes. Doing what I urged would've helped him immensely in 1992, but that wasn't how George Bush was wired. Not when his country's interests were somewhere else.

Les Csorba, White House staff:

One of my favorite personal memories of 41 was taking my father, a 1956 Hungarian Freedom Fighter, to the last Bush White House Christmas party in 1992. Still bruised from the President's defeat just weeks earlier, I was taken by surprise by the meaning of this moment—I was escorting my father, a blue-collar construction worker, to meet a President. Both these men had risked their lives in the fight for freedom versus tyranny. One was shot down in 1944 and found himself floating in the Pacific in a life raft surrounded by enemy forces. Years later, the other was tossing Molotov cocktails at Soviet tanks and fleeing deportation trains taking Hungarian teenagers to labor camps in Siberia.

As we approached the President and the First Lady in the

receiving line, I panicked: "What is Dad going to say?" With just an eighth-grade education, he sometimes had difficultly articulating his thoughts. I was nervous for him. But I let it go, allowing the moment to occur on its own. After they were introduced, my father, still speaking in a heavy Hungarian accent (he sounded a lot like Arnold Schwarzenegger), said, "Thank you for what you did to liberate my country and my people."

Without hesitation, the President pulled him in closer and said: **And thank you for all you did, sir.**

It was perfect: The one who took on the brutal tanks of the Soviet Empire and crawled across the Austrian border to come to America was now standing next to the statesman who had ended the Cold War.

In calling my dad "sir," I was profoundly moved by the President's graciousness and gratitude. A photo was quickly snapped, and we were escorted to the next room. The photograph became one of my father's prized keepsakes, but the moment remains one of my life's precious possessions: a tribute to the two heroes in my life.

Dante DeLorenzo, summer lad:*

No matter who you are, or what you do, you are never too big to serve others.

All his life, President Bush always found time to serve his community and his country. Whether it be his lifelong career in public service, volunteering for the Navy right after his eighteenth birthday during World War II, or his countless charitable organizations, President Bush always found time to put others before himself.

---

* President Bush's nickname for the high school and college boys hired every summer to do odd jobs at Walker's Point.

Throughout high school and college, I was involved in several groups that focused on community service and engagement because President Bush taught me the importance of giving back.

David Demarest, White House staff:

In January 1993, after President Bush left office, I found myself unemployed. Two old friends of mine (Ken Smith and Brian Tierney) put me on modest retainers with their firms to help me pay my mortgage. These were friends at a time when friends are needed most.

While I was working at Ken's firm one day, the receptionist came into my office and said, "There's someone on the phone who says he's George Bush. Who do you think it is?" I chuckled and said, "It's probably George Bush." She raced back to her desk, flustered, and transferred him to me.

The President got right into it:

**Dave, it's time for me to get out there and make some money. Probably the best thing I can do is some speeches. How much does a speechwriter get for writing a speech?**

I said, "Sir, you don't have to pay anyone to do a speech for you. There are a lot of talented folks more than willing to do it gratis."

He insisted: **Really, how much is the going rate?**

I could see he was like a dog with bone, so I replied, "Sir, the going rate is more than anyone should pay for a speech. I heard one writer say she was getting $5,000, and that's ridiculous."

**Well, would you be willing to do some writing for me?**

I said that of course I would, but before I could continue, he said:

**Then it's settled, $5,000. Come on down to Houston and let's talk about it.**

I thought, "That sly dog. He knows I'm out of a job, and this is his way of helping me out. Pretty smooth."

I flew down to Houston and was directed to show up at the home where he and Mrs. Bush were living temporarily. It was evening, and a torrential rainstorm was underway. I could see a car in the driveway with people in it, and I assumed they were Secret Service. But no one got out. I waited in the car in front of the house wondering what to do—should I just go knock on the front door? That seemed like a prescription for getting roughed up by an agent lurking in the bushes. Undeterred, I walked up to the door and rang the bell, expecting anyone but the President to answer. Wrong.

**Hi, Dave, good to see you, come on in. Pardon the mess. We're pretty much buried in boxes. What can I get you?**

Okay, this was just surreal—"What can I get you?"! This man was President of the United States just a few days ago.

"Sure. What are you drinking?"

I thought: "Where are the stewards, the staff?" He was playing greeter, bartender, and party host. Quite a new reality for an ex-President.

I stammered something about a scotch, and he was on it, opening box after box. The more he rooted around in the kitchen, the weirder it got. I had to intervene to put a stop to his search, so I amended my request to a beer. That he had in the fridge.

I took a lesson from this odd moment. This was not just his "style," it was who he was: relatable, gracious, sociable, warm. I saw how comfortable this man was in his own skin. Never taking himself too seriously, never looking in the rearview mirror, always looking forward. Rare qualities then, rarer today.

But that was only half of it. He got genuine satisfaction from helping others. He was thoughtful and caring, but by means of being quiet and unpretentious.

The following day I met with him in his office and talked

speeches. I ended up doing his first domestic speech and his first international speech—each for the absurd price of $5,000.

Barbara Hackman Franklin, cabinet secretary:

In 1972, while I was in the Nixon White House, I met George and Barbara Bush for the first time.

He was our ambassador to the United Nations. My job was spearheading President Nixon's effort to advance women in the federal government.

During the 1972 campaign, I gave Ambassador Bush some campaign buttons—NIXON with the female symbol through the O. He wrote me a very supportive, handwritten note, thanking me for the "absolutely essential buttons." The fact that he understood what I was doing and encouraged me really counted. Not every man I met back then was so inclined.

In 1992, as secretary of commerce, I traveled to China at the request of the President, becoming the first member of the cabinet to visit China following the events in Tiananmen Square in 1989. Both the political left and right were angry with China, and many did not want the US-China relationship normalized and the economic relationship renewed. And, of course, Clinton, who had just won the election, had been critical of President Bush's posture toward China during the campaign.

Needless to say, I was taking some major hits in the press.

The President's handwritten note, dated December 22, 1992:

**Well Done in China. Don't worry about the chicken criticism. You did the right thing. You got some business, and you did what I asked you to do and did it well. The critics are my regular carping critics who hate my policy. You just got caught up in that. So thanks! Have a great Christmas.**

This note made a huge difference to me because, frankly, I was feeling a bit bruised. What made it worse was that there was no time to explain what we had accomplished because we all left office just weeks later. His message underscores that doing the right thing is always the right thing regardless of the hits one takes.

George H. W. Bush's standards were high and his integrity was impeccable. He was ever gracious, kind, and humble.

### C. Boyden Gray, White House staff (from *41ON41*):

He made it easy for me to be the ethics officer of the White House because his ethics were so much better expressed than mine... The President never raised his voice, that I recall, and never really lost his temper. He would just give this look—this withering look—and people would just quake, and that would be the end of the conversation usually.

*Boyden died while I was writing this book. When I heard his daughter, Eliza Gray Summers, tell this story—one of 41's favorites—in the eulogy of her father, I asked her if I could put it in this book.*

"At a long national security meeting at the White House, the team was getting restless. Brent Scowcroft had fallen asleep.* My father watched as a note from President Bush made its way slowly around the table. When it reached him, Dad saw his name on it. He sat up straight in his chair, preparing himself to read an important note from the President. He opened it. It said, 'Question: How do you titillate an ocelot?'

---

* Brent, who worked impossible hours, was famous for nodding off during meetings. President Bush established the Brent Scowcroft Award and gave it out annually to the member of his team who 1) fell asleep the most soundly during a meeting and 2) had a good "recovery," meaning they woke up and pretended they were awake the whole time.

"A minute later, another note made its way down the table.

"It said, 'Answer: You oscillate the tit a lot.'

"A weakness for blue humor was a trait my father shared with the forty-first president. That—and a fondness for driving speedboats dangerously fast along the coast of Maine."

Joe Hagin, White House staff:

One of my most powerful memories of 41 comes from a staff meeting held the morning after Ronald Reagan's 1981 inauguration, our first official day in the White House. We assembled in the beautiful huge and ornate ceremonial office of the vice president, in the Old Executive Office Building, just across the driveway from the West Wing of the White House.

We were excited, somewhat in awe, and a little intimidated by our surroundings.

41 was typically gracious and welcoming, thanking us all for joining his team. Toward the end of his remarks to the staff he grew somewhat stern as he outlined his expectations. He explained that we were there to support President Reagan, his staff, and his agenda. That there would be no alternate agendas coming out of the vice president's office, no second guessing, and above all no leaking. We were there to support the President, period.

He closed his remarks with a thought that I carried with me all of my years working in the White House, and that I have passed on to young staffers. He spoke of the great honor and privilege that it was to work on behalf of the American people and the President in the White House complex; how special it was and how blessed we were to be working there. He challenged us all by saying that every morning when we walked through those White House gates, if we did not experience a sense of awe and respect for where we were and what we were doing, if we began to take it all for granted, that should be a sign to us that it was time to move on to another job, in another place.

## Ede Holiday, White House staff:

He taught all of us the lesson of the importance of humor when the weight of the world is on your shoulders, and how personal interaction and social graces can change everything.

One day at the White House a hand-typed invitation was sent to only the women on his senior staff:

**You and You alone, no spouse, no friends, are invited to a dinner in the residence.**

We, of course, were thrilled. When we got off the elevator in the White House residence, we were greeted with a woven rug with a portrait of HIM! It was the gift of some Chinese official, and we all laughed.

The dinner was about ten or so of us, all women except the President and Brent Scowcroft. Believe me, our fellow male senior staffers would have loved to have been there.

But it was his way of validating that we were important to him and valued. To my knowledge the unique invitation and dinner were never reported in the media.

## Cynthia Johnson, vice presidential staff photographer:

I was on the plane with him when he got the word that President Reagan had been shot. When we landed at Andrews, some people—including the Secret Service, citing security concerns—felt he should helicopter to the White House, landing on the South Lawn as only the President does. But the Vice President made the decision that he would chopper to the Naval Observatory* and motorcade to the White House from there. He didn't want to jump into the White House as though he was ready to take over. Hello, Al Haig!† Decorum. That was George Bush.

Ron Kaufman, White House staff:

In late 1977 I was searching for a candidate for President that I could support in 1980.

Ambassador Bush was coming to Boston to speak to a group of students at Harvard. I somehow managed to sneak in the back door.

I was blown away by his mastery of the issues, both domestic and foreign policy. Not to mention his extraordinary life experiences. But it was his answer to one of the last questions that made me fall in love. One bright young lad (as 41 would say) got up and said:

"Ambassador Bush, you have had an amazing life. Yale baseball team captain, successful businessman, congressman, RNC chair, ambassador to the United Nations, envoy to China, head of the CIA. Which of all the experiences were you most proud of?"

He answered without hesitation: **That's an easy one. My kids always come home.**

He had me for the next forty-five years!

Politics and governing can be an all-consuming career. Especially if you are blessed with working for a great American and end

---

* Official residence of the Vice President.

† Secretary of State Al Haig raised eyebrows the day of the Reagan assassination attempt when he walked into the White House Briefing Room and declared he was in charge.

up in the White House—I mean the White House! Putting it all in proper perspective is almost impossible.

But through it all, my compass always remembered: My kids always come home.

Bobbie Greene Kilberg, White House staff:

In December 1988, the President-elect invited me to his office to offer me the position of deputy assistant to the President for Public Liaison. I was deeply honored and excited, but I had to tell him that I could not imagine taking on such responsibilities with five children, the youngest being only one year old.

George H. W. Bush sat me down to explain how he was committed to having senior women on his White House staff and throughout the government. We discussed in depth how we were going to make this work. Somehow, we were going to control my work hours and my specific assignments by having the best backup staff in the White House.

He noted that the daily 7:30 a.m. senior staff meeting could usually be attended by my deputy since those sessions were really just show and tell. He would try to keep my working in the office on the weekends to a minimum—and largely succeeded in doing so. He also said that I could avoid overnight trips on Air Force One by taking the trips to Peoria and leaving the exciting international and West Coast trips to my staff, which made me the most sought-after boss in the White House. Further, he encouraged me to bring my kids to as many official White House events run by my office as possible so they would understand why what their mother was doing was so important.

The President-elect said he realized that I would never be part of the "inner circle" who were always there very late into the night.

The very nature of the balancing act of working directly for a President while raising five kids precluded that. (My husband, Bill, was hugely helpful as a dad, but still...) He said he knew this was a trade-off that women with children had to make all the time and men rarely had to make. But he was determined to set an upward path for women and wanted me to say yes and participate in that. I did say yes, and the four years with POTUS 41 were the absolute highlight of my professional life.

Keep in mind he was nearly sixty-five years old when he became President. I cannot think of many other men in that era, of that age, and of that generation who genuinely thought that way and who put their commitment into practice. Only a person of exceptional caring and character would have taken the time to consider me and to always check in over the four years to make sure it was working. He genuinely cared.

Lucy Lamb, White House staff:

I wasn't senior staff, but President Bush treated all of his staff with such respect and created an atmosphere that it felt like everyone was on a level playing field. Case in point: His personal penned letters. I have seven. I treasure each and every one but especially the one dated October 6, 2010, where he responded to an invitation to attend my father's funeral at Arlington Cemetery. President Bush wrote:

**I cannot join you and yours on October 12, but I will be there in spirit saluting a great American who served his country and who loved his family.**

President Bush was a true patriot who appreciated our military and understood the price of freedom.

★   ★   ★

John Magaw, director of the US Secret Service from 1992 to 1993*
(from *41ON41*):

One of the things that was very important to the Secret Service
and endeared both Mrs. Bush and the President [to us] was that on
any holiday it was always important to them that the agents who
were going to be traveling with them had time with their family.
So on Christmas or Thanksgiving they would never leave to go to
Kennebunkport, or go to Texas, wherever they might be going...
they would never leave until the evening to give [us] time with our
families.

*Fred McClure, head of legislative affairs for President Bush, writes about his
veto of the Civil Rights Act of 1990. It was a controversial decision, as sup-
porters felt it would have made it easier for litigants in discrimination cases to
win. However, Harvard law professor Charles Fried, in a* New York Times
*op-ed, called the bill "a public relations flimflam perpetrated by a cabal of over-
zealous civil rights plaintiffs' lawyers." He concluded by saying that the Presi-
dent should "veto this bill in its present form."*

*Here is Fred's take:*

Our argument against the bill was that the changes would force
employers to adopt quotas for hiring women and minorities to
avoid costly litigation on charges of discrimination. The Supreme
Court cases had limited the rights of employees who had sued their
employers for discrimination. The proposed legislation was intended
to reverse these decisions by changing the burden of proof, making

---

* Technically, President Bush would not have been John's boss. But of course John
would say he was.

it easier for litigants. Our argument was that if the burden of proof was changed, business would react simply by adopting quotas and say, "Look at our numbers. We're off the hook."

The challenge for the administration was that we got somewhat boxed in because it was named "civil rights legislation." The Congressional Black Caucus had come unannounced—though not to the press—to the Northwest Gate of the White House and asked not to see the President but me. Not only was I responsible for the President's congressional relations, but I was also the highest-ranking Black at the White House. It was my longest walk ever to the gate. As I met the caucus, cameras flashed.

It was a Friday, and the President had gone to Camp David. Early Saturday morning I got a phone call from him. He was really concerned.

**Did you see the paper this morning?**

I said, "No, sir, I'm not up yet. I haven't gone out to get the paper."

**Well, we probably need to talk, but I'm just going to go ahead and tell you that I hope that this is not putting you in a very difficult position because of what we're doing on the civil rights legislation.**

He was looking at the *Washington Post* and saw me above the fold receiving this petition from the members of the Congressional Black Caucus. The President cared deeply enough about me personally that he called to inquire about my emotional well-being. And then he followed up with this handwritten note:

**Dear Fred,**

    **You and I have not discussed the Civil Rights Bill. Let me just say for certain I know this has not been easy for you. I can guarantee you that it's a tough one for me, but I have been thinking about you, and**

**Lou Sullivan, Connie, and Art.*** **I hate to see friends troubled and hurt.**

**Fred, you are doing an outstanding job, and I hate to see your life complicated by something of this nature as I assume it is.**

> **Hang in,**
> **Warm regard,**
> **GB**

The President's empathy—his ability to understand and share my feelings—was a hallmark of his character. His loyalty to those of us who were acting on his behalf was demonstrated by his reaching out directly to share his concerns.

Brad Mitchell, White House staff:

President Bush was always thinking about others, how they were doing, and how he could bring them together as one team. No matter if you were a junior staffer (like me) or a senior aide, he made you feel like a special and important member of his team with a role to play.

It was a cold, rainy Saturday in March 1989 and I was working in my office when President Bush's personal secretary, Patty Presock, let me know that President Bush and his family were going to watch a movie in the family theater that afternoon, and the President was inviting folks working that Saturday to join him if they could take a break.

So that afternoon, with about ten other staffers, I watched a movie with the President and Mrs. Bush in the White House theater.

---

* Dr. Louis Sullivan was secretary of Health and Human Services. Connie Newman was the director of the Office of Personnel Management. Art Fletcher was chairman of the Civil Rights Commission.

It was gestures such as this that helped build a collegial, collaborative, and high-performing White House team that would serve the country well in the coming months and years. It's a lesson I use in my work with CEOs and C-suite executive leadership teams to this day.

Larry Mohr, White House physician:

On Sunday afternoon, April 26, 1992, I was on Marine One, returning to the White House from Camp David with President and Mrs. Bush. Also on board was the President's grandson George P. Bush, whose birthday was the previous Friday. During the flight President Bush reached into his briefcase and handed some note cards and a pen to his grandson. He then proceeded to tell George P. to write a thank-you note to each person who had given him a gift for his birthday. He also instructed his grandson to write the notes during the thirty-minute flight, so he could send them right after returning to the White House.

Those who knew President Bush knew that he was a prolific note writer. Most of these notes were written to his numerous friends in acknowledgment of how much their friendships meant to him. I loved that he was teaching this important personal quality to his grandson that Sunday afternoon.

The President's lesson of that day made a huge impact on me, as well. It helped me to understand the importance of acknowledging, cultivating, and celebrating the many friendships that have blessed my own life.

Ginny Mulberger, White House staff:

Rather than tell one of my many stories, I'd like to share a letter that President Bush wrote to my son in 2005, when he was eight. John had written him a note asking him why he wanted to be President.

In a simple handwritten letter, President Bush demonstrated what his motivation was throughout his life: to do good.

> **Dear John,**
>
> **You asked me a tough question. I am not sure how I got interested in becoming President.**
>
> **I did a lot of different government jobs— Congressman, UN Ambassador, envoy to China, Chairman of the Republican National Committee, Director of Central Intelligence—and then Vice President.**
>
> **When Vice President, I had already run for President, losing to President Reagan. As Vice President, I felt I could help the country and do good things as President. So I ran again in 1988 and won, and I loved it.**
>
> **Good luck to you, John.**
>
> **George Bush**

*In July 1989, the President of the United States stopped in Poland and Hungary en route to the G7 Economic Summit in Paris. Democracy was on the move in both countries, "busting out all over," as President Bush wrote in his diary.*

*Bonnie Newman of the White House staff shares a very specific memory from the trip:*

Throughout the trip the crowds were enormous, with people lining streets, hanging from windows, waving flags, and tossing flowers in the path of the motorcade. It was overwhelming to behold as Eastern Europe surged toward freedom and the Berlin Wall teetered.

Our flight into Budapest was delayed due to the weather. As evening fell, we landed as torrents of rain blew across the tarmac. Remaining on the plane to change into an evening dress for the state dinner, which was to follow a welcoming ceremony in Kossuth Square, I arrived just as the President, in the pouring rain, stepped forward to speak.

What appeared to be tens of thousands of people—soaked to the skin from waiting all day in the rain—went wild, vociferously applauding and cheering the President.

It was a chilling and thrilling scene to behold, even as the evening grew increasingly wet and dark. As the President stepped forward and tried to quiet the cheering crowd, an older woman in the front of the crowd caught his attention. She was drenched. Suddenly, the President, also drenched, removed his raincoat, handed it to one of the nearby Secret Service agents, and motioned toward the soaked woman. The crowd went wild!*

As an observer in that moment, I could not have been prouder of the man who was our President.

For the rain-drenched Hungarian people, who had stood for hours waiting to welcome the American President, they bore witness in that moment to the soul of the man and to the spirit of America. It was love at first sight.

Years later, while serving as the executive dean at Harvard's Kennedy School, I shared the story of this experience with students during a seminar on public service. My purpose was to illustrate the

---

* An addendum to this story, as told by the President's aide Tim McBride: The coat actually belonged to a Secret Service agent, who had given it to the President. I had left the President's raincoat on Air Force One. The President gave the agent money for a new coat and a signed photo of him wearing the coat.

noble nature of public service and the impact of soft power on the lives and freedoms of people around the world.

After I returned to my office, my assistant told me one of the students asked to speak with me. As I recall, his name was Peter Szoldan. He wanted to share that as a teenager, he, too, had been in Kossuth Square on that dark and rain-swept night!

He explained that his father brought him and his brother from their village to Budapest—despite the distance and the weather—because he felt it important that they see and hear the President from the United States of America, who he felt was a beacon of freedom and opportunity.

For Peter, the night proved to be transformative. He recalled how listening to the President and seeing the response of the Hungarian people inspired him to reach for what could be.

More than a decade later, I was awed by the serendipity that had brought this young Hungarian, now a student at Harvard University, and me together and our memories, gratitude, and admiration for the man we called Mr. President.

A man who one dark night in Budapest inspired a nation and at least one of its children to shed the shadow of communism and search for knowledge, for freedom, and for opportunity.

Gregg Petersmeyer, White House staff:

If empathy is the ability to understand what another person is experiencing and feeling, and compassion is taking action to help, George Bush was equally brilliant and accomplished at both.

Two important times in my life I experienced George Bush's empathy and compassion for me. The first came after Watergate when Bush was in China. The second came fifteen years later when I was in a dark place and needed much greater help.

Two months after President Nixon resigned, President Ford sent Bush to China. In the summer of 1975, he and Barbara invited me to come and stay with them for a month. Our paths had crossed lightly but repeatedly during the Nixon years while he held important positions and I was just starting out. But he liked young people, and we became friends.

In the months that followed Watergate, Bush and I corresponded frequently. He knew the depth of my disappointment in Nixon's culpability in the Watergate cover-up and how dispirited I was by the viciousness Watergate had unleashed in Washington and in politics generally.

So in one of his notes, George Bush raised the idea of my coming to stay with him for a while in China. I was by then a graduate student at Oxford, and I know Bush thought it would be a kind of resetting experience for me. He had zero responsibility to do such a thing, but he knew I was hurting.

At dinner one evening, seemingly out of the blue, although in hindsight I realized it wasn't an accident, George Bush said: **I don't care if I ever see Richard Nixon again. He lied to me, and friends don't lie to friends.**

The first sentence got my attention. It was its purpose, I'm sure, since Bush did see Nixon again (and he probably knew he would). It was the second sentence that was the real message and here is why I think George Bush decided to tell me this that evening: It was to help me sort out my loyalty to Nixon; he knew I needed permission to let go of those parts of loyalty that are not required.

George Bush felt strongly that trust is the foundation of a friendship. Lying to a friend is unacceptable. In a powerful and shorthand way, that is what George Bush was saying to me at dinner that night. He knew it would help me, and it did.

Fast-forward twelve years later to a Sunday afternoon in the fall of 1987. I was living in Denver, having moved there from New York a few years earlier to join a new energy company. My phone rang, and on the other end of the line was Vice President George Bush.

He was calling to ask me to be his Colorado state chairman for his 1988 presidential campaign. I was very surprised. I had attended a few meetings about the election with Neil Bush, who then was living in Colorado and to whom Bush had introduced me when I moved there. I had no experience running a statewide presidential campaign, not to mention one in a high-risk swing state. Moreover, I didn't really know people in Colorado and with considerable demands at home and at work, I had no free time.

When George Bush picked up the phone at the Vice President's residence that Sunday, none of these things mattered to him. Although I didn't realize it at the time, the call was not about me helping George Bush. It was about George Bush helping me.

In early 1985, my wife had died at the age of thirty-three of a long and devastating illness. We had three children, all under the age of five. Two years later, I was still putting on a brave face. The children were doing well under the circumstances, but putting one foot in front of the other was about all that still seemed possible for me at the time.

When the Vice President called me that Sunday afternoon, he mentioned none of this, but he knew all of it. How did he know? Because his life had been shattered by death when the Bushes' daughter Robin died of leukemia at age three.

He knew how hard it was to stay positive with the bone-crushing pain that would come in bigger waves than anything you could have imagined yourself withstanding.

George Bush picked up his phone and called me because he wanted to help me move forward. I said yes.

After the election, I agreed to move to Washington with my three children to join President-elect George Bush's White House staff as an assistant to help him establish Points of Light as a part of his presidency.

It was the greatest honor of my life to head up this important initiative for him.

Advancing the very idea of Points of Light itself took character on the part of George Bush. In the beginning (and in some quarters, for quite a while), the idea of Points of Light was satirized. But Bush stuck with it from his inauguration forward, and he never stopped. He saw the challenge as being about a movement and not a program. A constant refrain from him was: **From now on in America, any definition of a successful life must include serving others.** As President, he created the first White House Office of National Service, to keep presidential leadership focused on service; created a nonpartisan and nongovernmental foundation with the help of some of the most prominent leaders in America called Points of Light; signed the bipartisan National and Community Service Act of 1990; and became the first President to each day formally recognize and thank a different individual somewhere in America voluntarily making a difference. The Daily Point of Light Award is still given out today, honoring more than seven thousand volunteers.

Less than two weeks before President Bush left office, the White House released a report called: "The Points of Light Movement: The President's Report to the Nation." Here is what George Bush wrote in his cover letter accompanying his report:

**Points of Light are the soul of America. They are ordinary people who reach beyond themselves to touch the lives of those in need, bringing hope and opportunity, care, and friendship. By giving so generously of themselves, these remarkable**

**individuals show us not only what is best in our heritage but what all of us are called to become.**

George Bush was that person for me, and for all of us. He would be so proud that Points of Light is thriving today. And we should all be grateful for the legacy of service he left behind.

<u>Roger Porter, White House staff:</u>

Even in the midst of an international crisis, a president's other responsibilities must continue.

After Iraqi troops poured across the border into neighboring Kuwait in August 1990, President Bush spent much of his August "vacation" in Kennebunkport meeting with a succession of leaders and advisers and putting together a coalition to reverse the aggression. But he still had to attend to other concerns.

So one day in August a call came to me and Dick Darman, the director of the Office of Management and Budget (OMB), that the President would like a day of briefings on economic and domestic policy. We left the next morning, and I dressed—as I did each workday—in a suit, white shirt, and tie. Dick was dressed in an open-collar shirt and sport coat. Preoccupied with the substance of the briefings, I thought little of his casual appearance.

When we arrived at Walker's Point* it became apparent to me that casual dress was the order of the day and that my business attire was unique. I had not brought a change of clothes since we would

---

* President and Mrs. Bush's summer home in Kennebunkport, Maine. It was purchased by President Bush's maternal grandfather, George Herbert Walker, in 1900. Shortly before he became Vice President of the United States, President Bush bought it from his uncle Herbie Walker, which prevented his widow from selling it to the Howard Johnson hotel chain. Walker's Point is now owned by the five Bush children.

be traveling back to Washington late that evening. I felt overdressed and out of place.

As we entered his residence, the President was seated at the far end of the living room. Others were beginning to assemble for the meetings that would begin in a few minutes. Quickly sensing my overdressed situation, George H. W. Bush strode across the room, took me by the arm, and ushered me into their ground-floor bedroom. He began opening drawers, pulling out polo shirts of various colors. Soon he found one he thought would look good on me and said:

**What do you think of this color? We will be pitching some horseshoes later this afternoon and you will feel more comfortable in this. You are welcome to leave your jacket and tie in here. We won't be starting the meeting for another five or ten minutes.**

He did not comment on my lack of forethought or that I was overdressed, but graciously sought to make me feel comfortable and at home. He helped me deal with a potentially embarrassing situation in a quiet and unobtrusive way.

All of us have found ourselves in embarrassing situations from time to time. The embarrassment usually does not last long and is quickly forgotten, but now, many years later, I still remember his thoughtfulness and kindness. It is the kind of help that a friend extends when they are sensitive to our needs, however modest those needs may be. It was a gesture that taught me a great lesson about how we should treat one another.

Mary Matthews Raether, congressional staff:

Mr. Bush was only the second Republican member of the House of Representatives to appoint a female legislative assistant. When I attended my first House committee meeting with Congressman

Bush, I took a notebook so I could do a write-up of the proceedings for our files. After the meeting Mr. Bush suggested I not take notes in the future as he did not want the others to think I was a secretary.

I learned that Mr. Bush intentionally named a woman to the job and that he intended to help me meet both our expectations for my future. He was the best boss I would ever have. He always saw the best in everyone and made sure we all had a chance to prove what we could do.

There was no better example of that than his relationship with Don Rhodes, who had been a volunteer in President Bush's 1966 congressional campaign and never looked back. Don was extremely hard of hearing and was a bit of a curmudgeon. He was famous for wearing the same scruffy blue jacket every day. But he was intelligent and indispensable to the Washington congressional office where he was a staffer.

When the Bushes realized how difficult Don's hearing was, Bar took him to a number of hearing specialists who all told the same story—not much could be done.

The relationship was unbreakable. Don was a third parent to the younger children whose parents were often on the road. He controlled the family checkbook, and during the Bush presidency, had unlimited access to any place in the White House. Don worked for the Bushes until he died in 2011.

The intense loyalty worked both ways. The Bushes spread Don's ashes over their own gravesite. He was, after all, family.

Sig Rogich, White House staff:

After I accepted the job in the White House, I was contacted by the CBS Sports director, Mort Sharnick. He said that George Foreman was going to come out of retirement, and Foreman's team wanted me to be an investor in the franchise. With my background as a longtime member and chairman of the Nevada State Athletic Commission, which governs boxing in our state, I think they thought I could be helpful.

I said I was flattered but that I couldn't do any business now because I was going to work in the White House. Foreman went on to win a few hundred million dollars with all of his endeavors. I would have had a significant piece of all of that.

The very next day Mike Agassi, who is tennis great Andre Agassi's father, called and said: "Andre will be turning pro and we would like you to oversee all of his endorsements."

I told him the same thing. Andre went on to become a superstar and made a fortune.

So about a year later we are flying to Russia or somewhere long distance, and the President called me up to the cabin on Air Force One to have a cocktail and watch a movie.

And after a while he asked: **Well, Sigley, tell me: How do you sum up your first year in the White House?**

I related the Foreman and Agassi stories and told the President that I would sum up my first year as "the $40 million misunderstanding."

He, of course, loved it and laughed heartily. I can still hear his cackle.

President Bush might not approve of my telling you this story—the word "braggadocio" comes to mind. But my point is this: I would not trade $1 million for one second of the time being on his team.

Often it was the simplest of moments that meant the most.


Diane Ruebling, campaign volunteer:

It was the early days of the 1980 campaign, and I was accompanying Ambassador Bush on a trip across my home state of Iowa. We had a driver that day, and I was sitting in the back seat with GHWB on a short trip from Mason City to one of the small towns nearby. We drove by a small lake, and he immediately pulled out one of his note cards and wrote a note. I asked him what he was doing, and he said he was writing to one of the boys and showed me the note. (I think the note was to Marvin but not sure.) What I remember was that it was just a short note, something like: **Just drove by a lake and thought about the last time we went fishing. Love, Dad.**

At the time, I was a young mother and the impression he made on me was significant. As busy as he was, he took the opportunity to reach out to one of his kids. It warmed my heart and stuck with me the rest of my life. The importance of family never diminishes, no matter how busy one is.

Brent Scowcroft, national security adviser (from *41ON41*):

He always had other people in his mind. And that's very unusual for someone who has struggled to reach the epitome of political power. You think of them solely preoccupied with self. He has never been that way. It never consumed him.

...My relationship with him is a treasure I can't even begin to describe. It has transformed my life, made it full and complete in a way that I never dreamed could happen, and to find someone so powerful and so likable providing me with opportunities that he did is just something that I treasure beyond anything words can describe.

He is simply a remarkable man, and he is a dear, dear friend. And my life is rich because of him.

Sichan Siv, White House staff:

That I made it from the killing fields to the White House in thirteen years is a tribute to George Bush.

In the spring of 1975, while he was the US envoy to China, I was working in dangerous situations in Cambodia, trying to save thousands of people fleeing the war-torn countryside. The United States, aware of Communist reprisals, told me when the time came, I would have only one hour to report to the embassy to be airlifted out of Phnom Penh. It was April 12, 1975. Despite the flawless evacuation by the Ford administration (not one life was lost), I missed the helicopter by thirty minutes. I was meeting a provincial governor trying to feed some three thousand stranded families.

Five days later, the Communist Khmer Rouge turned the country into a land of blood and tears, killing everyone who had not been with them in their so-called revolution. My mother gave me her wedding ring, a scarf, and a bag of rice and told me to run. "No matter what happens, never give up hope," she said.

I rode a bicycle for three weeks across Cambodia but was captured near the Thailand border. Put in forced labor camps, I worked eighteen hours a day on a bowl of rice. I wondered if I would survive, but I prayed daily that I would see freedom.

On February 13, 1976, thirteen days after George Bush became CIA director, I jumped off a truck and ran, walked, crawled for three days, having nothing to drink or eat; nothing to guide me except the sun, the stars, and the moon. I was severely wounded in a booby trap, but managed to limp to Thailand, where I was jailed.

After teaching English to fellow refugees, I managed to immigrate to America, arriving in Connecticut with my mother's scarf, an empty rice bag, and two dollars. I picked apples there, then in 1977 went to New York to drive a taxi.

I later learned that my mother, sister, brother, and their children—fifteen family members altogether—were killed by the Communists.

In 1981, George Bush became Vice President, and I graduated

from Columbia University. On July 13, 1988, as a dais guest of President Reagan in the Rose Garden,* I met George Bush for the first time. The thought never crossed my mind that a few months later I would work for him, and he would become the most influential person in my life.

On February 13, 1989, exactly thirteen years from the day I jumped off that truck in the Cambodian jungle, I started working for the forty-first President of the United States. While my mother gave me life and my wife, Martha, gave me love, 41 taught me about leadership and how to be a complete person.

I learned mainly from watching him. For example, I was impressed how he managed to keep communications open with Beijing after the Tiananmen Square massacre on June 4, 1989; yet he received the Dalai Lama at the White House.

He quickly digested the eighty-two-page report on Iraqi atrocities in occupied Kuwait I sent him on December 14, 1990, and did not stop talking about it.

He was among the first to congratulate me after his son George W. Bush asked me to represent America at the United Nations. He started calling me Mr. Ambassador.

In October 2018, Jean Becker informed David Bates, Shirley Green, Fred McClure, Chase Untermeyer,† and myself that when President Bush died, we would accompany "41" on Air Force One for his last earthly journey to Washington.

---

\* The occasion was Captive Nations Day. Captive Nations Week is observed every year in solidarity with nations living under authoritarian rule.

† All former White House staff who lived in Texas. I was very happy I could give them a ride to President Bush's state funeral in Washington, DC. Unfortunately, they had to find their own way home. Air Force One was full of Bush family members on the return flight.

The flight with President George W. Bush, Secretary James Baker, and of course "41," was quite emotional. I realized I was the only person not born in the United States.

He once wrote to me:

**When we think of you, we think about an outstanding leader and public servant; we think about honor, decency, and integrity; we think about service to others.**

I would say back to him: "Thanks for your life, love, and leadership. Until we meet again, I am blessed you are beside me. Whether or not we can see each other, I always feel your spirituality. In serving God and Country, I give thanks in my prayers for thee."

Dorrance Smith, White House staff:

The Queen of England was coming to the White House in May 1991 for a state visit.

**I have an idea**, the President said. **We should take the Queen to an Orioles baseball game! It's our national pastime, and I want to take her to Camden Yards.**

I knew from past experiences that this "idea" was a direct order. So I dutifully said, "Great idea, sir; let's do it."

Fast-forward to May 15 as Marine One departed from the South Lawn with the President and Her Majesty en route to the Baltimore Orioles versus the Oakland Athletics baseball game. Seated next to each other in the owner's box, they had a front-row seat for all the action. Problem was, well, there was very little action, which left the President in the role of explaining innings with no runs, or a bloop single, or double plays. After five innings the score was 2–1 Athletics. There were no grand slams for the Grande Dame. Our national pastime was proving to be our own sticky wicket—a tricky or awkward situation. Patience was indeed building character!

The Queen noticed the Orioles third-base coach, bandy-legged Cal Ripken Sr., who was pacing back and forth in front of her. She asked the President, "What does that gentleman do?" Gamely the President said that his job was to either stop the runner on third base or signal him to continue on to home base to score a run. She said curtly, "Do you mean to tell me that is his entire lot in life?"

With little hesitation the President turned, pointed at me, and twirled his index finger, the signal to start up Marine One. Destination: White House South Lawn. Minutes later the fading lights of our national pastime were in the rearview mirror.

What did I learn from this presidential misadventure? Maybe even when you are the most powerful person in the world, ideas don't always work out.

Kristin Clark Taylor, White House staff:

Shortly after my mother died, Vice President Bush called me into his office. As I walked in, what I remember most is the expression on his face. I'll never forget that face.

His head was cocked just a tiny bit. He was nibbling the inside of his lower lip. His gaze was intentional and intense, his focus gentle and loving. He asked me how I was doing; how I was holding up since losing my mama.

My tears came then, but not really in a torrent. They fell gently, kind of like a soft rain. I told him how much I missed my mother, how broken I felt, how hard it was to live and breathe in a world without her.

What he said next gave me strength and mighty comfort. He talked to me about faith, standing strong in it; about family, pulling them close around me; and about the importance of wrapping the most wonderful "mama memories" around my shoulders and wearing them like a comfortable cloak, letting them bring me comfort.

I'd walked into his office that morning assuming he had a media-related question or concern. But he didn't want to talk about the media stuff at all.

He only wanted to see my face and ask if I was okay.

In that single moment—and in countless moments thereafter—he taught me vital life lessons about sympathy and empathy, about faith and friendship, about loyalty and grace—and about the power and glory of love.

All these beautiful lessons began to weave themselves into the fabric of my daily life in a way that I could actually *live* them and pass them on to my children.

Looking back, I see with startling clarity that George H. W. Bush was able to teach me all these things because he *was* all those things.


Pete Teeley, campaign spokesperson:

The ordeal began innocently enough: I had a dull pain in my right side. The diagnosis was an inflamed appendix. No big deal. A pretty routine surgery.

The next thing I remember was waking up in a darkened room. I hurt badly and sensed something was seriously wrong. But I was too exhausted to pursue the thought. I just wanted to sleep.

At about 7:30 in the morning, the bedside phone rang, jarring me partially awake.

**Teeley. How ya feeling?**

It was George Bush calling.

"I really feel bad, I'm sorry, I can't talk now," I mumbled, and dropped the receiver back into the cradle.

I thought to myself, "I just hung up on the President of the United States."

Later that morning the surgeon would explain how he'd been surprised to discover a tumor and had to remove a one-foot section of large intestine, along with the appendix and the lymph nodes for biopsy. Three had tested positive for cancer. If he was surprised, I was stunned and frightened.

The entire situation grew stranger still. A week to the day after the first surgery, I went under the knife again, this time to untangle a twist in my colon.

"It will take twenty minutes. Don't worry about it," the surgeon told me.

Apparently, he had failed to mention to the anesthesiologist that I had been throwing up black bile all week. When it happened again during the operation, the fluid slipped into my lungs, essentially drowning me and causing aspiration pneumonia to set in. I was moved immediately to intensive care.

Despite massive doses of intravenous antibiotics, the pneumonia held fast. That night the pulmonologist conceded I might not survive.

That word got back to the Oval Office.

Finally after seven days I regained consciousness, to find a nurse on the edge of my bed. "You've been through a terrible time, but you made it. You're going to be all right."

Because of the breathing tube down my throat, I couldn't talk.

"It's Friday," she added.

"Friday," I thought. "The day of the operation."

No, it was Friday a week later.

Two days later, my two intensive care nurses told me what the doctors had not: "You wouldn't be alive today if it were not for President Bush. When he heard you might die, he sent his doctor here. That changed everything."

I wasn't surprised. Knowing President Bush, he did this for me not because he was the President, but because I was his friend.

And he didn't stop there. He called a few times to check on my condition. One call even brought some levity.

The phone rang at the nurse's desk.

"President Bush is calling. He wants to know how Mr. Teeley is doing," the nurse said to another.

"I can't talk to him," she said.

"Why? You're the head nurse."

"I know, but I am a Democrat."

A few days later I was moved out of intensive care to a regular room.

There was a commotion in the hallway with nurses and others gathering. In walked First Lady Barbara Bush.

"Well, I can see you're getting better," she said. It was a touching visit and one she mentioned often, referring to it as the "time we almost lost him."

President Bush's help did not end when I left the hospital. He sent his doctor to my home to put me in the most advanced clinical trial that was then enrolling patients. The trial was a smashing success, and it became the most successful treatment for colon cancer for at least the next decade.

Thirty-two years later, I remain thankful for the love and thoughtfulness of George and Barbara Bush and the decades of life to enjoy with my children and my wife, Victoria. I am living proof that character matters.

*My editor encouraged me to share my own hospital story, so here goes:*

*In 2005, after not feeling great for weeks, I had an emergency hysterectomy at Maine Medical Center in Portland, Maine. The pain-causing culprit* *was a benign fibroid tumor that had grown into the size of a volleyball\* and was wreaking havoc in my body, including shutting down all my bodily functions. I would not share this rather personal detail if it were not key to the story.*

*The morning after the long, complicated surgery, I woke up to find the forty-first President of the United States in my room. (Mrs. Bush came later, so we could have "girl talk.")*

*He was there when my surgeon, Dr. Hector Tarraza, followed by a large group of residents, came into my room to report on my surgery. He was taken aback to find President Bush sitting there, and as professionally and gracefully as possible, told President Bush he was there to discuss my medical condition and it might be best if he left the room. Before I could answer, President Bush assured them he was family and did not need to leave.*

*Although I was in a morphine-induced state, I still remember with incredible clarity two things he asked during the briefing:*

- *He asked if he could see the tumor, wondering if I didn't want to see it too. I really did not. The tumor, thank heavens, had already been dissected to confirm it was noncancerous, so it was not available for viewing. President Bush was oddly disappointed.*

- *Dr. Tarraza explained to the residents that what finally made me realize I had a serious medical problem was the shutting down of all bodily functions. Again, President Bush was fascinated. **Number 1 or number 2?** he asked. Dr. Tarraza looked at me to see if I wanted to answer. "Both," I told him, as I clearly remember pushing the morphine drip at this moment in time. **Fascinating**, President Bush replied.*

---

\* The staff named the tumor "Wilson," after the volleyball that kept Tom Hanks company in the movie *Castaway*.

★  ★  ★

Paula Trivette, White House medical unit nurse:

It was customary for the White House nurse to remain in the medical unit in the evening until the President retired for the night. Generally, President Bush would stop in the unit and tell us to head home. One night, after a state dinner had ended, he opened the medical unit door and said:

**Paulita, come out here. There is someone I want you to meet.**

I walked into the foyer to be introduced to actors Don Johnson and Melanie Griffith. President Bush quipped to me:

**I just want you to know that I know important people too!**

His sense of humor is what kept us all going, even during the longest of days.

William Webster, former head of the FBI and the CIA, and his wife, Lynda:

We have been privileged to meet and work with many extraordinary people over our combined eighty-eight years in Washington, DC. While many have left impressions, good and bad, none have impacted our hearts and lives as much as George H. W. Bush and his life partner, Barbara. Outlined below, in no particular order, are a few lessons gleaned from our time with both.

- Be loyal.

Being CIA director wasn't easy. In four and a half years in the role as director of Central Intelligence, Bill witnessed the first Gulf War; and a coup attempt on Soviet leader Mikhail Gorbachev and eventual fall of the Soviet Empire, to name just a few key issues of the day.

Bill or the agency in general was often the target of sniping in the press or even within the inner sanctums of White House senior staff. Having had the position himself years earlier, the President remained loyal and supportive of Bill and of other senior CIA staff with whom he had close respect and, yes, affection.

- Play to win.

Bill was director of the FBI when he became acquainted with then Vice President Bush, and those encounters were often social, including on the tennis court. Bill quickly learned that the Vice President was a polite but fierce competitor. He admired that, and the fact that the Vice President and later the President arrived at a game ready to be competitive—not only with others but with himself.

- Support your boss.

When President Reagan asked Bill to move from the FBI to CIA, Bill was often at the White House to brief the President and Vice President Bush. It was during those meetings that Bill observed George Bush as he interacted with his boss. He offered advice when appropriate, but once a decision was made, he supported the President, even if he didn't agree with the decision. Bill never saw or heard of Vice President Bush ever carping about a decision that wasn't to his liking. He was loyal to the core and checked his ego at the Oval Office door. Whatever advice he gave the President, Vice President Bush did it in private.

- Be a good listener.

George H. W. Bush listened to the opinions and advice of others. While he didn't always follow a given piece of advice, he certainly took it into consideration.

On a personal scale, "wife of," Lynda, always appreciated that when speaking with the President, he always appeared to be listening. As tempted as he might have been, she never saw him look over her shoulder to see who else more interesting or more "important" was in the room.

- Be a good loser.

The President's tough loss to Governor Bill Clinton in '92 was handled with extreme class and grace after what was surely a crushing blow. That the Bush-Clinton "odd couple" would become such close friends later was an example we should all follow.

- Don't brag.

If there were any two people who deserved to toot their own extraordinary accomplishments or tout their A-list friends and acquaintances, it would be President and Mrs. Bush. We never heard them do so. They felt more strongly about the "we" than the "me" in life.

- Respect the rule of law.

In his role of FBI and later CIA director, not once did Bill see President Bush ever consider working around the law or ignoring it completely, even in circumstances when it would have been far easier to ignore legal implications or entanglements. President Bush knew that ignoring our precious rule of law would lead us down a road to eventual societal disintegration.

- Love well.

To be married, and happily so, for seventy-three years is accomplishment enough; but to do so through multiple jobs, a myriad of moves, six children—including the loss of one precious daughter—and very public lives is an achievement matched by no other couple we know.

Living life with honor, honesty, loyalty, and integrity was paramount to Barbara and President Bush. How to instill this back into our American discussion and life should be what drives each of us daily.

*I encouraged my fellow East Wingers (I was one of Mrs. Bush's deputy press secretaries during the White House years) to contribute their stories, even if we technically worked for the First Lady and not the President.*

Ann Brock, scheduler:

The best thank-you I have ever received came from President Bush after the November 1997 dedication of his library and museum. I was blessed and very lucky to have been the director for the opening, and according to President Bush, was his "Library Czar."

After all of the festivities came to an end, I was called to come down the hall to his office at 10000 Memorial in Houston, where he gave me a letter. This letter told me of a plan, a plan that involved me being booked to fly to Tucson, Arizona, where I was to be a guest at the Canyon Ranch Spa. I was to **go forth to Arizona... bearing with you the lasting thanks from this former something or other...**

Well, geez, when I read this letter, I still tear up with such gratitude and love. No one knew how to say "thank you" better than he did.

He also could give great advice. I asked him to introduce me to a cowboy, and he said: **You don't want to date the cowboy; you want to date the owner of the ranch where the cowboy works.**

★　★　★

Julie Cooke, director of projects:

I am a better person for having been in George H. W. Bush's orbit for thirty-five-plus years. I couldn't help but be influenced by his kindness, his sense of joy, his humanity, and his values of loyalty, faith, and service.

I remember when as Vice President, he halted his motorcade in a driving snowstorm to give a ride to a lonely stranger struggling in the snow on Massachusetts Avenue in Washington, DC.

A month after losing the 1992 election, he invited comedian Dana Carvey—who became famous for imitating the President on *Saturday Night Live*—to come to the White House to cheer our down-in-the-dumps staff.

Knowing of the cancer treatment for the child of one of his Secret Service agents, he shaved his hair off in solidarity with the little boy who had lost all his hair.

I learned to pursue music more fully by seeing President Bush delight in the music of the Oak Ridge Boys and George Dvorsky,★ among so many others.

Watching him skydive out of an airplane and drive his beloved boat like a bat out of hell off the Maine coast reminded me of the value of having fun and living fully.

And knowing of his generosity for thousands and thousands of people in need, and his deep love and pride for his family, each day prompts me to try to think more of others than myself.

President Bush—and of course, Mrs. Bush too—are daily voices in my ear: Did I do something good today? Did I take myself too seriously? Did I laugh? Have I given more than I have received?

---

★ George Dvorsky, a Broadway actor/singer, was a favorite of the Bushes.

I will be forever grateful for those lessons by the example of a great man.

<u>Sondra Haley, deputy press secretary:</u>

President Bush was known for spontaneously inviting folks out on his beloved *Fidelity*.* I learned to hold on tight since he loved to thrill his guests with speed. But one time we stopped; the fishing poles came out; and the boat bobbed and bobbed and bobbed. I made my way to the bow, taking deep breaths until I vomited. I thought I was discreet, but soon after felt President Bush at my side. He handed me a tissue and said:

**Welcome to the club. I once threw up on the prime minister of Japan.**

He was the best at easing someone else's embarrassing moment with compassionate humor.

<u>Carol Powers, photographer:</u>

Technically, I was not an East Winger; I was one of the White House photographers who just happened to be assigned to the First Lady, so I felt like a member of the Barbara Bush team.

But on Christmas Eve 1990, I was detailed to travel with President Bush to Camp David aboard Marine One. Upon landing, he jumped in a golf cart and asked me to join him. He was anxious to get to the gym where his kids and grandkids were playing wallyball.

---

* The name of President Bush's powerboat, which he kept in Kennebunkport, Maine. His boat will be mentioned nine more times in this book. *Fidelity I*, which he had when he was Vice President and President, is now on display at the George Bush Library and Museum. The older President Bush got, the faster his boats got. *Fidelity I* was a cigarette boat with two 280-horsepower engines. His last boat, *Fidelity V*, was a Fountain boat with three 300-horsepower engines.

While there he got a phone call, and as it was my duty, I followed him to the phone that overlooked the court. You never knew when a historic moment might occur. When he hung up, he turned to me and said, **They just got Noriega!**★ Then he said, **Shhh**, and went back to watching wallyball.

I was now a trusted adviser!

*I knew I could count on some of the members of President Bush's advance teams to come up with a few stories. (And what, exactly, is an advance person? Someone who travels in advance of the principal and organizes the logistics of the trip, including press coverage. They are a hardy bunch.)*

David Anderson:

In my four-plus years working with him, I never saw him not treat anyone with respect. Granted I had limited—compared to many, many others—access to him, but I got to see him on the road with "real people." He was always genuine. He was never full of himself.

When the President traveled, he always asked to meet any Daily Point of Lighters who might be living nearby. As a lead advance person, I had the privilege of escorting them to stand under the seal of the President on Air Force One to wait for the President to depart the plane. I specifically remember the children who were selected. He usually spent more time with them than the elected officials at the bottom of the stairs.

What I learned is that moments matter. Whether the President of the United States or just a regular person on the street, those

---

★ Manuel Noriega had surrendered to the Vatican embassy in Panama City. He gave himself up to American troops on January 3, 1990.

moments matter and can make a difference—even if you are not aware of it at the time.

When Walker's Point was severely damaged after a nor'easter* came ashore in New England in 1991, I was part of the team that went up with them and spent the day cleaning out the house. I will never forget sitting on the floor with the President going through his books (most of which had deep personal meaning and were signed); shoveling out mud; and searching for personal items in their bedroom that most likely had been washed out to sea. It was a traumatic day.

Within just a few days of our return to Washington, I received an envelope with a personal note from him thanking me for my help. I know he typed it because someone I know in the office said he typed all of them on his own typewriter (remember those?). I was amazed that he would take the time to write me a note after the horrible days he had dealing with this personal tragedy. But more importantly, it taught me how important the personal messages and "little things" we do make the biggest difference. We should all mourn the lost art of note-sending!!

Now that I'm a grown-up, a father, and a CEO, I realize there was so much more I learned from him, by watching him from afar.

Top of that list would be how to make decisions: Have the courage to make the difficult decisions; don't let outside pressure push you into making wrong decisions.

As an entrepreneur for twenty-five-plus years, I have faced more situations and decisions than I can count where this came into play.

---

* This storm came to be known as the "Perfect Storm," and a George Clooney movie about a fishing boat and its crew that was lost in the storm was based on it.

My go-to phrase when faced with a difficult decision to this day is: "Do what's right."

Antonio Benedi:

In the early 1980s while traveling overseas with Vice President Bush, he told me this story after meeting with some leaders that were very self-promoting.

He was in middle school where he played on the soccer team, and one day after a critical game for the championship, his mother asked him who had won the game. President Bush proudly told her he kicked the winning goal! His mother sat him down and with a firm tone told him that he didn't kick the winning goal on his own. She told him that the whole team was responsible for the winning goal. She also said, "George, don't be a braggadocio."

I truly believe at that moment President George H. W. Bush learned a life lesson that would stay with him until he died. President Bush never took credit for all his accomplishments. He gave the credit to the people around him. What a selfless life he led.

Gordon James:

I was one of the advance people who went to Kennebunkport every August. The first summer was relaxing with the only tension coming from the fact the President couldn't seem to catch a fish.

The second summer was very intense. Operation Desert Storm was in the early planning stages. The days were now filled with personal visits from coalition heads of state. The helicopter landing pad was busy with arrivals and departures from Logan Airport in Boston.

On one particular day, the request came from the press office to have a joint media availability with a visiting head of state on the compound. I was smart enough to ask Mrs. Bush if it would be okay. It was, after all, their private home. Of course, she agreed.

I don't remember who the visiting head of state was, but I do remember going to the front door of the house to get the President. He opened the door dressed in a flannel shirt with a knit tie squared off at the bottom and a can of Coors in his hand.

I think I said, "Did you get dressed in the dark? This is not going to work."

He took my suggestion and at least changed shirts and put the beer down.

He was the Leader of the Free World, but he was still a guy. I was glad he was our guy.


Rob Schuler:

One of the trips of President Bush's in which I was called on to assist was in 2004 when golf legend Jack Nicklaus asked him to play in the Morgan Stanley Pro-Am, which kicks off the annual Memorial Tournament at Muirfield Village Golf Club in Dublin, Ohio.

President Bush was just a week away from his eightieth birthday and was coming off a grueling travel schedule that would have challenged someone who was fifty years younger.

But when he arrived in Columbus, Ohio, President Bush was insistent on helping off-load his luggage from the jet and get it into the cars—in spite of the fact that there were plenty of folks half his age willing to do so.

The next morning was an early start, and he was still clearly tired. Muirfield Village, with its steep hills and rough terrain, is an unforgiving course for both golf and the golfer. While the club has a rule against carts on the course, they made an exception for

President Bush, and we were given strict instructions to get him into the cart and not to let him walk.

For the most part, we were successful, until the last hole. As he was being encouraged (more like begged) to jump in the cart after his drive and avoid climbing the long, steep hill on this 417-yard par 4, he looked over and said sternly: **It's important to finish strong.**

As he strode up the final hill to the green, the large, assembled crowd was certainly enthusiastic about his strong finish.

After the long, exhausting day of play, President Bush was running on fumes. But that night he was expected to participate in the very prestigious meeting of the Captains Club for a private dinner and discussion. (The discussion was considered so secret and sensitive, we had to negotiate to get permission for a Secret Service agent to be within earshot of the meeting. The "secret" topic: "The Golf Ball, Advances in Technology, and How This Will Change the Game of Golf." It was agreed that the agent on duty would not be an avid golfer to assure he would be a disinterested party.)

President Bush was dragging—as was the presentation, I think— but he knew how important this was to his host. Finally, President Bush apologized to a not-very-pleased Jack Nicklaus and excused himself from the remainder of the meeting. As we were leaving for the golf cart to take him back to his villa, he asked if we could swing by the dinner that Jack's wife, Barbara, was hosting for her friends. He entered to the complete surprise and delight of the group.

President Bush told Barbara he was dead tired and had to excuse himself from the Captains Club dinner but could not miss the opportunity to visit with her and her friends before heading to bed. He was sincere in his warmth and praise for Barbara and her charitable works and took the time to speak to each of her friends and pose for impromptu photos. Barbara was glowing that a former President of the United States made a point to visit her and her friends.

As we were heading back to his room, someone in our group commented that "was one of the smoothest things I've ever seen— there is no way that Jack can be annoyed with you for leaving early when Barbara floats in and tells him how you made her night in front of all of her friends."

President Bush looked over and said: **You don't get to be President of the United States without learning a thing or two.**

Bruce Zanca:

George Bush taught me to take the high road.

In October 1987, Vice President George Bush was preparing to announce his presidential candidacy. *Newsweek* magazine published a cover photo of Mr. Bush at the helm of his boat with the headline "Fighting the 'Wimp Factor.'" At the time, I was a twenty-seven-year-old press aide to the Vice President. Really, I was a press-wrangler. My job was to take care of the press pool, which traveled with the Vice President on Air Force Two.

Vice President Bush, Mrs. Bush, their family, and their staff were all upset about the *Newsweek* cover and article. Margaret Warner wrote the piece. We all thought the article and the cover treatment was an uncalled-for cheap shot.

Shortly after the article was published, we made an overnight campaign stop in suburban Detroit, Michigan. We arrived in Detroit early in the afternoon, and then the motorcade took us to a historic hotel in Grosse Point. That afternoon Bush conducted local television interviews and had some administrative downtime before the evening campaign event.

The assembly time for the motorcade was 5:30 p.m. in the hotel parking lot for a 5:45 p.m. motorcade departure. Margaret Warner did not show up on time. When advance director John Keller called me on the walkie-talkie and asked me if I was all set for departure, I told him I was missing a reporter, but we should still depart. I said I would arrange for a car to bring her to the next event. I wasn't about to make the Vice President and Mrs. Bush wait for the reporter who penned the offending article. I also admit that I was angry about the story and thought a little retribution was appropriate.

When we got to the event site, word got around to the staff that I had left Margaret Warner behind. Almost instantly, I was summoned to the holding room where Vice President and Mrs. Bush were waiting for the event. I went to the holding room and the miffed Vice President said:

**Zanca, did you just maroon Margaret Warner?**

I said, "She didn't report on time. She knows the rules. So yes, I left her. I got her a ride, and she's on her way; she won't miss anything."

**We are not vindictive, Bruce. That is not how we roll.**

I was embarrassed and put in my place. I said, "Yes, sir, I apologize."

As I was leaving the room, Mrs. Bush said to me with a wink, "Good job, Bruce; I would've left her too."

All those years ago, George Bush, as he always did, led by example. Even though he must have been mad about the article, he required that we do the right thing. He showed me it was correct to take the high road. Today I long for character-centered leaders like the forty-first President of the United States.

*Knowing that the former staff of President Bush might not necessarily be objective in their storytelling, I reached out to a group of people who were known to be pretty tough on the forty-first President: the journalists who covered him before, during, and after his presidency. After all, they were witnesses to history, too. Here are some of their observations:*

Rita Beamish, Associated Press:

President Bush was gleeful, to the point of zealotry, when it came to his many outdoor sports—whether rounding the links in "aerobic golf" (the self-proclaimed Mr. Smooth famously quipped, **We shoot for time**); lunging across the tennis court; casting for "big blues"; or revving his speedboat over the sea.

But in parallel with his kinetic gusto was a second trait: the relish with which he wrapped others into his competitive fun. He pulled not just family, friends, and professional athletes and entertainers into the fold, but people of all stripes. He was as likely to drag in the likes of John Major and Boris Yeltsin to the horseshoe pit as to encourage the prowess of administration officials and White House cooks and groundskeepers into his horseshoe competitions.

When he learned that I, a workaday reporter who covered him every day, was a runner like him, we struck up a chitchat about our shared affinity. Very soon I found myself occasionally invited along on his runs—an experience that was simultaneously surreal, journalistically compelling, and comfortably fun.

On trips to Kennebunkport, the sports mania kicked into high gear. Bush's boat *Fidelity* might roar by with the low-key national security adviser Brent Scowcroft or the Danish prime minister gamely hanging on. Bush's sons, longtime political friends, or Canada's Brian Mulroney would show up as multisport wingmen. When the more staid French president came to visit, everyone wondered how Bush would lure him into the fray. François Mitterrand in fact declined the chance for a *Fidelity* zip-about, but Bush later recounted that all was not sedentary: Bush got him out for a walk in the woods.

Journalists learned to gear up for Maine duty: running shoes for when Bush spontaneously invited the press pool on his dawn runs; hats and gloves for his winter power walks; umbrellas for weather-be-damned outings. One downpour found Bush riverside, intent on breaking a multiday fishless streak—with soggy, discouraging results.

Nearly three decades younger than Bush, I didn't truly appreciate his vigor until the years flowed by. I realized that I had internalized the inspirational bar he set, monitoring my own progression decade by decade until I was still proudly running in my sixties, as he had.

On a 2008 visit to Boston, my husband, Paul, and I day-tripped to Kennebunkport with our two daughters. We arranged to meet up with our friend the great Jean Becker. But on arrival she told us Bush was at loose ends out at Walker's Point. Learning we were in town, he invited us over.

Now slowed in gait but typically cordial and chatty out by his pool, the former President was eager from the outset to get us on the water. Bent on piloting *Fidelity*, he waved off a staffer's observation that conditions were a bit choppy. We piled onto the boat.

That day left an enduring image: The aged athlete standing at the helm, hands gripping the boat wheel, smiling as he joyfully bounced *Fidelity* over the waves, seemingly heedless of the Secret Service agent at his back with one hand on the President's belt and the other ready for any lurch. Beneath a gleaming sun, a chilly breeze blew across the sea.

We zoomed to the town harbor, where Bush slowed into the channel. He merrily waved to people onshore, calling back to those he seemed to know. The water, his boat, Kennebunkport—his happy place. There was no mistaking the town's most famous resident: radiating in the outdoors and enveloping everyone around him in his ebullience.

★ ★ ★

<u>Tom Brokaw, NBC anchor (from *41ON41*):</u>

Like all journalists who've worked in Washington or covered politics, we were all students of the presidency, and at this stage in my life, I've come to certain conclusions. One is that it's very helpful to have had a lot of life experiences. Not just political experience, but George Bush went to war, came home to Barbara, then went to Yale, then he went to Texas to try to be an oilman. He bumped up against a lot of realities that a lot of people need to know about if they are going to run the country...

I believe in my lifetime the most underestimated President has been George Bush.

<u>Ann Compton, ABC News:</u>

It was the defining moment of his presidency.

Hours after Saddam Hussein sent Iraqi tanks across the border to invade the oil-rich kingdom of Kuwait, the President of the United States helicoptered back to the White House from an urgent gathering of his war council at Camp David. George H. W. Bush had made no public statement, but everyone knew the United States was the only global power capable of leading allied forces to repel the attack and stabilize the Persian Gulf and its supply of oil.

The President strode from Marine One up the South Lawn to the huge gathering of reporters and cameras awaiting his first words. He did not disappoint:

**This will not stand. This will not stand, this aggression against Kuwait.**

**...I want to see the rest of the world join us, as they are in overwhelming numbers, to isolate Saddam Hussein.**

I blurted out that his longtime ally King Hussein of Jordan had just flown to Baghdad, where the king embraced Saddam. The photo was splashed across on the front page of the *Washington Post*.

The President's reply was sharp. Fierce. He said with an edge to his voice:

**I can read. What's your question?**

I stood mute. It was a tone I had never heard from George Bush during more than a decade of covering him. The moment passed. The President moved swiftly inside. We all understood the gravity of the moment. I took no offense.

The next morning, President Bush prepared to announce he was sending his defense secretary to the Middle East with the promise of American boots on the ground to force Iraq out of Kuwait. It was war.

I was summoned to the press secretary's office. Marlin Fitzwater handed me a small white envelope with my name handwritten on the front and the words "It's personal" underlined, twice.

The small note left me stunned.

**Dear Ann,**

**You did a great job yesterday. I hope my response during our press to-and-fro was not offensive. I wasn't too happy with my reply.**

**All Best,**

**GB**

Below his initials he had drawn a happy face—wearing a sad frown.

I have saved that note all these years and even showed it to my children when they got older. The quality of grace and respect for another person's feelings were remarkable even in moments of incredible stress.

I often tell the story when invited to speak to groups about the presidency. I even brought the letter itself with me when I retired and Brian Lamb interviewed me on C-SPAN about the decades of White House coverage. I explained that I had never heard President Bush "bark" at anyone.

Then came another letter:

> **Dear Ann,**
>
> **You're much too young to be retired, and it's hard to imagine the White House press room without you there. But you deserve the break, and I can tell you from firsthand experience that when you leave a big job there is an exciting life thereafter.**
>
> **Now about that "bark." I am horrified! Are you sure it wasn't just a little yelp? In any case, have you forgiven me, dear Ann??**
>
> **Barbara and I send our warmest regards and congratulations on a job superbly done. You're the best, Ann Compton.**
>
> **Sincerely,**
> **George Bush**

The word "grace" has a reaffirming strength to it.

Yes, Mr. President. I not only "forgave" you long ago; I continued to admire the grace with which you lived.

Maureen Dowd, *New York Times*:

We live in a world where many Republican politicians love to hate more than they want to work together. But President Bush was a model of reaching out to those who disagreed with him or criticized him. President Biden tries to do that, too, but President Bush was the charming master of the game.

Most presidents cut me off as soon as they get into office and read my columns about them. They just abruptly drop me from the White House columnist briefings. Sometimes I think they find it harder to take criticism from a woman, because underneath all the civility and modernity, they still don't think women should have power over their image or livelihood. I've seen famous male columnists criticize presidents, in print and in person, and the presidents get annoyed but don't cut them off. But with me, it's different. They take it very personally; I refer to it as "the Castration Sonata."

President Bush never cut me off, no matter how annoyed he got. He would vent about me in his famous "blue notes." And once he sent Marlin Fitzwater and Brent Scowcroft to have dinner with me in Houston on New Year's Eve, and Brent said, "We have a favor to ask. Can you please stop calling the President goofy?"

But President Bush was exceptionally fair to me, as a journalist and as a woman. He told me clearly what he didn't like and what he thought I had gotten wrong. And he teased me about his ambivalent "love/hate" feelings toward me, even joking that he had had to consult a psychiatrist, which, of course, we know he would never do. As Jean Becker, his chief of staff after the presidency, used to joke: "You two need couples counseling."

He put some jabs in the little notes he sent to me over three decades. Here are samples, all written after he left office:

**I like you. Please don't tell anyone.**

**Darn you, Maureen Dowd.**

**Sometimes I found it better around my family to go 'Maureen who?'**

He would sign a letter he had typed, **Love**, and then scratch it out and write in **not quite there yet**.

But he never interfered with my ability to do my job, and he always kept the door open to friendly relations. With Poppy,* there was decency and sweetness.

When my mom died at ninety-seven in 2005, he sent me a kind email that made me cry:

**It hurts to lose a parent. It hurts an awful lot. When my own Mom died, I went up to Greenwich to check on her. She was close to death and her breathing was so labored that I literally prayed to God, as I knelt right there by her bed, that she would go on to heaven. She was prepared to do just that. I hope your own Mom had a peaceful passing; and that she felt joyous about going on to heaven. Heck with politics. Heck with the NYT and all my hang ups about it.**

He never lost sight of the fact that humanity was more important than ideology. And unlike President Biden, who cut me off for writing a mild column about Hunter Biden's vicissitudes, President Bush was able to tell me that he didn't like my tough coverage of W.'s presidency and the misbegotten Iraq invasion (in my opinion), without icing me completely.

In one note complaining about my coverage of W.—and humorously wondering why he still liked me, given that coverage—President Bush wrote another sign-off that made me mist up:

**Put it this way. I reserve the right to whine, to not read, to use profanity, but if you ever get really hurt or if you ever get really down and need a shoulder to cry on or just need a**

---

* 41 was named for his maternal grandfather, whose children called their father Pop. Therefore, young George H. W. Bush acquired the nickname Poppy.

friend—give me a call. I'll be there for you. I'll not let you down. Now, go on out and knock my knickers off. When you do, I might just cancel my subscription.

But he never did. He was against cancel culture before cancel culture existed! He just was not a vengeful, sniffy, begrudging person. He was, in a word, classy.

Jamie Gangel, NBC and then CNN:

Not long after President Bush was diagnosed with vascular Parkinson's disease, my family and I had dinner with the Bushes near their summer home in Kennebunkport. He was still in excellent shape, but he told me what the doctors warned him was coming.

**I will miss golf**, he said, and paused, then added with determination: **But I can still do plenty of other things!**

I couldn't help but think back to 1993, how in order to get the first interview with him post-presidency, he ran me ragged playing golf, fishing, swimming, and running—all in the rain.

He wiped away a couple of tears. I did my best to hide mine.

The notion that this competitive athlete, who could easily finish off four sports and four challengers before lunch, would no longer be able to do that seemed inconceivable. And frankly, at the time, I just could not imagine how he would handle it. I should have known better.

For the last ten years of his life, George Herbert Walker Bush taught us his greatest leadership lesson by example: Live every moment to the fullest. While the notion of being confined to a wheelchair might make most of us want to pull the covers over our heads and hide away, George Bush never missed an opportunity to go out. Just ask his chief of staff Jean Becker the four scariest words that began every day: **I have an idea.** Those ideas might include going to an Astros baseball or a Texans football game; going to the theater to see a favorite musical; or of course jumping out of perfectly good airplanes.

Whether it was flipping the coin at the Super Bowl or hosting all the former presidents and Lady Gaga for a Hurricane Harvey fundraiser, there was no stopping George Bush.

In his book *Power and Destiny*, historian Jon Meacham tells a story about 41 as he was nearing his ninetieth birthday. A hurricane was approaching Walker's Point with 50 mph winds. The Big House★ at Walker's Point was boarded up, and everyone got ready for the worst.

At one point Jean could not find 41. She finally found him outside, sitting on his scooter, looking out at the stormy sea. The Secret Service agents could barely stand, the wind was so strong, and Jean struggled to get to his side. When she finally did, she shouted through the wind, "What are you doing, sir?!"

His answer was pure George Bush: **I can't see anything from the house. I don't want to miss anything.**

He would tell all of us that is exactly how we should all be living our lives: Make sure you don't miss anything.

<u>Gene Gibbons, Reuters:</u>

A few days after my wife, Lynn, died in 2012, President Bush, then eighty-eight, telephoned to express his sympathy. His call, at a stage of his life when time was his most precious asset, was enormously comforting at the worst moment of my life. He knew me, but not that well. So it certainly would have sufficed had he asked his staff to send a letter of condolence and left it at that.

Not Bush. He went the extra mile. Selflessness was part of his character, a trait I saw often while covering his presidency. Giving of oneself

---

★ What everyone called President and Mrs. Bush's house on Walker's Point.

takes effort. Yet it would go far toward shaping the kinder, gentler America that was 41's "vision thing." He practiced what he preached.

Once during a visit to Maine, we briefly discussed an article in the *Atlantic* by Joseph Nye that described him as one of the three great modern foreign policy presidents. FDR and Ike were the others. I remember Bush saying he was honored by the encomium* but didn't deserve it because he just wasn't in the same league with Roosevelt and Eisenhower. I can't imagine any other president I covered, including Jimmy Carter, showing such humility or even pretending it.

I plead guilty to hagiography.†

While I know empirically Bush wasn't perfect, the only thing I can think of to fault him for was his sometimes lack of good PR, but even that was endearing. The two examples I most vividly recall are these:

- During a visit as Vice President to NATO headquarters in Brussels in the late '80s, he said Detroit could **learn a lesson from Soviet tank mechanics**, infuriating the US auto workers union.
- After agreeing to "revenue enhancements" as part of a budget deal, he was out jogging and replied, **Read my hips**, pointing to his butt, in response to reporters shouting questions about whether he'd violated his **"read my lips—no new taxes"** pledge.

Linda Lorelle, anchor at Houston's NBC affiliate:

It was May 4, 1995, and my assignment was to "toast" the forty-first President of the United States at a fund-raiser for a local charity.

---

* Encomium: A speech or article that highly praises someone.
† Hagiography: Idealization of someone.

Never mind that I hadn't met him. My role as an evening news anchor at Houston's KPRC-TV landed me the invitation, my reporting apparently having caught the eye of George and Barbara Bush.

Four of us were set to toast him, including the legendary heart surgeon Dr. Denton Cooley.* I was terrified.

I needn't have been. That famous 41 charm and grace were on full display, immediately putting me at ease. It was the beginning of a series of extraordinary encounters and events that, over the next twenty-three years, led to—dare I say it—a friendship with President and Mrs. Bush.

Growing up on the South Side of Chicago, I never imagined I'd have a file of personal notes and memorabilia from a US president. Some are handwritten, others on official letterhead. All treasured memories that reveal the essence of George Herbert Walker Bush.

One great example: His willingness to call in a favor to Apollo 13 captain Jim Lovell on my behalf. President Bush asked his good friend to donate his services as a keynote speaker to help my education nonprofit raise scholarship funds. We raised a record amount of money that year.

Then there's the day Jean Becker called to say, "President Bush wants to have lunch with you. He wants to make sure you're okay."

The news of my rather sudden departure from KPRC in 2006 was the talk of the town. If you read Jean's first book about 41, *The Man I Knew*, you know President Bush loved good gossip, so there was a bit of that in this. But more than anything, he was genuinely concerned about me.

The three of us met at his favorite, secluded lunch spot. Every few minutes or so I pinched myself. "Am I really having lunch with

---

* Dr. Cooley performed the first successful heart transplant in the United States.

President Bush, who wants to know how he can help me take the next step in my career?!"

And it wasn't just lip service. He continued to check in and I kept him updated.

On the night he died, I pulled out the "Bush File" and sprawled on my bedroom floor as my old TV station blared in the background with news of his passing. The letters, scripts, and photos brought back cherished memories as I smiled through my tears.

The week that followed was unforgettable. Emceeing the City of Houston's tribute to our beloved 41. Witnessing the outpouring of love and respect across our nation and around the world. Attending the funeral to say goodbye.

As I sat in St. Martin's Episcopal Church, surrounded by former presidents, dignitaries, and Bush family and friends, I was transported back to the night I met our forty-first President. How he vanquished my nerves in one fell swoop by just being himself: Kind. Gentle. Compassionate. And funny as hell.

Later that night I found the script I had meticulously written so as not to make a fool of myself:

"To President Bush: On behalf of the children we are helping tonight, thank you for coming home to Houston, for your continued leadership, for truly being a part of this community, for showing the children of Houston that you care."

And from the little girl who grew up on the South Side of Chicago, thank you for being my friend and showing us all the best of humanity.

Peter Maer, CBS News:

In February of 2005, former Presidents Bush and Clinton, at the behest of President George W. Bush, embarked on a goodwill mission to Asian countries devastated by a massive tsunami. For a reporter who had spent years covering both men, it was amazing to witness up close the developing friendship between the two former political foes.

Mr. Bush's incredible sense of humanity was so evident at disaster sites and behind the scenes on that long journey. At a stop in Indonesia, the two former Presidents saw rubble that was once a thriving village. A sad little man described how his entire family had been swept to their deaths. His wife and children were gone.

"Now they live only in my heart," he said through a translator. Bush and Clinton offered words of condolence. On the long flight home, I had an opportunity to chat with Mr. Bush. (President Clinton had left the trip as he traveled to other stops in Asia.) As we gazed out the window to the dark Pacific waters below, we recalled the Indonesian man's plight and the devastating losses of so many others the two leaders encountered. There I was, discussing the fragility of life with a man who survived being shot down over the Pacific in World War II and later suffered the loss of a beloved daughter. He knew so much about the blessings of life itself.

I shared a phrase my grandmother and mother often recited at times of loss: "Man plans. God laughs." I explained it was an old Yiddish phrase.

**Yiddish you say**, said Mr. Bush. **Very interesting.**

Shortly after I returned to my seat in the back of the aircraft from the Air Force fleet, Jean Becker approached with an astoundingly generous offer from the forty-first President. Mr. Bush invited a weary reporter to use the only bed on the plane, but he wanted me to know he'd be seated in an adjacent chair. I declined the poignant offer but to this day I marvel at how a former President could be so very considerate.

★ ★ ★

Diana Walker, *TIME* magazine White House photographer:

One learns a lot about the character of the President when one watches him every day!

President Bush was always gracious to the photographers and in some cases he gave us nicknames. I was Lady Di.

All of us had our own code of ethics. One thing some photographers did to get a little more action between the principals at a summit, for instance, was to call out for the two leaders to shake hands. I completely disagreed with this practice. Shoot what you see, period.

I had traveled on the Bush press plane to visit the famous shipyard at Gdansk, Poland, on July 11, 1989. Of all the places we went on this presidential trip, this stop was the most newsworthy because Lech Walesa, the Solidarity leader and opposition leader, was to meet with the President. (Walesa would become the president of Poland in a matter of months.)

I had talked the press people on Bush's staff into allowing a small pool of photographers to go behind Bush and Walesa up onstage, showing the huge crowd of dockworkers and press in the background. Making sure I had the right lens and the right film, I nervously waited with the rest of the press pool for the two men, with their wives, to arrive at the riser.

I will never forget the feeling: I depressed the shutter on my camera and it went nowhere. My battery was dead! Feverishly, I took the lens off another camera, shoved it in my pocket, and got the wide lens off the dead camera and onto a working camera! I lifted my camera to my eye, and of course, the four principals had turned back to face the huge audience before them. *TIME* would not have the picture of the week after sending me there! This was not good. I was a wreck!

Never before had I done something like this, and never again did I do it. I called out to the President of the United States: "Mr. President, sir, please, just one more time?!"

The President turned to Walesa and the ladies, urging them to turn back around so they could wave to the people waving to them from the tall building behind.

**How's this, Lady Di?!?!**

I was saved. All of us within earshot could not believe what President Bush had done for a photographer at such a historic moment.

Of course I have never forgotten. I sincerely knew at that moment what I had always thought, but if I needed proof this was it: What a totally good guy President George Herbert Walker Bush was.

*Next up: The members of the small but mighty staff who took care of 41 during his post-presidency.*

Barbara Knight, staff assistant:

One day while I was working in the office, President Bush sat on the corner of my desk, and said:

**Barbara Jr., I'm going to have lunch with my bride today, but let's call the boss and see what's on the menu.**

I was thoroughly amused and completely game as he dialed and put Mrs. Bush on speaker phone.

**Bar, I'm here with Barbara Jr. and she knows I'm coming home to eat lunch with you, but we wanted to see what was on the menu today.**

To which she answered very matter-of-factly: "Peanut butter and jelly sandwiches." I was dying inside but he was so happy and simply said something along the lines of **Okay, see you soon!**

I thought it was just precious that he was taking time to go home and have lunch with his wife, knowing he had to be back in the office for afternoon meetings. He was as excited about the sandwiches as he would have been a gourmet meal for two reasons: He lived life with gratitude every single day, and to the very end, he was head over heels in love with his wife.

Melinda Lamoreaux, staff assistant:

If I had to pick just two things I learned from President Bush, they would be:

- Live life with creativity and humor.
- Always look for ways to transform the ordinary into extraordinary.

Many people probably envision the office of a former President to be a rather stiff and formal place. This was not the case at the Office of George Bush—OGB as we called it! The OGB staff were some of the luckiest people in the world because our boss chose to make the ninth floor at 10000 Memorial Drive* a place where every day was a new day. The saying "never a dull moment" described the possibility that the next visitor might be a former world leader or an equally important meeting to discuss an "idea" that President Bush wanted to share with the staff. The atmosphere in our office was exciting and upbeat because of one very special person—George Herbert Walker Bush!

Oddly, the example I am going to use is his love for the famous book character Flat Stanley. Over the years, we received hundreds

---

* The address of President Bush's office in Houston.

of Flat Stanley letters from young students around the country. For context: Flat Stanley was created as a project to increase children's reading and writing skills as they document where Flat Stanley has "visited" around the world. Students would mail a paper "Flat Stanley" to selected individuals and ask them to journal the places and activities of Flat Stanley's adventures.

President Bush took great interest when Flat Stanley arrived at the office. He loved the chance to give "Flat" a trip around the office of a former President. It would have been easy to ask one of us to throw "Flat" back in the return envelope and say he was here for a day, but that would be way too ordinary and rather boring. George Bush was the consummate leader of living life to the fullest—even on behalf of a fictional character from an unknown letter writer.

Below is a reply from President Bush to a young student named Katie, who also happened to be the daughter of former White House staffer Ginny Mulberger. So it's possible Katie's Flat Stanley got VIP treatment. My only regret is we can't share the photos of Flat Stanley that President Bush took to send back with this letter.

**Dear Katie,**

**Boy am I lucky or what!**

**Flat Stanley, neatly folded, is attached to this letter. He can fill you in on the details; but here's what happened.**

**When Stanley got here everyone was very excited. They liked his striped pajamas. They liked the look on the guy's face. Only two people here thought he looked like a bit of an over-confident lad—a wise guy. The rest fell madly in love with him.**

Anyway, I hope he enjoyed his day. I tried to show him interesting things about the office of a former President of the United States.

First, the flat one took his turn at answering the phone. He helped at the front desk with phone calls. Stanley had trouble dialing with those mittens on, but he got "operator assistance" and the AT&T lady did the heavy lifting.

Flat Stanley seemed to be interested in the Secret Service, so he got briefed by the agents here at the office. He tried out the Sig-Sauer automatic pistol that the agents carry. He almost shot the glutes off an aging volunteer here—just an accident. I told Stanley not to worry. I am heavily insured.

Later today I am going to my Presidential Library at Texas A&M where I will shoot an A&E TV film with David Frost. Stanley tried to get himself invited to go to A&M, but frankly he is so energetic that I get a little tired around him, so we flushed him reluctantly telling him "No, Stanley, you can't go. We are folding you and sending you back to Katie." The guy seemed crushed, not about being folded but about not going.

But later he smiled when I showed him my new cowboy boots. The boots are made by my friend Rocky. They show the seal of the President. On the bottom of the presidential seal it says Air Force One. Flat seemed to like the boots and tried them on. They were too big. I worried that his paper feet might get blisters.

Katie, do any of your classmates know how to work email? I am not bragging but I do! I showed Flat Stanley how to do email. He was very interested. He stayed glued to my computer screen. (Get it? Glued! He was really taped on with scotch tape!).

I am going to miss the Flat Man. When he got here, I was not too pleased. I didn't know what his heartbeat would be, what he'd really be like, but I got to like him. Now here he is back. I hope he tells you he had a good time. He didn't get in the way exactly, but he sure probed into a lot of different areas. But why not? He's a young guy and there's a lot of exciting things to learn. I wish I were Flat Stanley's age. There's so much wonder ahead for him, so much love.

I think Stanley is really looking to the future. I tried to tell him about when I was President of the United States. He was not at all interested in that. He simply wanted to talk about Big League Baseball and about what he wants to be when he grows up. He first told me he wanted to be a guy who dissects fish and frogs. But then, as I showed him around, he decided "I will become an email expert. People will 'consult' with me and pay me big bucks." Flat Stanley learns fast.

Love,

**George Bush**


Nancy Lisenby, assistant to the chief of staff:

Like most people, I learned from President Bush by watching him. Here are a couple of examples.

- When you must correct people, do it gently—especially if you're in a position of power.

President Bush was leaving the office in twenty minutes and Jean was desperate for him to sign some letters inviting a few sports stars to speak at an event at his presidential library. He couldn't make up his mind on whom to invite (he knew so many) and when he finally did, we had minutes to spare.

Linda Poepsel, who headed up correspondence, was swamped with her own last-minute letters, so Jean asked me to get them printed out. She had already written them; all I had to do was change the names and addresses for each person, then rush them in for him to sign. Easy-peasy.

After I put them on his desk, he called me back and said oh so gently:

**I think we need to change one of these.**

I had "Dear Clyde"* at the top, but someone else's name and address at the bottom. I was mortified. Thankfully, he had caught it, or I probably would have mailed it out. As I apologized profusely, I just remember his gentleness. He did not give me a look like I was an idiot. He did not make me feel any worse than I already did. He just softly said: **Good thing we caught it.**

- Don't pile on when someone is down.

Unfortunately, I've seen people chewed out by powerful people. (Sorry, I won't say who.) People in power need to really consider their tone and words—something 41 knew how to do so very well.

A prominent Democratic politician was all over the headlines for

---

* That would be Houston Rockets basketball star Clyde Drexler.

doing something unethical but not illegal. He was getting fried in the press.

41 wrote him a short, handwritten note. I was helping Linda run off his correspondence before mailing it out and when I saw whom he'd written, I remember thinking to myself: "I hope 41 told him what a bad thing it was he'd done." Instead, the note said: **Hang in there. I know you're a good man.**

- Stand by your commitments.

41 was supposed to travel out of state to give a speech somewhere. He came to the office that morning and was sick as a dog: diarrhea, vomiting, upset stomach. Of course he wouldn't cancel the trip. I was in his office doing something and kinda scolded him, "Sir, you are too sick to travel—you really shouldn't be going blah blah blah."

He looked at me with that humble look he had and said, **Well, they are expecting me, and it would be disappointing if I canceled, so I must go**.

It was not only his comment, but it was also the way he explained his position to me in such a humble way. He really was the kindest man.

Jim McGrath, speechwriter:

I was on the road with 41, driving either to or from an event, when he asked about the recent dissolution of the Neumann-Roussel public relations firm. Pete Roussel had been a longtime staffer from the 1960s and 1970s and was a close friend; Roxann Neumann had also become a good friend. Neumann-Roussel had done a lot of work for us, including managing publicity for the opening of the library.

I could tell he was probing for the inside scoop and what led to the breakup. I knew the details, but I feigned ignorance and told 41 that I was trying to stay out of the friction and fray between two dear friends.

I'll never forget what he said next:

**That's a very good policy, one I learned the hard way. I remember when my old business partner John Overbey told me he was leaving his wife, who was an entirely unpleasant and disagreeable woman. I was instantly supportive and told John why I thought it was a good idea, and what I thought of his wife. A week or two later they were back together and working things out. Things were a little awkward between us after that, so I decided I would never again stick my nose in where it wasn't needed!**

Laura Pears, scheduler:

In 2006 I accompanied President Bush as his personal aide to attend the Safari Club International Convention in Reno, Nevada.

Typical of his crazy schedule, President Bush had returned to Houston just the day before from a trip to Pakistan, where, as a special envoy for United Nations secretary general Kofi Annan, he had visited the regions devastated by an earthquake.

I rarely traveled with 41, but it was decided that his aide, Tom Frechette, needed a break from his duties.

After delivering the keynote address at the black-tie dinner, President Bush returned to his suite at the Silver Legacy Hotel and Casino for a brief visit with Vice President Dan Quayle and General Norman Schwarzkopf.

Finally, he actually got tired and decided to retire for the evening. But first he gave me $20 to go to the casino with General Schwarzkopf and learn how to play blackjack.

Needless to say, I was a bit intimidated to go gambling in Reno with a war hero.* And that was before we sat at a high rollers table. But as the evening wore on, I gained confidence and ended up winning $100. I thought I had won the lottery.

The next morning, I greeted President Bush with a full recounting of the evening and proudly paid him back.

He was very creative and delighted in putting together people who otherwise would never interact with each other. He was the master at this!

His goal was always to bring everyone around him some joy.

Linda Casey Poepsel, director of correspondence:

George H. W. Bush was possibly the most thoughtful person ever.

I was among the White House support staff who traveled to the Malta Summit. President Bush and Gorbachev had concluded their sessions and were preparing to leave the boat. Staff were positioned alongside the departure path in bleacher-like stands about five rows high. I was in the last row. Midway down their path, 41 turns and says something to Gorbachev and then looks up and motions me to come down. Surely he meant someone else! But it was me. I came down, and he introduced me to Gorby. I was in such a state of shock that I don't even remember his exact words. I wanted so much to ask him why me—lowest staffer on the totem pole—but we never discussed the incident. He just always did have a soft place in his heart for the "little guy."

Then again, I'm not sure President Bush ever realized he had long ago stopped being one of the little guys.

In 1989, President and Mrs. Bush spent the July Fourth holiday in Kennebunkport. A friend of the Bushes arranged to have a rather

---

* General Schwarzkopf had led all coalition forces in Desert Storm in 1991.

large fireworks display at Walker's Point—something the entire community could enjoy. Unfortunately, the fireworks left behind quite a bit of debris.

So the next morning, President Bush came down to the shed next to the staff office and gathered up brooms, dust pans, et cetera, and asked me to meet him at the tennis court. Mrs. Bush had already cleared the court, and President Bush and I started sweeping up the driveway, making small piles of debris as we went. At one point, he came over to where I was sweeping and gathering, and without saying a word, he bent down and held a small pink dustpan while I swept my pile into it.

The President of the United States holding a pink dustpan . . .

Mary Sage, receptionist and special projects:

I think that 41 was the first President to use a laptop computer.

When he left the White House at age sixty-seven, he enjoyed using his laptop computer with fun fonts and a laser printer. Although he continued to handwrite many thank-you notes, he also loved pecking them out on his computer.

In 1999, when a good friend offered President Bush ten BlackBerrys, Jean Becker told our computer consultants that she didn't want anyone's email on the front page of the *New York Times*. They assured us that the BlackBerrys were secure, and we gave them to President and Mrs. Bush, their aides, and staffers who wanted to use them.

President Bush embraced it and had a great time with the instant replies. At his son's 2001 inaugural parade, President Bush was photographed standing watching the parade while using his BlackBerry. He loved communicating with family and friends using his laptop, BlackBerry, and later his iPad and iPhone.

We were honored and blessed to work for a parachute-jumping, BlackBerry-addicted former President.

He taught us you are never too old to learn new tricks.

*How addicted was 41 to email, the internet, his computer, and all his other devices? He wrote this note to his good friend* TIME *magazine writer Hugh Sidey in 1999.*

**Dear Hugh,**

It's 11:05 a.m. here in Houston.

I feel horrible and alone—unloved and even scared.

Why? might you ask. Well Michael\* just rushed in and said our E-Mail must be closed down for 4 days. He announced, firmly almost defiantly, "Our server will be turned off in exactly five minutes."

No time to notify family and friends, no time even to say goodbye to my wife of 54 years, Barbara. Cut off as if Norad† had told us a theater nuclear weapon was coming right here to suite 900, and here alone, in exactly five minutes...

Michael was too busy rushing from office to office to explain why, but it has to do with a nationwide virus. Some evil little computer nerd out there is spreading a virus; and to hear Michael tell it, if we

---

\* Michael Dannenhauer was the acting chief of staff while I was putting together President Bush's book of letters, *All the Best*.

† North American Aerospace Defense Command, based in Colorado Springs, Colorado.

don't turn off our server and close out our own E-Mails
in five minutes disaster could strike.

This virus might come right into my machine and
wipe out all my files, all 'documents sent.' Michael
tells me if it strikes, then virus-laden messages will go
out to everyone in my global file and in my Personal
Address file. Every single person in those files will get
a contagious message; and then their modems, their
e-mails will crash. It's that serious. It's like Armageddon
and there's nothing even Bill Gates can do about it.

... Twelve months ago I was a Fax man or a phone
man. Now I e-mail everyone in the office and tons of
people outside the office. I am hooked. I know how
to hit the "reply" button and to use the paper clip
that lets me forward documents. I can spell check and
thesaurus words. I can use color and different fonts to
emphasize things... I even listen for the little chime
that quietly sounds when an incoming e-mail hits
my modem. When I hear it I look for that tiny little
envelope icon on the bottom right hand corner of my
IBM. It comes right on, saying by its very presence
someone is writing you, someone cares.

... It's 11:15 AM. We are now shut down, off-line,
disconnected from each other, alone in a world that
is still tough in spite of the implosion of the Soviet
Union.

When I was a kid we didn't have TV. We didn't
know about faxes or computers. And, of course,
Al Gore hadn't even made his contribution to
connectivity back then.

**But then came E-mail right into my life. I resisted at first . . . I had not then discovered the absolute essentiality of e-mail, but our server has been down now for 6 minutes and I feel lonely and lost.**

**Call me . . .**

**George**

Margaret Voelkel, a volunteer in the Office of George Bush:

I volunteered for President Bush for nearly forty years, beginning in 1979 when he first ran for president. Over the years, I helped address and mail Christmas cards, opened mail, and updated addresses in the database. When he lost the election in 1992 and came home, I came into his Houston office at least once a week, often more. I was in charge of all requests for autographs. He sometimes would pretend to be grumpy about autographing photos, books, hats, golf balls—just about anything. But then again, he was happy to do it. He had a hard time saying "No."

The work wasn't exactly exciting, but we loved it. President Bush always made time for the volunteers, coming back to our workspace and telling us stories about his travels and some of the famous people he met. And he always had a joke or two.

He taught all of us how to live life with joy.

*We're going to give the final word in this chapter to two different groups of people: the women who served as Barbara Bush's personal aides over the years; and the men who served as 41's.*

*As President Bush would say: Ladies first. I challenged Mrs. Bush's former aides to abandon the themes of humility and 41's big heart and focus on humor. They were, after all, a frequent target of his good-natured ribbing. They loved it. And they even learned a thing or two.*

*I should add these women were more than personal aides. They did every-thing for Barbara Bush: scheduling, correspondence, press relations, trouble-shooting. And maybe once in a while buy a pair of pantyhose.*

*For both the women and the men, the years they proudly carried the title "personal aide" are in parentheses.*

Becky Brady Beach (1978–1981):

When then candidate for President George H. W. Bush and Mrs. Bush were hosting a lobster cookout in Kennebunkport, I was in the kitchen trying to help their cook, Paula Rendon. I am from the Midwest—Iowa—and not familiar with cooking lobster. I'm not even sure I had eaten lobster. Anyway, I had no idea what I was doing.

Then Mr. Bush came into the kitchen and gave me a cooking lesson:

**If the lobster starts screaming, the water may not be hot enough.**

I nearly passed out. But it was a lesson learned.

Maybe a more valuable lesson came from a conversation we were having one day on the campaign trail for Vice President. We were talking about a lot of things.

**Becky, remember to give back to our country whenever you can.**

I took the advice to heart and later founded the Puppy Jake Foundation to provide service dogs to wounded veterans.

Kim Brady Cutler (1981–1985):

I cannot remember when I was tagged with the nickname "the General" by then Vice President Bush, but it was most likely in a holding room somewhere when I was telling him what he had to do next—yes, ordering him around like a general.

Whenever I went to visit them, right to the very end, he always greeted me with that incredible twinkle in his eye: **General, how the heck are you?!**

In 1996, President Bush was the honorary chairman of the Presidents Cup golf tournament, held that year in Virginia, and I was enlisted to do the advance work. President Bush invited General Scowcroft out for the day, and at one point, President Bush yelled out, **Hey, General**, and both Scowcroft and I answered, "Yes, sir?"

The look on the President's face was priceless as he saw Scowcroft looking at me wondering what was going on, and me turning an embarrassing shade of red! Never one to miss the opportunity to inject humor into a situation, the President took great joy in explaining the different rankings he gave to us generals—we were all in hysterics—and I am pretty sure Scowcroft squeaked by with seniority in the end.

President Bush loved to see the humor in things big or small and always put those around him at ease. I have a copy of a quote on my desk by Edward Everett Hale: "Look up and not down; look out and not in; look forward and not back; and lend a hand."

It reminds me every day of our fearless leader. They are words President Bush lived by, and through example, he taught us to live by them as well.

And, of course: to remember to see the humor in life.

Elizabeth Wise Doublet (1985–1987):

I was sitting with Vice President Bush on Air Force Two, and we had a long conversation about what I would do and should do when I left my job to finish college and go to graduate school.

He was the person who gave me the most support then, and during some important moments later in my life. On this occasion, he taught me a song, a Shaker song.* I often sing it to myself to try to make it a rule to live by. I can't hear it without thinking of him. It goes like this:

> *'Tis the gift to be simple, 'tis the gift to be free.*
> *'Tis the gift to come down where we ought to be,*
> *And when we find ourselves in the place just right,*
> *'Twill be in the valley of love and delight.*
> *When true simplicity is gained,*
> *To bow and to bend we shan't be ashamed,*
> *To turn, turn will be our delight,*
> *Till by turning, turning we come 'round right.*

## Casey Healey Killblane (1987–1989):

He amazed me how he could be so forgiving. The press was not nice (I didn't think so, anyway), and yet he invited them to Walker's Point every summer for a press picnic. He loved to tease and joke with them, always seeing the other side of the story.

I learned that sometimes you can help change the story. For example:

His first summer as President he just couldn't seem to catch a fish. One day he convinced everyone today would be the day. He hinted that maybe a good send-off would help. So on the back porch we all started drawing posters. Even Mila Mulroney† made a couple. We

---

* Per the Smithsonian website: In the 1800s, Shaker music was part of the worship life of the Shaker faith community and became some of the best-known American folk melodies.

† Wife of then Canadian prime minister Brian Mulroney. They were both visiting at the time.

all gathered on the dock and absolutely gave him a huge send-off. Funny thing is, I don't remember if he caught one that day or not. The press loved the whole scene, and it became the story.

The pictures, the story, and the memories are about the fun and always having hope. And George H. W. Bush always had hope.

### Peggy Swift White (1989–1993):

President Bush taught me a valuable lesson regarding Grey Goose vodka martinis. We were having a late-night snack at the Bull & Bear in Manhattan following a political fund-raiser in 1997. General Scowcroft, who was staying at the hotel but not a part of the event, was invited to join us. They each ordered a martini, and I followed suit. With a twinkle in his eye, President Bush said:

**Don't ever drink more than one of these in public until you know you can handle it.**

I did, and I can't.

### Quincy Hicks Crawford (1994–1998):

President Bush taught me that when you get an idea to do something, don't overthink, just do it. Have people over. Write someone a letter. Pick up the phone and reconnect with an old friend. Bring a little levity to every situation. If you can make it into a corny contest, do it. If it can be turned into a funny award, create it. If you have enough people for a bracket, then, by all means, compete. Take a landlubber on a really fast boat ride. Leave a big tip. Stop the car and help someone find a lost dog. When the opportunity arises or the proverbial lightbulb goes off, embrace it.

President Bush did something for someone every day, and everyone loved him for it.

★ ★ ★

Kara Babers Sanders (1998–2000):

George Bush knew the key to a happy marriage is a happy wife. And how to keep her happy? Always take her calls.

One hectic afternoon, I was covering the front desk at the Office of George Bush when all phone lines literally lit up at once. The simultaneous callers: General Colin Powell, Secretary James A. Baker, and Governor (at the time) George W. Bush. I was about to dart into President Bush's office to ask in what order he wanted to take the calls when the fourth phone line rang. Yes, it was Barbara Bush. When I told President Bush just how in demand he was, his answer without hesitation:

**Put Bar on—tell the others I will call them right back.**

I never forgot how he prioritized his wife—that day and always.

Which is why it should be no surprise that in the spring of 2000, George Bush had an idea: to plan a "modest surprise" party for Mrs. Bush's seventy-fifth birthday in Kennebunkport—a town the size of a postage stamp. The details of the celebration were quickly and secretly arranged. And after considerable deliberation, we settled on a "containable" guest list of family, close friends, and former staff. Invitations were issued and were followed up quickly by stern missives from the former President to stay away from downtown and Ocean Avenue for fear of spoiling the surprise.

We were rolling merrily along until one day George Bush utters the words we all knew to fear: **How can we make this even better?** While McDonald's may have coined the drive-through question "Would you like to supersize that?" George Bush was truly the original supersizer.

With a wave of his conductor's wand, the "containable" guest list rapidly reached global proportions—from a Saudi prince to his local barber. Suddenly the whole world was invited to the "little lobster bake." And in the middle of all the details was George Bush. He executed a picturesque sunset arrival to the party by motorboat. He charged all his children to stand and deliver rousing, humorous toasts. He tapped A-list entertainment to keep the evening rolling. And he even directed and played a starring role in humorous skits written and performed by grandchildren and former personal aides. It was a magical night.

Thanks, President Bush, for showing us how to always make things "even better."

Brooke Sheldon (2000–2003):

You have to go with the flow. That's what I learned from 41.

After a speech in sunny, beautiful southern Florida, President and Mrs. Bush, Tom Frechette, and I boarded our private plane back to Houston. The pilot informed us that the weather in Houston would not allow us to depart, and we would have an unexpected overnight stay in Florida. This unwelcome news was met with jeers and moaning, but we eventually grabbed our bags and cell phones and began to make arrangements to spend the night.

On the way to the hotel, President Bush decided we needed to stop at Walmart and pick up some supplies. So we all entered Walmart and went our separate ways to get overnight toiletries. We met up at the checkout lane where 41 stood across from a cashier, as any father or grandfather would, and waited as we all placed our items. 41 lovingly questioned: **Brookie, did you remember to get a toothbrush?**

Amanda Aulds Sherzer (2008–2010):

In 2009, Mrs. Bush underwent major heart surgery in which her aortic valve was replaced with that of a pig. Truth be told, President

Bush was a nervous wreck about the surgery. Mrs. Bush was his everything!

To ease the tension and make her laugh, President Bush would playfully "oink" at her. He would call to her, "Sooey, sooey," and ask if she felt like corn for dinner. At Mrs. Bush's annual literacy fund-raiser, A Celebration of Reading, he even brought a real pig onto the stage (Sidenote: The pig was not potty-trained). His claim was that this pig's relative was the heart donor, and we needed to show our thanks.

President Bush taught me the benefit of bringing laughter to every situation—even the most stressful ones.

## Hutton Hinson Higgins (2010–2014):

President Bush taught me to believe in long shots.

On a Friday afternoon, when I happened to be alone at the office, he wanted to get the International Space Station on the phone. 41 had faith that I could figure it out. After an hour of phone calls to former astronauts, I called up to the house and let him know that I had the International Space Station on the blinking line.

Yes, for me, that was a moment.

This might surprise you, but he also taught me to be bold with fashion. He walked out one day to do an interview, wearing a fully sequined jacket from the Oak Ridge Boys. I must have given him a look, as he said:

**You never said which jacket I had to wear.**

## Catherine Branch (2014–2017):

My first memory and impression of President Bush took place on my fifth day on the job. As one can imagine, my nerves were high as the new aide.

It was a Friday evening, and I arrived at the Bushes' house for my final mail folder drop-off. President and Mrs. Bush were sitting in their den watching television when I heard a noise coming from the guest bathroom a few feet away. The toilet was overflowing at a rapid pace onto their hardwood floors and out through the hallway.

My smile-and-keep-calm face turned on as I silently kicked my heels off and ran to find a plunger to stop the water from overflowing. Water was everywhere. President Bush asked what all the commotion was.

I got up from my hands and knees to calmly inform my new employers that their toilet had overflowed, but the situation was under control. Mrs. Bush was horrified. President Bush slowly smiled at me and then quickly invited me to join them for dinner. He insisted, Mrs. Bush insisted, so I accepted their kind offer, dried myself off, and joined them for dinner with a TV tray in front of me.

My immediate reaction to the dinner invite was surprise. I had just started the job, and they barely knew me. But even at age eighty-nine, President Bush's ability to show care, warmth, empathy, and humor around a stressful (for me!) situation was part of his DNA. The toilet jokes that ensued after this incident were an extra fun treat for him too.

*We'll end with stories from some of 41's personal aides who, except for his wife, likely knew President Bush better than anyone. They were by his side in good times and bad; when elections were won and lost; when history was being made—or sometimes when fish were being caught; as he jogged down the beach or lay in a hospital bed fighting for his life. His aides were always there.*

## David Bates (1978–1980):

I had the privilege of spending a lot of time with President Bush as a friend of Jeb's growing up; as the President's personal aide when he first ran for President; and later when I worked for him when he was Vice President and President. I never recall his giving me any advice, but I learned how to conduct myself personally and professionally by observing him. He led by example.

President Bush taught me:

- To treat everyone with kindness and respect. He treated the most junior hotel staff person the same as he treated a wealthy supporter and donor.
- To do your duty and pursue excellence in whatever you're undertaking. I remember when he was first running for President, we would get on the plane after a nonstop day of campaigning, but he would never take the briefcase off his lap and have a beer until he had finished with his paperwork, including writing thank-you notes. He was the same after he was in office.
- To maintain the highest ethical standards. I remember in August 1980, shortly after he became the vice presidential nominee, then presidential nominee Reagan asked him to travel to China and Japan to showcase the foreign policy credentials of the ticket. When we were in Tokyo at the Okura Hotel, he had a massage after a long day of meetings. Afterward, I remember him emphatically telling me, more than once, to make sure that he paid for the massage out of his own pocket, rather than having the campaign pay for it.
- To always put your country first. When facing difficult decisions as President, I remember his saying: **Let's just do what's right (or best) for the country.** He was a selfless patriot.
- To be a grateful person. He never failed to thank those who helped him. And he was always grateful for the blessings in his life, which he expressed through his deep faith.

★ ★ ★

Donald Bringle (1983–1984):

One of my favorite times with the Vice President was when I had the opportunity to ride with him in the limo. He would talk to me about people I did not know. He would explain to me the kind of people they were, and the roles they were involved in. These discussions were never political in nature. They centered on the character and integrity of the individual, first and foremost. Were they good men and women? Were they trustworthy and team players? Were they loyal? Did they value their families? These were the characteristics he valued in others.

An intern had just joined the Vice President's staff, and one day when we were out running, he mentioned the young man, stumbling over the first name.

"Do you mean Muliufi Hannemann?" I asked him.

He looked at me very surprised and asked how I knew the name. I just happened to have been at the Iolani School in Hawaii with Muliufi when we were both in middle school. Though a staunch Democrat who would later run for several offices in Hawaii and serve two terms as mayor of Honolulu, Muliufi was welcomed by the Vice President in such a warm and gracious manner. He was a young man of high quality and accomplishment, and character.

Again, Mr. Bush valued character and integrity above all else—much higher than political affiliation. He was an excellent judge of character and expected the highest ideals to be adhered to by others, and himself.

Tim McBride (1985–1990):

In 1988, during Vice President Bush's campaign to become President, my dad was diagnosed with pancreatic cancer. The Vice President knew the gravity of my dad's illness and often asked how he was doing.

In late October, during the final weeks of the campaign, the Vice President made a campaign stop in Dearborn, Michigan, less than ten miles from where my parents lived. During our visit, he quietly pulled me aside and insisted that I drop off the campaign for a few days to stay behind and spend time with my father. It was crunch time, and I didn't feel I should leave my job.

**I'll be fine. Don't look back and regret not spending time with your dad. Years from now, that time together with him will mean far more to you than anything we do the next couple of days.**

I spent the next couple of days with my dad. It would be one of my last visits with him—he died a couple of months later. More than three decades have passed and my memories of the final weeks of the 1988 campaign have largely faded, but those days with my dad in late October are among my most vivid and cherished memories of him.

Thank you, President Bush.

Fast-forward to January 20, 1989, one of the warmest Inauguration Days in American history. As he was walking down the steps of the White House toward the limo for the ride to the Capitol with President Reagan, the President-elect pulled me aside to tell me he would not be wearing his winter coat for the swearing-in ceremony; consequently, when we arrived at the Capitol, I left the coat in the trunk of the presidential limo.

In the minutes before he was to be escorted out on the podium for the official swearing-in, the President-elect noticed Mrs. Reagan bundling President Reagan up with a scarf and heavy overcoat. The President-elect turned to me and asked for his coat. I reminded him it was in the limo and there wasn't enough time to get it before the swearing-in. He urgently said to me:

**You've got to go get it. I can't go out there looking more vigorous than the President.**

Knowing there was no chance I could get to the limo and back before he was escorted out to the podium, I offered him my overcoat for the march down the steps of the inaugural platform. I have always marveled that on this most important day of his life—like every other day—his first thoughts were for the "other guy."

Bruce Caughman (1990–1991):

The story I'd like to tell is about the importance of family.

When I was the Air Force military aide to the President, I accompanied him on foreign and domestic travel, serving as the primary emergency action coordinator for all military assets supporting the President and providing on-the-scene interface for all military support matters.

When word got out that the personal aide to President Bush was looking to leave for another job in the administration, several of the current staff members began "putting their name out there" as being interested in the position. I was an active-duty military officer, and the thought never crossed my mind as one who would—or even should—be considered for the position.

As time drew closer for the departure of Tim McBride, I began to hear my name as one being considered for the position. It was hard to believe since I hadn't talked to anyone or shown any interest in the position. I'd always had a good relationship with the President and Mrs. Bush, and whoever replaced the current aide would have big shoes to fill, as Tim was beloved by the family.

Following a visit to Camp David by Soviet president Mikhail Gorbachev—during which I was the primary military support coordinator—I was called into the Oval Office to meet with the

President. He told me that after discussing it with his family, he wanted me to serve in the role of his personal aide. He was looking for someone who could do the job and also someone the family felt comfortable being around.

Family was extremely important to President Bush, and during my time around the Bush family and especially serving in the role as the personal aide, I was treated like family by every one of the Bushes. There were many rising stars among the staff members the President could have selected, and I was humbled and honored to be the one the family felt most comfortable with to serve in the role.

Another lesson I learned from the President is no matter how high or important your position, show appreciation for those who work for or provide support to you. On many occasions I witnessed the President showing thanks through personal notes or a signed photo, or through his kind words of appreciation.

Hearing a word of thanks from the most powerful person in the world makes you want to work even harder.

Gian-Carlo Peressutti (1996–2000):

I often think of my tenure as President Bush's aide as getting a graduate degree in multiple disciplines. This story fits that bill. The masterclass is leadership, one of 41's favorite topics.

President Bush was about halfway through the reception and photo op at an event in Indianapolis when panic hit me. I was fairly certain the copy of the speech he was to deliver in about an hour never made it off the airplane. Panic turned to paralysis when I fished his speech box out of my bag and found that it was empty.

The reception concluded and the Secret Service and I shepherded President Bush into his holding room for a bit of downtime before he hit the stage for the main event. It was now or never. I had to tell him. He was in a familiar pose—seated, legs outstretched, arms down by his sides, head back and eyes closed. Somehow, I found my voice.

"Sir, I think I left your speech on the airplane."

I heard the words leave my mouth but felt eerily disconnected from them.

President Bush opened his eyes, but his posture didn't change. He didn't even raise an eyebrow. His tone was neutral. It was neither urgent, nor angry, nor accusatory.

**Well, what are you going to do about that?**

My response was more reflexive than declarative.

"I'm going to get it before you hit the stage."

He said nothing in reply and just simply closed his eyes again.

The next forty-five minutes or so were a blur. After I confessed to the agents what had happened, they arranged for a state police vehicle to whisk me back to the airport and onto the tarmac to our borrowed, private plane. I bounded up the stairs and grabbed the speech from the seat pocket where I had tucked it after 41 dictated revisions during the flight. The police car was rolling again in seconds.

With about fifteen minutes to spare, I arrived back in the holding room to find the former President exactly as I had left him. He looked over at me, gave a nearly undetectable smile, and didn't ask a single question. As showtime approached, he stood up and I handed him the speech box. He never even opened it as we made our way to the stage.

President Bush's response to my error exemplifies how he so naturally embodied strong leadership. Through this episode and so many others like it, he taught me how good leaders support their team, trust their people, and have faith in the processes they've put in place. 41 quietly acknowledged that everyone makes mistakes and emboldened me to not panic and to embrace the chance to make it right. And then to move on. Throughout this whole episode, President Bush uttered only nine words, but the lesson he imparted has lasted for decades.

Tom Frechette (2000–2006):

It seemed that nearly every day President Bush would do something for others that he would have viewed as a small gesture but that in reality had a significant impact on the recipients.

He had tremendous respect and appreciation for the members of his Secret Service detail. In 2013 a member of his security team had a three-year-old child, Patrick, who was diagnosed with leukemia and had lost his hair through chemotherapy treatment. 41 noticed one day that the first few agents he saw that morning had shaved their heads and asked why they all had done so.

The answer: Patrick's father had shaved his head in support of his son, so the agents shaved their heads in support of their colleague.

Upon hearing the reason, he immediately decided he would shave his head as well. That very minute.

Some of his staff were concerned (and rightfully so) that Mrs. Bush maybe should be consulted. His answer:

**She'll find out soon enough, right?**

This was classic George Bush. He was not concerned with his own appearance, nor what Mrs. Bush might think (nor anyone else for that matter). His only focus was on how he, too, could join them in solidarity to support this courageous young boy.

The photo of a bald George Bush holding the bald Patrick led the evening news that night and ended up on the Times Square jumbotron.

Another of my favorite stories began with a dinner held in honor of Chinese president Jiang Zemin in Houston, marked with the typical grandeur and ceremonial splendor.

Throughout the evening President Bush, as always, was generous and thoughtful. At the conclusion of the dinner, he accompanied President Jiang as they left the dais and escorted him to his motorcade to send him off. As he turned to walk toward his own motorcade, he encountered a large group of hotel staff, who had been previously barricaded for security reasons, enthusiastically waving and greeting him.

In true George Bush fashion, he veered off course and headed for the large kitchen where they were gathered, warmly shaking hands, posing for pictures, and engaging in brief conversations with each of them.

This was an all too familiar scene, for he was the same person in public as he was behind closed doors. It made no difference to him whether the person was a president, a CEO, a member of hotel staff, or a sanitation worker. All were shown the same graciousness and respect.

Everyone met the same George Bush.

Coleman Lapointe (2012–2015):

President Bush had the ability to be present, and in return, connect with people on a very personal level.

I was fortunate to begin working for him and Mrs. Bush at the age of fifteen, starting at Walker's Point as a "summer lad," as President Bush used to call those of us hired to work in the yard and run errands.

By then his White House days were over, and he held the title Former Leader of the Free World. During these post-presidential years, even when he wasn't traveling, he kept his days full. Despite a sometimes-grueling schedule, he rarely appeared fatigued, and maintained mindfulness enough to connect with those around him with genuine excitement and interest.

To me, it was not his accomplishments that I admire the most, but his appreciation of others, his patience with his loved ones, and his ability to be present in every moment. Whether hosting an old friend like Mikhail Gorbachev, "Gorby," as he called him; or sitting on the back deck of Barnacle Billy's with Billy Tower,★ he treated each encounter with utmost respect and importance.

It's these characteristics I wish to emulate, and as my family continues to grow, it's these characteristics I wish to instill in our children.

*Note: The last personal aide was Evan Sisley, who was at President Bush's side when he died. Evan's thoughts about 41 can be found in chapter 7, the chapter about death and dying—and about faith.*

*Longtime Bush staffer and friend Chase Untermeyer decided to share his "lessons learned from George H. W. Bush" by summarizing a talk he gave nearly twenty years ago.*

*Chase's list is the perfect wrap-up of this chapter. It's a checklist on how to be a good boss—and a good leader. So he gets the final-final word in this chapter:*

- Write short, handwritten, personal notes.
- Clean out the in-box and answer all phone calls by the end of each day.

---

★ Barnacle Billy's was one of President Bush's favorite restaurants in Maine, located on the water in Ogunquit, Maine. Although he did like the food, his favorite thing was that he could pull up to the restaurant in his boat. Billy Tower was the owner.

- Presume competence and loyalty in subordinates and let only their actions persuade you otherwise.
- Be friendly and polite to everyone, especially "little people."
- Let your people go and pursue their own goals but keep them in the circle.
- Defeats can become victories.
- Take "bad" jobs. (Example: 41 really, really did not want to leave China and come home to head up the CIA when President Ford asked him to do so. He assumed it was the end of his political ambitions. Next to being President, it became his favorite job.)
- Another version of this: Take the hand you've been dealt without complaining and make the most of it. (Example: BPB swearing she always wanted to live in Odessa, Texas.)
- Nice guys can finish first.
- Be on time.
- Make the other person feel as if he/she is the only person in the room.
- Don't hold grudges or otherwise dwell on the past.
- Don't make personal attacks.
- Show loyalty up and loyalty down.

---

# CHAPTER FIVE

# FAMILY AND FRIENDS FIRST
## *Heart*

I will always be grateful for the lessons of kindness I learned from my beloved dad.

—*Doro Bush Koch*

*We've talked a lot so far about what it was that made President Bush such an effective leader: Character, Courage, Decisiveness, Loyalty.*

*Maybe it's time we talk about that very big heart of his.*

*He would be the first to tell you that whether he was flying off an aircraft carrier in the South Pacific; playing baseball at Yale; drilling oil wells in Texas; heading the CIA; or being President of the United States, his life mantra never changed:*

*Faith, family, and friends.*

*For his Yale fiftieth-reunion book, he and the others were asked to write a short essay about who they were after fifty years:*

**Well, I am a happy man, a very happy man. I used to be a government employee, holding a wide variety of jobs. So many, in fact, that my wife Barbara became fond of saying "Poor George, he cannot hold a job."**

... Yes, I am the George Bush that once was President of the United States of America. Now, at times, this seems hard for me to believe. All that is history and the historians in the future will sort out the bad things I might have done from the good things. My priorities now are friends, family, and faith.—George Bush.

*We will talk about faith in the final chapter; this chapter is all about his big heart, as shown through stories shared by his family and friends.*

*We'll start with family.*

*It was from them he drew his peace and strength. As he once wrote about Kennebunkport, where the very large extended Bush-Walker clan gathered every summer:*

My sons and daughter all come home to this special place. So do our grandkids, cousins, brothers, sister, nieces, nephews. They all come home to Kennebunkport, Maine, for this is our anchor to windward. When the storms of life are threatening it is here that all of us get comfort and strength. When we seek tranquility or say our prayers for peace we come here. It is here we count our many blessings.

*Here are some of the family's stories and thoughts about the man whom they considered not only their dad/gampy/uncle/cousin, but also their patriarch.*

Doro Bush Koch, daughter:

When I was a mother of two children and newly divorced in my twenties, Dad taught me the importance of unconditional friendship and love.

Understanding that a divorce is never one-sided, Dad immediately reached out to my former husband the summer after our divorce for a round of golf. This gesture of kindness had a ripple effect that spread across our family and his. It turned something that was very painful and raw into something more bearable. It set the tone for how our families would engage with each other from then on. In fact, it was the seed of kindness from which many other kindnesses have grown. I will always be grateful for the lessons of kindness I learned from my beloved dad.

### Lizzie Andrews, granddaughter:

Gampy* was the best role model. He treated everyone in the room as his equal, was kind, humble, and always had a funny joke up his sleeve. As a step-granddaughter, I was pretty shy when I first joined the family, but he always made me feel just as special as every other grandchild. I always admired his quiet confidence and his unique ability to make those around him feel loved and included.

### Noelle Bush, granddaughter:

Gampy always taught me to be humble; to be a hard worker; to go to church; and to pray every night.

### Pierce Bush, grandson:

I learned about how not to take yourself too seriously, and that celebrity status doesn't mean very much compared to your relationships with your friends and family.

At the end of the day, people are just people.

I learned this lesson when we went to the Super Bowl in February 2002 in New Orleans right after 9/11. Gampy was flipping the

---

* The Bush grandchildren called their grandfather Gampy and their grandmother Ganny.

coin to start the game with legendary Dallas Cowboys quarterback Roger Staubach. The evening before the big game, we got invited to the NFL owners party at the D-Day Museum, now the official National WWII Museum. It was an amazing experience with a special tour before the dinner led by historian Stephen Ambrose himself.

There were all kinds of hotshots at this event, and as a precocious fifteen-year-old, I was a bit overwhelmed by it all. Gampy could tell, and he pulled me aside during the cocktail hour.

**Hey, Pierce, this is what I like to call name-dropper's paradise**, he said, nudging my side with his elbow. Scanning the room, he observed Rupert Murdoch, the owner of News Corp, eating an appetizer off a tray right in front of us. He pointed to him and said, **Pierce, does Rupert know you yet?**

U2 singer Bono was there, too, and Gampy asked the same question.

**Does Bono know you yet?**

It was such a funny way to frame up asking if I had met these famous people, and it certainly made me less intimidated to be at this fancy party that I had no business being at!

Gigi Koch, granddaughter:

My favorite thing in the world was being able to spend the summer with my grandparents in Maine. I remember one rainy afternoon, Gampy asked my mom and me what we were doing. He said he was taking out *Fidelity* and told us to bundle up. I remember being slightly surprised and feeling just a little hesitant. It was pouring outside! My mom, who takes after my grandfather in her love of being on the water and her sense of adventure, was all in. So we put on our rain gear and headed out to the boat with him. The seas were big and rough and it was still pouring rain. That didn't stop us from flying. Gampy loved being on his boat more than anyone I know, and he loved bringing that joy to others, even if it meant coming home soaking wet. He turned ordinary moments into the most fun.

Lauren Bush Lauren, granddaughter:

My grandfather was so many things to so many people, but to me he was simply a loving grandfather.

Even though he was President of the United States, he continued to move through the world with a lot of humility and love. Of course my vantage point as a granddaughter was of my grandfather not in the Oval Office (though we grandkids could be known to sneak in there from time to time to snoop around), but my grandfather was out of the spotlight more during Sunday taco meetups in Houston after church, on family trips, and during summers spent in his beloved Maine. And during this time, he never took himself too seriously. He was present and enjoying life—his boat, his dogs, his family, and lots of constant competitions and activities from tennis, backgammon, horseshoes, and more.

He had an ongoing challenge to the grandkids that the first grandkid to beat him in a set of tennis would be rewarded with $100, or BIG folding green as he would call it. I was in high school and had recently joined my tennis team, though an average player. But Gampy was in his late seventies, so I thought that I had a pretty good shot of beating him simply because I could still hustle for the ball and had that youthful endurance on my side.

We started our game at Walker's Point, and soon there was a crowd gathered to watch. He was still agile but not able to run for the ball like he used to. But what he could do were lots of strategic and artful drop shots and lobs. Between the crowd of family and friends watching and Gamp's tricky shots, I was not on my A game.

Then a few games into what I remember being a somewhat tight match, he put on a baseball hat that had an angler fish going through it with a tail that would flop when you pushed a button. It was the final straw of distraction that caused me to lose the match. But it was all in good humor and fun!

Now that I am older, I can appreciate even more how he purposefully created special moments and rituals with family and friends that were filled with joy and humor, which is something I now aim to do with my family and friends. My tennis match with Gampy was also a life lesson in how to lean into your strengths, which in my grandfather's case were a big cheering crowd, lobs and drop shots, and a funny fish hat. And that win or lose, it was more about the fun of being together.

To this day the tennis court at Walker's Point, now converted to two pickleball courts, is still where my family gathers daily in the summer for some fierce but friendly competitions. Gampy's spirit lives on.

### Ashley Bush LeFevre, granddaughter:

The men in my family are not afraid to cry.

I've watched my dad, Neil, completely break down over an emotional episode of *Touched by an Angel* (or pretty much any toast he gives to someone he loves). My brother, Pierce, lost it at both my sister's and my wedding. My uncle George famously sheds tears on the national stage from time to time.

And then there's my grandfather—Gampy, the original crier. The one who showed them—all of us—how to feel these intense emotions life throws at us. You don't sweep it under the rug to look more powerful, more in control, more effective. Instead, you embrace the sadness, the joy, the heartbreak, the tears.

Ten years ago, at one of our favorite Tex-Mex restaurants, I was asking Gampy about his life, posing questions like: "Who was your best friend growing up?" He'd either respond right away or direct me to Ganny. My grandmother was Gampy's historian, remembering the smallest details of his life—of their life.

But one question hit harder. I asked my grandfather: "You've lived such an incredible life, is there a memorable event that stands out among the others?"

I thought it was a no-brainer: the day he was elected President of the United States! Instead, he sat in silence for a long beat. I was getting ready to ask Ganny what hers was when I realized my grandfather was crying. He was no longer sitting at that table, but deep in thought about someone, something. He finally looked up at me, tried unsuccessfully to compose himself, and then through tears recounted the harrowing day he lost two of his crew members during World War II.

I remember the waitstaff at the restaurant being alarmed, and quickly forgoing the water service. Gampy was eighty-eight years old when I was quizzing him about his extraordinary life, but the memories of his twenty-year-old self were so vivid, so fresh. The heartbreak so real.

**Not a single day passes where I don't think about those two men who lost their lives too early.**

Gampy was a young Navy pilot when his aircraft was hit by enemy fire. His two crew members, Lieutenant Junior Grade William White and Radioman Second Class John Delaney, did not survive. It was an emotional touchstone that undoubtedly shaped the rest of his life. And instead of trying to forget that horrifying incident, Gampy made sure he thought about it every single day.

To witness a man who has lived such a powerful and extraordinary life be so vulnerable and grieve so publicly was such a testament to the kind of leader he chose to be: compassionate, thoughtful, resilient. By example, Gampy encouraged all of us to live deeply, to feel everything, and to not be afraid when the tears start rolling.

Ellie LeBlond Sosa, granddaughter:

Gampy taught us about the importance of a hard-earned dollar from a young age. He would ask us if we wanted to make some "folding green." My cousins and I would jump at the opportunity because: (a) We loved our Gampy; and (b) we would use the money to buy candy from the candy store in Kennebunkport.

He'd pull his socks off and hand us the lotion, and we'd get to work, massaging his tired feet. After we were done we were pumped when he'd hand over a couple of crisp dollar bills. Looking back, I think we should have charged more!

Jody Bush, sister-in-law:

Right after George dropped out of the presidential race in 1980, he and Barbara hosted Neil's first wedding in Kennebunkport. I know they were pretty down—I think everyone thought George's political career was over. But on Neil's wedding day, George erased his ego, erased all thoughts of himself. He was the groom's father. He wanted it to be a day of celebration for his family; not about him. I have never forgotten that.

Billy Bush, nephew (from *41ON41*):

He's so compassionate and kind and giving and always thinking about somebody else. And he'll always put himself last . . . you can't be around President Bush and not come away a better person yourself. It's impossible. He'll rub off on you.

Jamie Bush, nephew:

Uncle George was President when my six-year-old Sam and I were down on the pier at Walker's Point. Sam was holding his $10 Cape Porpoise hardware store fishing rod, expecting to catch a fish any minute. It would have been the first fish ever caught from that pier.

The Leader of the Free World walked through on his way to his office when he paused and then came out to us, curious, as he'd never seen anyone fish there.

**Whatcha doin', boys?**

"Fishing!" says Sam.

**Can I look at your equipment?**

The President takes the rod, examines it closely, and says: **Want to come up to the house? Maybe I can find you some equipment that might improve your chances.**

When we get there, Uncle George starts going through the hall closet looking for stuff, meanwhile handing Sam various items like the Bulls NBA championship ball signed by Michael Jordan and the team, and similar hardware from other teams, saying: **Would you hold this, Sam?** All the while Sam's eyes keep widening. Uncle George puts together a tackle box of his own equipment and gives him a rod. **Here you go, Sam; see if this makes a difference in your luck.**

Then he casually said: **By the way, Sam, Roger Clemens\* is here for lunch tomorrow, wanna come up for some horseshoes?**

Sam didn't hear the word "shoes," as he was out the door on his way to the pool shouting, "Mom? Mom!!! Roger Clemens is COMING HERE!!!"

---

\* Roger Clemens was the star pitcher for the Boston Red Sox at that time.

Sam was never the same, especially as we walked around the last few holes on the golf course with Clemens and Uncle George the next day; then Sam was invited to play horseshoes for five to ten minutes with Clemens and the other Sox.

My takeaway was this: "When you care for/love the least of these, you care for Me." Uncle George had the gift of seeing every single person as more interesting than himself and treating them as such. There was, for so many of us, as his mother designated him, almost no "self" there. Remarkable, always.

Later that summer Sam was summoned to the Big House one evening because Bucky (Uncle George's brother) had told the presiding bishop of the Episcopal Church in America that Sam did a great rendition of Cab Calloway's "Minnie the Moocher." Picture Sam leading Bishop Allen (on his knees), singing, "Hidee hidee hidee hii! Hodee hodee hodee ho!" with Uncle George seated nearby, vodka in hand, smiling that beatific smile. Those were the days.

Alexander "Hap" Ellis, nephew:

In the spring of 1989, I was contacted by a good friend whose brother had been shot in cold blood with two other young civil rights activists in Mississippi in 1964. Books and even a Hollywood movie have chronicled this shameful moment in our history.* My friend asked if I would be willing to reach out to my uncle to see if the President would welcome the three families to the White House to commemorate the twenty-fifth anniversary of this terrible tragedy.

The President agreed, and the families gathered in the Oval Office on June 23. I was in Boston and remember thinking I needed

---

* James Chaney, Andrew Goodman, and Michael Schwerner were killed by the Ku Klux Klan in June 1964, which became known as the Mississippi Burning Murders.

to watch the nightly news, as this surely would be a great moment for the families—the Oval Office, after all!—and hopefully for the President.

Well, it certainly was the lead story, but not the one I envisioned. Instead, the story was how family members (not my friend, thankfully) used the meeting, particularly the photo op and the informal press gathering outside afterward, not to memorialize the tragedy of twenty-five years ago, but to press a political agenda and challenge the President's motives. I was horrified. I immediately called the White House and got through to my aunt, and despite her reassurances, I felt sick to my stomach.

Not three days later, a two-page letter arrived from the White House, wherein my uncle found a way—as he always seemed to do—to say that while he was disappointed, he was not surprised because a meeting in the Oval Office and then with the press corps outside is a rare opportunity for national publicity. He further wrote: **I am inclined to discount what was fundamentally, in my view, a rather discourteous performance.**

It was yet another example of one of his core leadership tenets: Always be willing to put yourself in "the other guy's shoes," even when that person is indeed discourteous if not right down rude. Not to mention his love of family, taking a moment to reassure a worried nephew.

Postscript: By return mail I promised never again to suggest a meeting in the Oval Office.

In the summer of 1991, it was my turn to give the President a little encouragement.

Notwithstanding the earlier, and stunning, success of the Gulf War, my uncle found himself dealing with an increasingly difficult economy and restless voters. I sent him a note saying, "In the words of a Nitty Gritty Dirt Band song, 'If you ever want to see a rainbow, you gotta stand a little rain.'"

Fast-forward to October, and Reba McEntire invites my aunt and uncle to the Country Music Awards. He tells Reba and the audience that he kept that line "under the glass" on his desk—underscoring how important country music themes were to him and Aunt Bar, and the country. Alas, campaigning in New Hampshire in early 1992, he used the line several times in his stump speech, and while usually citing the band correctly, at one stop he called the band the "Nitty Ditty Nitty Gritty Great Bird." Unfortunately Maureen Dowd was there, covering the campaign for the *New York Times*—and yes, of course, it was on the front page the next day.

But I do think that the refrain from the Dirt Band's "Stand a Little Rain" is quintessentially my uncle.

Robin Ellis, Hap's wife:

The first time I met President Bush and Aunt Bar was almost fifty years ago.

My second date with my future husband was a traditional Sunday barbecue lunch at his aunt and uncle's house in Washington. Uncle George was RNC chairman at the time.

He was at the grill cooking burgers and dogs, and Aunt Bar had cooked up her traditional mixture of two kinds of Campbell's soup. (I think it was a combination of pea and tomato.) And maybe a Bloody Mary was offered also.

I was immediately made to feel completely at home. In the years since that day, the acts of kindness, graciousness, thoughtfulness, loyalty, love, and sense of humor that Uncle George has shown to me, Hap, and our children and daughters-in-law, and even grandchildren are endless.

Just recently Hap and I pulled out a bottle of a very special wine Uncle George had brought with him to an end-of-the-summer dinner at our summer home in Kennebunkport. On the bottle—in gold, indelible ink—he had written:

**Hap and Robin—'til we meet again. G.B.**

Jim Pierce, nephew:

In 1990, we had a conversation as Uncle George, Aunt Bar, and I traveled from the White House to a political event. His son Neil had been the target of a massive media witch hunt solely because Neil had served as an outside director to a large Colorado-based savings and loan bank that had failed.

The media and certain members of the opposition party were playing "gotcha" with one of the President's children.

He asked me how I thought Neil was doing, and as he asked the question, his eyes welled up. I told him Neil was just fine, and he would weather the storm. But the pain on his face told me all I needed to know. The Leader of the Free World was feeling the pain only a parent could know.

At the time I was unmarried and children were not part of my life. I saw how he was hurting because of what he saw as an injustice being foisted upon his son. As I think back on that conversation, I do so as the parent of adult children. What I now realize is that they are always children, and no matter how much they mature and embrace their own journeys into adulthood, the basic parental gene never turns off. No matter what is happening in and around one's life, family comes first.

Uncle George was the Leader of the Free World. Family came first.

★ ★ ★

*It seems appropriate to let his wife of seventy-three years have the last word. After all, she usually did.*

Barbara Bush (from *41ON41*):

When we were first married, I had no idea what my life was gonna be. Might have scared me if I'd known...I'm thinking nobody in the world has ever had the life I've had. I've had none of the responsibilities and all the joys of being the wife of George Bush...The other day we were talking about different leaders that we knew—I knew every one of them. Good, bad, or indifferent, thanks to George Bush. I mean, that's amazing.

...We say we love each other every night. And then we fight over who loves the other one more. And that's always a nice argument. I win.

*And then there were his friends—thousands of them. If he were here, he would not approve of my separating staff, colleagues, acquaintances, and yes, even the journalists from this group of friends. He considered them all friends, as they did him. I hope he forgives me for this transgression.*

*Just how strongly did President Bush feel about the importance of friends? He wrote this letter to James Baker and Bob Mosbacher\* one day after lunch.*

**February 5, 2009**

**Dear Jim and Bob,**

**As I headed back to the office after our lunch today, I had a serious thought. I wanted to share it with you.**

---

\* Robert A. Mosbacher Sr. served as President Bush's secretary of commerce after helping him get elected in 1988.

All three of us have had power lunches with famous people. As John Connally★ once put it, "I have dined with kings and potentates."

But the lunch we had today was simply a lunch between dear friends. We didn't have an agenda and none of us were trying to get our photo taken by that intrusive, persistent camera lady, who has become a minor pain in the a - -.

All we had was the joy of real friendship and what a treasure and joy it really is. I am a very lucky guy and I know it. And I want to be sure you two know that I feel that way, and that I am grateful to you both— always will be.

We have all sat at "head tables," but our little table today trumps any head table in the world. When I say my prayers tonight, I will give thanks for the friendships we share and honor.

George

*When I reached out to some of 41's friends and asked them if they wanted to write something for the book, they immediately started filling up my in-box. It was great fun reading all their stories, but there was one problem: Many of them did not address their assignment: What did you LEARN from George Bush?*

*Then I finally realized that all their stories, although very different, were about one very important lesson he taught us:*

*How to be a better person.*

---

★ The former governor of Texas, he was wounded while riding with JFK in Dallas when the president was assassinated.

*There are stories about his big heart, about his humility, about his sense of humor.*

*And how he lived life with joy. He truly believed we were meant to have fun.*

*Here are some of the people who made his life sing—sometimes literally.*

### Duane Allen, one of the Oak Ridge Boys:

41 found out that I love to fish, so he told me on a certain day we were going fishing—Joe Bonsall, Donna Sterban,* and me.

We had barely gotten out of the cove on *Fidelity* when 41 pushed the hammer down and off we went to only God and 41 knew where. It was full throttle. The Secret Service agents were trying their best to keep up in their boat.

It wasn't long before we saw the seagulls flying over a certain spot, so we locked down, set our hooks, and got in place with our rods and reels. I got a huge hit immediately, but the fish broke my line. So I reeled in the line and the lure was gone. Immediately 41 handed me another rod and reel, took the one I had, and said, **They are hitting your bait. You catch the big one while I fix your line.**

For a moment I could have cried. It was more important to 41 for me to have a great time than it was for him to spend his own time fishing.

He reminded me at that moment so much of my daddy. I learned so much from him about how to treat others and how to just be a good man.

### The Reverend Ed Becker:

While my sister Jean was President Bush's chief of staff in his post-presidency, I visited her in Kennebunkport almost every summer. Lucky for me, I was often invited to go out on boat trips with

---

* Joe is another Oak Ridge Boy and Donna is the wife of Oak's Richard Sterban.

President Bush. He was an expert boatman who had been plying the waters of the Atlantic Ocean off the coast of Maine in various types of boats since he was a small child. Watching him at the helm of his boat was like watching a master painter at work at his easel.

One Sunday afternoon President Bush phoned Jean to report that a pod of whales had been spotted close to the coast and he was going to go find them. His daughter Doro was "in"; would we like to go? Of course we said yes!

The reports certainly proved true. We were surrounded by whales. Very large whales. The whales were so close to our boat that we were able to recognize that the same whales that were surfacing and then diving back into the water on the port side of the boat were surfacing and diving again on the starboard side of the boat, and vice versa. So it was obvious that the whales were going back and forth under *Fidelity*.

It was very exciting—we had never had such an up-close whale-watching experience. President Bush remained cool and calm, looking from side to side and watching the whales as they surfaced and dived back into the water. I remember Doro also remaining very cool and calm, just like her father. After about a minute or so, President Bush slowly moved the boat forward and drove us out of the area. Jean and I continued to be very effusive about our excitement at having just experienced the best whale-watching ever.

Afterward we did wonder if there had been a possibility that we might have been in some danger of a whale causing the boat to capsize. Jean asked President Bush about it, and he assured her that we had not been in any significant danger. And we knew that we had been in the best possible hands with President Bush at the helm. Of course we were safe.

Then a couple of weeks later, there was a report of a couple drowning off the coast of South Africa after a whale tried to surface under their boat and capsized it. Jean and I then realized: Yes, we could have drowned.

Looking back on it, I think President Bush knew that there was at least some risk of a whale capsizing our boat that day, and that he just coolly and calmly assessed the situation and moved us to safety as soon as he knew the best way to do so.

What character lessons did I learn from President Bush from that whale-watching experience? One would certainly be, when possible, to stay calm and keep cool under pressure.

More fundamentally, though, another character lesson to be learned is to have faith and trust in God. I think that the reason why President Bush was able to keep cool under pressure that day in the middle of a pod of whales—as well as at so many other times of his life—was because of his faith. I do not remember President Bush speaking a single word that day while we were in the middle of a pod of whales. Nor do I think I ever had a single conversation with President Bush about his faith. But all of us who knew and loved him knew from his actions and the way he lived his life that he was a man of deep faith who seemed always to trust in God.

Jeff Benson, Navy captain:

As a proud graduate of the Bush School, some of the lessons I learned from President Bush have been a guiding light during my career as a Navy officer.

1. Leadership under fire.

During World War II, 41's bomber plane was the last to land before other fighter planes began the next landing cycle. As he got out of his bomber, the following aircraft stalled on landing and flipped over next to him. Before the aircraft fell into the water, the blades on the plane killed one sailor by slicing him into three pieces. Bush remembers a chief petty officer on the flight deck vividly saying, "Clean up this ship and let's get going." He wrote and talked about this incident numerous times, and the importance of "leadership under fire."

As the captain of a destroyer deployed in Japan, I experienced several tense situations in the Taiwan Strait and South China Sea. I often reflected on 41's comment about leadership under fire, a characteristic I feel he demonstrated many times in his lifetime, including when he was shot down. I retold 41's story to the ship's crew during an extended deployment as a reminder that you must persevere and keep going in the most challenging situations.

2. Political civility and kindness.

In a time when negativity and attacking the other political party seem to drive current politics, 41 consistently demonstrated over his career acts of civility and kindness as a leader.

In 1969, after President Nixon's inauguration, President and Lady Bird Johnson departed Andrews Air Force Base for Texas. At the time a congressman from Texas, 41 was the only Republican at the airport to wish them off in person. Regardless of party politics, 41 believed in political civility and respected the office of the President. When asked why he was at the airport, he said: **He [President Johnson] has been a fine president and invariably courteous and fair to me and my people, and I thought that I belonged here to show in a small way how much I have appreciated him. I wish I could do more.**

This story impacted me during a class with 41 while at the Bush School. There will be disagreements about political issues, but respecting each other, regardless of the political party, is what makes our democracy great.

Dana Carvey, comedian and actor:

One memory of 41 that for me exemplifies his character happened on Election Day 2004. His son George W. Bush was running for reelection and was facing a close race with the Democratic nominee, John Kerry.

My phone rang and on the other end I heard 41's familiar drawl:

**Hi, Dana, George Bush here. How ya doing?**

"Well, um, hello, Mr. President. I'm doing fine, thank you. Uh, isn't your son running for reelection today?"

**Well, yeah, he is. But how are you?**

I admit that I was surprised to hear from him on this particular day. We had done a number of events together, but he didn't often call me at home. I thought it must be an emotional and dramatic day for a father whose son was running for a second term as President of the United States. Why would he be thinking about me?

**Bar and I saw you on TV last night and wondered how you're doing. Everything going well in your life? Family all healthy?**

"Everything's going great, Mr. President. Thank you for asking."

**Good, good, that's good—just wanted to hear your voice, Dana.**

I couldn't help but ask, "And, uh how's the election going?"

**Well, Florida's tight, but looking good. We'll see how it goes. Anyway, God bless you and your family.**

"Thank you, Mr. President. And thank you for the call. I hope all is well with you."

**We are blessed. Goodbye now.**

* * *

Ray Chambers, businessman and philanthropist:

In telling this story, I am wonderfully reminded of President Bush as a deeply caring, authentic human being, leader, and man with good humor.

It begins in 1988 with the phrase "a thousand points of light." The inspirational notion in his convention speech was not campaign jargon for George H. W. Bush. It was his profound belief that volunteers could do an incredible amount of good for the country and for each other. He affirmed that we all possess a warm, bright point of light within us; one that spurs us to help one another.

Born from a luncheon conversation I had with one of the new President's ambassadors, Joseph Zappala,* the idea for the Points of Light (POL) Foundation soon became more than a dream. The ambassador introduced me to White House staffer Gregg Petersmeyer, and together we outlined its mission and objectives. Consequently, I had my first meeting with President Bush to discuss the vision, and he asked me to be the founding chairman of the organization. During our conversations about it, the President became almost ethereal with the idea of spreading the light ever further by having more and more people become volunteers. It was core to his way of thinking, and it inspired the entire board, which included former Michigan governor George Romney; John Akers, CEO of IBM; Roberto Goizueta, CEO of Coca-Cola; and many other hugely bright individuals.

President Bush was such an inspirational leader. He was a true living example of a Point of Light. He was a beacon to me of how positively one could live their life, accomplish something as great as being President of the United States, carry the nation through a war

---

* He was President Bush's ambassador to Spain.

with nearly 40 allied nations joining us, and all this time keep his ingrained decency, gentleness, and kindness. It never left him.

Tony Dill, head of the Army's Golden Knights:*

One of my colleagues was asking about the tandem jumps the Golden Knights made with 41, and he told me about his interaction with President Bush that was twenty years earlier than mine.

When Chuck Fox was a junior in high school in Iowa,† he and three of his classmates volunteered to help with an event at the Des Moines Civic Center in the run-up to the Republican Caucus in 1980. They were asked to help guide candidates around the skywalks and other parts of the event.

He remembered that all the candidates and their staff were moving around but no one interacted with the helpers. 41 finished up a speech in one of the nearby rooms, and when he came into the hallway, he stopped and shook hands with all the helpers and thanked them for being there. Chuck was awestruck that someone running for President would take the time with the volunteers. His kindness made a huge impact on a kid from Iowa.

I relayed to Chuck that the forty-first President had not changed. I told him how gracious 41 was every time we saw him, and it didn't matter which VIP or dignitary was present, if he saw our soldiers, he would come over to talk to them.

George Dvorsky, singer/actor:

Their first big public outing after the Bushes left Washington in January 1993 was to see a production of *Brigadoon* at Houston's

---

* The Golden Knights is the Army's demonstration and competition parachute team.
† Chuck is now a senior director of technology.

Theatre Under the Stars (TUTS), where I was playing the leading role of Tommy Albright. After the curtain came down, the cast was asked to stay onstage to greet the former President and First Lady. How stunned was I when President Bush walked up to me singing, "Almost Like Being in Love," which was one of my favorite songs that I sang in the show, so naturally I joined in.

This began a truly wonderful friendship because my career often took me to Maine's Ogunquit Playhouse in the summers and then more shows at TUTS over the next twenty-five years. They would come backstage at intermission to say hello (and to use my bathroom). They would have all of the privacy they needed.

It wasn't long before they invited me to sing at numerous parties both at Walker's Point and at varying venues in Houston. I was told to keep my mini concerts to under twenty-two minutes because President Bush wasn't shy to say, **Okay, let's wrap it up** at the twenty-five-minute mark.

The man loved his music, and how thrilled was I that MY music was a part of that.

Being the last person to sing for him at Walker's Point in September of 2018, I had my twenty-two minutes carefully planned. But this time he kept saying "more" after every number. I hadn't planned "more" so I looked at my accompanist and said, "Let's do this one or that one." I threw in "Almost Like Being in Love" and was amazed to see President Bush, sitting in his wheelchair, singing right along with me just as he had done twenty-five years earlier in Houston. It was an unforgettable moment recaptured.

Dr. John Eckstein, Mayo Clinic:

President Bush emailed me before 43's inauguration asking me if there was anything he could take to prevent his crying at the ceremony. I said no, first because there wasn't a medicine that could guarantee he wouldn't cry other than a general anesthetic! But more importantly, I said, "Mr. President, you have every reason to shed tears of joy. Let them flow and let the whole nation see what a good, caring, and proud father you are at this momentous event. The American people will love you more than they already do."

I think he worried the moment called for stoicism and not tears, and as always, he wanted to do the right thing.

The night before President and Mrs. Bush began their annual examinations at Mayo Clinic in Arizona, they would frequently invite Diane and me to dinner, usually at Morton's Steakhouse. The four of us would have a wonderful conversation and a delicious dinner. Invariably, as soon as other restaurant diners recognized the Bushes, they had no hesitation to come over and ask for an autograph, have their picture taken, or just to chat. Not once did either of them refuse any of their requests or show any irritation. They made each diner feel like the "most important person in the world." To us, it demonstrated their character and their humanity.

This may be a little too personal, but I think 41 would be okay with my sharing it.

Whenever I did President Bush's physical examination, the final "act" was the prostate/rectal examination. President Bush would always say, **John, do we really have to do this?** And I would say, "Yes, sir—we do."

Before we began, he would head to the bathroom, which was down the hall of our long corridor at Mayo. We would walk out with him, and he would tightly hold his medical gown, which was open in the back behind him. When other patients were walking up or down the corridor, many would recognize him, and those that did would often say "Oh, wow! President Bush, can I shake your hand?"

With that, he would release the back of his gown to shake the hand of the happy patient! And with that, his rear end was wide open to the entire world behind him in the corridor.

Just like in the restaurant, President Bush showed his friendliness, his character, and his willingness to always be the magnanimous person he was all the years that I knew him.

Mike Elliott, a member of the Army's Golden Knights:

Why one more jump?

That question had to have popped into the heads of 41's family when they were informed that he wanted to take a tandem skydive on his ninetieth birthday. I was even a bit surprised after watching his health struggles from afar.

But I got the call from Chief of Staff Jean Becker telling me the President planned on taking this jump and that he wanted me to be his jump instructor. This would make the third time he and I would fall through the skies together.

The two previous times jumping with our forty-first President were through the United States Army Parachute Team, the Golden Knights. By the time I received this call, I had retired and established a parachute team called the All Veteran Group so I could continue to share the skills I had learned in the Army.

Why did he pick us?

Why did he pick me?

I realized the former world leader trusted me. We had developed a bond, given our passion of flight together. And when you tandem jump with someone—well, you do become close. Very close. Literally.

It gave me a feeling of pride, of honor, and a myriad of emotions I struggle to even vocalize.

I was reminded of our two other jumps when I shared the skies with our former president. The first was in College Station, Texas, for the rededication of his library. This jump was a secret—a secret he kept from even his Secret Service.* I remember sitting in his office planning the jump with our Golden Knights team commander, Lieutenant Colonel Tony Dill, and our sergeant major, Michael Eitniear. I had to pinch myself.

I thought to myself: "Here is a young kid from Linden, North Carolina, who only saw presidents on television. He never had a clue that he would be standing arm to arm with a former world leader, much less discussing strapping him to me and falling from over twelve thousand feet in the sky, placing the President's life literally in my hands!"

The most amazing thing to me was that he was so incredibly kind. So generous. And displayed a smile that showed he was a true giant. It showed he had an amazing character.

And as you well know, character matters.

A day prior to the library rededication jump, Mrs. Bush—or the Silver Fox, as 41 called her—wanted to meet "the guy" and the team that would be taking her husband up twelve thousand feet in the sky. I remember waiting in the foyer of the building across from the library and seeing her coming down the stairs.

She came up to the team, and the sergeant major and the com-

---

* I do know why he didn't tell the Secret Service. He knew they would feel obligated to report the planned jump to their boss at Secret Service headquarters, who likely would tell the President of the United States, George W. Bush. 41 felt his son had enough to worry about so didn't need to know his dad was jumping again. Tony Dill remembers that President Bush told the Golden Knights that during his career, even with the CIA and through his presidency, no one was ever able to keep a secret until this event and he was truly impressed and grateful.

mander introduced themselves and then, as if frozen in time briefly, both of my leaders turned to look at me and pointed in my direction.

"Ma'am, this is Sergeant First Class Mike Elliott. He is going to be 'the guy' that is going to tandem jump with your husband."

I remember looking down at her with a massive smile on my face because she was such a beautiful, radiant vision that embodied what mothers look like as they are smiling at their children. I knew she was going to give me a hug, so I reached down to hug this sweet woman, and she looked up at me and said, "If you hurt him, I will kill you. All of you."

I laughed a little bit because she had a fun little quirky smile on her face, but it definitely pumped up my mind quite a bit to take extra measures to ensure the tandem jump would go off without a hitch.

And that it did.

Afterward, the President addressed all of us who were there:

**Just because you are eighty years old, doesn't mean you have to sit in the corner and slobber all over yourself. Get out and live. Live your life. Do things that drive you.**

And that message sank into my mind. Another lesson learned from this great giant of a man on this earth.

Leading up to his eighty-fifth birthday, the commander and sergeant major received another call from the chief of staff, telling us the President wanted to jump on his birthday, this time in Maine.

A few days before, the advance team, consisting of myself and my good friend Dave Wherley, arrived to figure out the landing zone. We picked Saint Ann's Episcopal Church, where the Bushes attended services every Sunday in the summer.

We completed our reconnaissance and informed the President we were done, that we had all of the answers we needed to ensure a safe operation and were ready for the show.

He looked at me and Dave and asked us what we were doing for dinner.

"Sir, we don't have any plans. We're just going to go do something at a local restaurant."

**Well, Bar and I would like to have you over for dinner.**

I looked at Dave and said, "Sir, absolutely. We'll be back at 6:35."

The night was surreal as we were sitting there with the Bushes and one of their grandchildren. The President asked us: **You boys want a drink?**

And again, I found myself pinching myself. I remember thinking: "Here I am, sitting down across from a former world leader and a former First Lady, having a vodka cocktail, and he's talking about the time he was shot down over the island of Chichijima during World War II."

The funniest thing is that the Bushes' dog Bibi was sitting beside me during the conversation, and as I was drinking my cocktail, the dog nipped me on my index finger.

I'll be honest. It was quite painful.

But I couldn't scream in pain because you just don't let that exit your system when a former President is telling you about the time he was shot down over enemy waters during World War II! It was not a time or place to scream. So I did my best to ignore it and smile and get my finger out of Bibi's mouth.

And then she did it again.

Finally, Mrs. Bush caught on to what was going on, so she stood up, walked out of the room, and proceeded to find a chew toy so Bibi would leave my fingers alone.

It is impossible to describe just how amazing it makes you feel being surrounded by a giant personality and the way he treats people, with an incredible family making memories so few have the joy to experience. The smiles and the jokes and the welcoming nature to make sure you feel part of the family.

President Bush wrote me after the jump:

**I am not sure I will ever come down from the high of that jump. I loved every second and now I can truthfully say that being 85 is no big deal. Everyone in this huge city of Kennebunkport seems to have met you and parenthetically seems to be in love with you. Many, many thanks for another fantastic day in my life. You are the best.**

Now back to that ninetieth birthday jump.

When you get the message that you are going to take the ninety-year-old former President in an airplane to fall from twelve thousand feet, there are a lot of things that happen mentally. You get a little nervous. Everything changes. Even the way you eat, your workout routine, your daily living changes because you want to make sure that you do your absolute best for him.

You do your best for anyone and everyone attached to you during a tandem skydive, but there is an added element when your passenger is a former President of the United States of America. And he's ninety. In a wheelchair with Parkinson's.

Our team flew up a few months prior to sit down and talk with him to see if we could make the ninetieth birthday dream a reality. I knew there would be challenges.

But I didn't expect this one: The day before the jump, I received a call from Jean Becker: "Mike, we need you over here at the office now."

I was thinking to myself, "My God, something must have gone terribly wrong." I immediately left the hotel and raced to his office to hear the news:

"Mike, Mrs. Bush is saying no. There's a big party planned for tomorrow night and she is not going to have it. No jump."

I replied, "Well, that's the First Lady. She rules the nest. I guess that means we're going to pack up our stuff and go home."

"No, Mike. We want YOU to go up and talk to her."

As soon as Jean told me that, I immediately thought back to the time the Silver Fox told me that if anything happened to her husband, she would kill me.

So I told her, "Okay, if you think that's going to help, then I'll be glad to speak with her."

"Well, you're very persuasive. You have jumped with her husband twice and if anybody can do it, you can do it. President Bush 43 went up and spoke with her. I went up and spoke with her and she is not having it."

So Jean and I headed up the hill to the Big House. As we got close to the top of the hill, we saw the President sitting there talking to one of his aides. When he saw us, he motioned us over: **Hey guys! What's going on?**

"Sir, your wife is saying no. She's not going to allow the jump to happen."

He sat up in his wheelchair: **I thought we had all this worked out.**

"Yessir, we thought we had it all worked out, too, but she changed her mind."

**Well, what are we going to do?**

Jean told him, "Sir, we want Mike to go up and talk to her. Mike is very persuasive and maybe he can change her mind."

So there I was, standing with the President, who had been in charge of so many world-changing operations—the end of the Cold War, Desert Storm—and I'm thinking: "He's going to put his foot down and he's going to fix this."

The President looked up at me and asked: **So do I have to go up and talk to her as well?**

We all got a little chuckle out of that. Jean said I should wait with the President while she let Mrs. Bush know I was coming to talk with her.

Ten minutes rolled by.

Jean walked out and back over to where the President and I were shooting the breeze. To our surprise, Jean told us, "She saw all of you standing out here and talking and told me she doesn't want to talk to anyone about this. She told me to tell you to take him on his jump, but he better not get hurt."

Knowing that was directed at me, all I could think was, "Man, if anything at all happens, I'm going to have to face Mrs. Bush!"

As Jean was telling us this, the door to one of the cabins on the property pops open and 43 walks out and over to where we were. He had paint all over himself from painting. He asked what the verdict was from his mom.

Jean Becker replied simply, "She said yes."

A little surprised, 43 asked, "Was she pissed off?"

Jean said, "No, she was not."*

43 looked directly at me and proclaimed, "Mike, you're the man!" And then proceeded to give me a high five and then walked right back to his cabin to continue the paint job.

The last jump wasn't the best landing, but I remember that smile on President Bush's face with everyone singing "Happy Birthday" to him for achieving a jump on his ninetieth birthday.

---

* Actually, I lied. I didn't think they could handle the truth. She was mad. But Mrs. Bush gave in because she knew this jump was important to her husband, and that he had a talent for getting his way anyway. With or without her support, this jump would happen, and she knew it. But she told me emphatically she did not want to talk to any of "them" about it.

I will never forget President Bush, and I cherish the letters he wrote to me as a friend. At one point, he said:

**Between you and I, to say we have a close relationship is an understatement.**

It didn't matter where I was from. It didn't matter the color of my skin. Because the character of this man was that he saw everyone as equals, and I am grateful that I had the opportunity to share our passion of falling through the sky at 120 miles an hour.

And that, my friends, is something I will never forget.

Bruce Gelb, ambassador and businessman (from *41ON41*):

I arrived at Andover in 1941...they did a form of hazing for new boys...This guy says to me, "Okay, I want you to go to my room. I got a big stuffed chair, and I want you to get that chair over to my new room."...I couldn't lift the damn thing..."I can't do it, I'm sorry, I cannot move that chair," I told him, at which point the guy got me in a hammerlock with my right arm behind my back and started to put pressure on it...I couldn't move.

Then I heard the words: **Leave the kid alone.** The guy dropped me like a hot potato, and the next thing I knew I'm standing there and he's moving his chair back to his dorm room. "Who the heck was that?" I asked. And the answer was, "That was George Bush... he's just the best guy in school."

...All I knew was I had a hero that has been a hero for my whole life.

Edward Gillespie, White House staff for President George W. Bush:

During my tenure as counselor to President George W. Bush, I would see the former President in the White House on occasion (more rarely than one might expect). Whenever 41 was there, he would go out of his way to be unobtrusive in any way. He did not want his presence to be a distraction to the staff. But he was never a distraction; he was a joy to be around. The former President liked to swap stories, pick up any good gossip, or hear a new joke (slightly off-color was a bonus).*

In December 2008, President Bush 43 delivered the winter commencement address at Texas A&M. A&M is home to President Bush 41's library, and the former President and Barbara Bush were there to welcome their son to campus. We were less than a month away from President-elect Obama's inauguration and the official transfer of power. The outcome of the recent election reflected President Bush 43's then low standing in the polls, and the country was still in the throes of the financial crisis. It was a difficult time in the White House, and it was uplifting for the president to be back in Texas and to see his beloved parents. And while his approval ratings may have been low in the latest Gallup survey, they were high in Aggieland!

The students loved the commencement speech, interrupting it with the kind of thunderous applause we had not heard in a while. It was a joyful occasion. After the ceremony concluded, 41 rode in "Stagecoach"—the presidential limousine—with the soon-to-be former president to see him off at the helicopter pad. (We had to chopper from College Station over to Air Force One at the Waco airport.) I watched from Marine One as President Bush hugged his father goodbye and turned to climb aboard to settle into his seat across from mine.

I was checking emails on my cell phone as we were lifting off

---

* Whenever President Bush was visiting his son, my email would light up like a Christmas tree as various White House staffers would report that the forty-first President was making the rounds. They loved it.

when the president leaned over, tapped me on my knee, and pointed out the window.

"Look at Dad," he said.

President Bush 41 was standing at full attention, one hand on the hood of the big black car to brace himself as he leaned into the swirling winds being whipped up by Marine One's furious rotors. Sand and grass were being blown up onto his blue suit and into his wind-whipped hair, and a Secret Service agent was positioned behind him like a quarterback in shotgun formation, arms up ready to catch the former President if he was literally blown over.

"He's paying respect to the office," President Bush 43 said as we looked down through the window.

I still get goose bumps remembering that moment as George H. W. Bush displayed not only a father's unconditional love for a son, but a war hero's respect for the presidency of the country he loved and served with such great distinction.

Dava Guerin, author:

It was one of those beautiful sunny days in Kennebunkport. The night before was filled with anticipation of meeting the Leader of the Free World. They came from all across the country, as far as Alaska and California, to spend an afternoon at Walker's Point. Traveling was no easy task for these young men and women. Some were obviously missing arms and legs, and others not as obvious, struggling with debilitating traumatic brain injuries.

Why were they there, you may wonder.

Several months earlier, 41 had offered to come out of retirement from writing forewords to pen a heartfelt message for my first book with my coauthor Kevin Ferris—now one of eight—called *Unbreakable Bonds: The Mighty Moms and Wounded Warriors of Walter*

*Reed.*\* Not only that, but President Bush suggested that we hold the book launch in Maine. Here is part of what he wrote:

**Every commander in chief before and after me would agree that working with our military is the single biggest privilege of being president of the United States. There is no harder decision we face than to put our men and women in harm's way; and there's no worse news to receive than someone has been killed or injured.**

So ten of our nation's heroes, many of whom had the most devastating injuries during the War on Terror in Iraq and Afghanistan, and their devoted mothers began the trek up the long driveway to literally meet their hero—not only the former President of the United States, but the youngest Navy pilot shot down in his plane over the Pacific Ocean during World War ll.

At the time, 41 had fallen out of bed and was wearing a neck brace. Before he met the group, I sat with him alone in his office and gave him a short briefing about the people he was about to meet. You should have seen his smile. As broad as Lake Michigan.

One by one, after being cleared by Secret Service, the wounded warriors began wheeling and walking up the driveway, some with their service dogs, expecting to see 41 in front of the house. That would not do. President Bush insisted his aide wheel him down the driveway so he could meet each and every wounded warrior, shake their hand, and give them a presidential coin. It was the least he could do to honor the service and sacrifice of those young men and women who, like 41, cherished service and were willing to fight and die for our freedoms.

And then there was the big surprise: As it turns out, George W.

---

\* Published in 2014 by Skyhorse.

Bush was in town visiting his parents. For most of these wounded warriors, the forty-third president was their commander in chief. They couldn't believe he and the former First Lady were there as well.

The day was magical for the entire group. One wounded warrior ended up proposing to his girlfriend with 41, 43, and both First Ladies cheering him on.

Another Army specialist said that meeting 41 in person was the singular most meaningful experience in his life. And the mothers could not believe how gracious and self-deprecating President Bush was, not to mention Barbara Bush, whom they were also thrilled to meet.

As if that were not enough, for our second book that Kevin and I wrote, called *Vets and Pets: Wounded Warriors and the Animals That Help Them Heal*, Barbara Bush offered to write the foreword, and both she and 41 invited us to hold our second book launch at Walker's Point.

By that time, 41 was not doing well, and it was painful to see his decline from just a few years earlier. Still, he wanted me to brief him, but this time I decided to read him a short letter I wrote letting him know how much he meant to me, and also his impact on the wounded warriors he had met during our last visit. As I held his hand, I could see he was struggling. Still, he insisted on being wheeled down his driveway, this time to meet fifteen wounded warriors, veterans, and the animals that helped them get through the trauma of war and their resulting visible and invisible injuries.

It was a sight to behold. The group surrounded 41, some putting their hands on his shoulders, others holding his hands as they escorted him in near formation and slowly made their way toward the house. It was as if the wounded warriors were now protecting the man who spent his entire life protecting them. They didn't want to let go.

Despite he and Mrs. Bush being surprised to see a potbellied pig and two wounded screech owls—one of whom had a major accident on 41's khaki pants—it was obvious to me that 41 was loving every moment. He was with his people. Maybe he was thinking about the men he lost when his plane crashed over the Pacific Ocean? Maybe he was recalling the decision to send young men and women to fight for their country during the Gulf War? Or maybe it was just as simple as this: President George H. W. Bush cared about people. He never put himself first. He remembered the little things and recognized in others their commitment to service. He was a champion of the little guy and those with disabilities who struggle to get through every day.

His impact on the wounded warriors and their mothers will last a lifetime. They've all told me that over and over again. What will I always remember? A President of the United States who befriended a thirty-year-old and showed her by example what character, empathy, loyalty, and service embodied. Character matters. And 41 chose to share that gift with countless heroes on the battlefield and the home front.

When he was lying in state in the Rotunda of the Capitol, two of the wounded warriors who met 41, along with me and my husband, had the honor of leading a group of people with disabilities to say their last goodbyes. There were plenty of tears. But they were tears of love and gratitude.

Charles Hermann, first director of the Bush School of Government and Public Service:

Having just celebrated its first twenty-five years, the Bush School already is a recognized leader among its peer institutions.

And no one did more for the school than its namesake. President Bush repeatedly spoke to classes, brought world-renowned figures to the school, pitched horseshoes with students, helped recruit new faculty, and dined with students and faculty.

I worried after he was gone that the school might lose some of its magic, but then I realized we just needed to work a little harder to continue to advocate for and teach two of the values that President Bush held most dear.

The first is easy to talk about because he spoke of it often and with passion: public service. He repeatedly told all of us—especially students—that public service was a noble calling. More powerfully, his life offered a dramatic, continuous illustration. The vast majority of Bush School graduates—in numbers much larger than any of its peers—are in fact pursuing public service careers.

A second essential value is not one he spoke about, but one he demonstrated throughout his life: to work with others holding different political views from his own and encourage them to join him in dialogue and compromise for the public good.

There are many examples of bipartisan cooperation, but perhaps the most dramatic was his friendship with Bill Clinton. Like every other person who has lost a position that they passionately seek, President Bush suffered personal pain and anguish. Yet, after President Clinton finished his term, the two men became friends, working together for good causes, especially raising money for victims of natural disasters.

I am proud that Bush School students strive to embrace these values manifested throughout the remarkable life of our forty-first President. But what about the rest of us? At a moment when the basic fabric of American democracy is imperiled by those unwilling to accept anything but their own unmoderated position, all of us need to emulate George H. W. Bush:

Not to think alike but to walk together.

★ ★ ★

Jeff Hoffman, member of the Points of Light board of directors and employee of Disney:

As board meetings go, when one is hosted by a former President of the United States, the anticipation is heightened.

The board was Points of Light, of which President Bush was the honorary chair. He had invited the board to meet at his presidential library, with a dinner the night before.

We started with a cocktail reception in his private apartment upstairs. He took us on a tour, and I would later find out that Mrs. Bush was not pleased that we went into his bathroom, as he did not tidy up (she was not with us on this occasion).

For the dinner, I was surprised to be seated next to the President. I'd already had a nice catch-up with him upstairs, so he was ready for a more substantive conversation. The topic he wanted to cover was helping me to grow the Disney VoluntEARS program globally. We already had programs in Paris and Tokyo because of Disney's parks there, and a solid program in London.

I was particularly focused on China. Disney was changing from a licensing model in both China and India to an operating model. I was working on bringing staff on in those countries and, in addition to our employee volunteer program, was about to start writing a corporate social responsibility plan for both countries.

This is to say that while my board colleagues were enjoying a nice social evening before the next day's meeting, I was being grilled and coached on what I needed to do to make this happen.

Who knew that the ambassador to the United Nations under President Nixon, the China liaison under President Ford, and of course the Leader of the Free World, would be a "senior adviser" to Jeff Hoffman regarding the expansion of Disney VoluntEARS throughout the world.

He may have lost the presidency, but he never quit being a leader, or caring.

Annie Kennedy, Walker's Point gardener:

It was an Indian summer kind of day at Walker's Point in the fall of 2017—the high season for transplanting and cutting down the perennial gardens. My uniform of red-and-white-striped overalls was, as usual, filthy, and my hands even dirtier. By midmorning I happened to be walking up the driveway when I saw the President in his wheelchair coming from the Big House toward the lower end of the property where his office was located. It was always a great privilege to "run into him," and share a few words or have him join the tune he heard me singing while I worked. (He swears he loved my singing and often joined me.) It was customary to offer an elbow bump because of my dirty gardening hands.

There were very few people on the point this late in the season, and the President looked less Kennebunkport-casual than usual. His golf shirt and khakis were replaced with an ultra-crisp long-sleeved button-down, and he was wearing pleated blue dress pants. For this reason I said, "President Bush, you must be on your way to see someone really important." Then he said: **That would be you, Annie.**

The complexion of my day changed to one of awe. Here was the former Leader of the Free World not making a distinction between his gardener and a person who most likely had historical significance. Although I had seen him greet many people, including me, with eye contact and "presence," this day was different as he verbalized how he sees it. It would have been so easy to wave and blow past the help. George H. W. Bush appears to have inherited that wisdom of presence to others at a young age, and he taught his family to look through this same rare lens. It really takes a form of "unlearning" to encounter people this way. However, if you strip your mind of the existence of power centers of fame, wealth, talent, and intelligence—you will see the garden of human light that he saw.

David McCullough, Pulitzer Prize–winning author and historian (from *41ON41*):

I have interviewed or known eight presidents, maybe nine. And what strikes one is how different they are from each other . . . I once said that if I had to drive from Boston to St. Louis with one of them, that the one I would pick to go with would be George Bush Senior because he's great company and he's entertaining and enjoyable to be with.

. . . I think he was just a natural-born leader. He wasn't a show-off leader, he wasn't an exhibitionist, or a stunning performer onstage. I think he was himself.

. . . I do think his real creed was service to the country, much more than being a political superstar, or getting reelected . . . he took defeat superbly, which is a real measure of one's character. He's really a great man.

Reba McEntire, country music singer and actress:

I'm not sure why we hit it off so well, but the first time I had any correspondence with President Bush was when I went to Washington to do *Christmas in Washington*.\*

I had just arrived at the venue when somebody handed me a message that said "call 41" with a telephone number on the message. I didn't know who 41 was, so I asked the person who gave me the message and they said, "President Bush."

---

\* *Christmas in Washington* was a holiday variety show attended each year by official Washington, airing from 1982 until 2014, first on NBC and then on TNT.

I didn't know what to think. So I called the number, and the President welcomed me to Washington. Wow!

It was the beginning of a wonderful friendship. I've been so blessed to go to their homes and have dinners with them and even got to go on a vacation with them. Now, I'm not saying that to brag. I'm saying it because I want you to know how special they were to me. They were so down to earth, funny, and very entertaining. I just couldn't get enough of them.

One time while President Bush and I were texting, he told me that they were going to the baseball game that night. He told me to be sure and watch when so-and-so got up to bat because he would wave at me. Well, I'm sure he told everybody that, but it sure did make me feel special.

When flying back from the cruise in Greece,* I went to where he was sitting and, kneeling by his chair, I told him: "I take a lot of vacations, but nobody's ever invited me on a vacation like this before." I told him how much I appreciated it. He was really something special.

Singing at his funeral was a gift, a hardship, and one of the greatest things I've ever gotten to do. It felt like I got to say goodbye in my own way.

Our friendship taught me that even if you are the leader of the United States of America, you can still have a wonderful sense of humor and a huge, loving, and giving heart.

That's a good scale to go by.

---

* The Bushes were frequent visitors to Greece. Not long after he left office, President Bush accepted an invitation from Greek businessman John Latsis to use his yacht, the *Alexander* (and later, the *Turama*), for a cruise around the Aegean Sea. President Bush's first instinct was to say no, but when he realized he was no longer a public servant and could say yes, he did so with gratitude and excitement.

★  ★  ★

Drayton McLane, businessman and former owner of the Houston Astros, and his wife, Elizabeth:

We first met President Bush when he was running for the US Senate in 1964, when the Republican Party was just emerging in Texas. He made a stop in Temple for a fund-raiser, and as we remember, there were only about twenty people there. We were greatly impressed with him at that first meeting.

Over the years we had several other opportunities to see him in large groups, as when he was a congressman from Houston, and particularly as Vice President. When he finished his term as President of the United States, he and Barbara moved back home to Houston, and we had the opportunity to renew our friendship. That was really the beginning of our close personal relationship.

Some of our best memories are from visiting them in Kennebunkport. We went every year for four or five days at a time over a fifteen-year span. There were several houses there on the compound, but they were very gracious and had us stay in their house with them. We always had a great time.

One of the most exciting experiences at Kennebunkport was when the President asked us to go out with him on his powerboat. He loved boating and particularly going very fast. Barbara warned Elizabeth not to go out with George because he would scare you to death. It was so important to him that we go for a ride with him that Elizabeth agreed to come along.

One of the Secret Service men on the boat took us aside and said he had to forewarn us: If the boat turned over, they were not there to rescue us; they were there to save the President. We were on our own! We did go fast; very fast. It was a wild ride. He liked to hit the waves sending the boat into the air, then come crashing down. As we returned to the dock, he hardly slowed down. He just sped in, turned the boat sideways, and we were perfectly alongside the dock. We were very thankful to get off the boat. Several other times Drayton went back out with him, but Elizabeth never went for another boat ride with President Bush. She and Barbara would often go to a movie instead. Smart.

Jean Becker, the president's longtime chief of staff, had an office in a two-story cottage right as you entered the property. We would go down to her office for a visit after breakfast, and we would not have been there fifteen minutes when the President would come strolling in. He would say, "I don't want to miss any of this." It would be just the four of us talking on all kinds of subjects. Each time we did that, year after year, he would always show up during our visits with Jean. He enjoyed the atmosphere of her office, and we would sit for an hour or two and just talk.

During the nineteen years we owned the Houston Astros, we gave the Bushes six seats in our Diamond Club level on the first and second rows, just behind home plate. The President loved sports in general, but baseball was his favorite. He could talk baseball all day.

They would attend almost all the home games before they left for Maine. One of the things that really stands out to me was every time the President and Mrs. Bush would walk in and come down to their seats, unannounced, the entire crowd in the stadium, forty thousand people, would stand, applaud, and cheer for them. They would leave generally at the end of the seventh inning. Again, the entire stadium would stand and applaud, without anyone saying anything as they exited. This shows the great respect that Texans had for the President and Barbara.

Every spring he would invite six of the active Astros players to come to his office for a BBQ lunch. He would ask each one of them to tell something about himself. These young men were twenty-two to thirty years of age and would never have found themselves in a setting alone with a President of the United States. They would just be in awe. Every year during Spring Training, players would quietly ask to be on the list for this year's lunch.

He frequently would bring interesting guests with him to the games. It was always fun to meet not only influential and accomplished people from all over the United States, but great people from all over the world that were visiting him. One time he had with him the lady who was the president of Latvia. The President asked if, during an inning break, we could have her introduced to the crowd. Our public announcer made the perfect introduction, saying we had with us a great head of state, the president of Latvia. The stadium erupted with cheers and applause. When they sat down President Bush leaned over and said to Drayton: **I bet not many of them know where Latvia is!**

Of course many times he would have his children and grandchildren with him. It was a great pleasure getting to know all of them. You could see the great love the grandchildren had for their grandfather and grandmother. They particularly toed the line when their grandmother spoke!

In our private discussions he would talk about what a great country this is. He was never critical of any sitting president or any former president of the United States. He was always positive about politics.

We spent a lot of time with them, and our lives were enriched by it. We could see the great love they had for each other, for their family, for Texas, and for all of America. They weren't just good people; they were the best of the best.

★ ★ ★

<u>Diane Melley, member of the Points of Light board of directors:</u>

President Bush possessed an incredible ability to make ordinary and powerful people immediately feel like his friend. That was true even if you'd never met him, were considerably younger than he was, or had policy differences with him. In all these circumstances, he led by being gracious, welcoming, and respectful.

As a mid-career IBM executive, I introduced him at a Points of Light National Convention in 2004, where he was presenting IBM CEO Sam Palmisano with a National Service Leadership Award. By that time in his life, I was among hundreds of people who had introduced President Bush at events, but he greeted me with sincere warmth and interest. While in the greenroom, he chatted and laughed with me, made the personal connection to me as an Eisenhower Fellow,* and lightheartedly poked fun at "Sammy" (my boss) and their respective golf games. I was instantly charmed and made more comfortable for my role in the program.

This secret power to put people at ease—to relate on a human level above all else—would play out in many other encounters I witnessed. He was particularly skilled at engaging with young people. I watched as he enthusiastically hosted roundtable discussions with Eisenhower Fellows from around the globe, displaying through attentive listening and pertinent follow-up questions that he valued the perspectives of these young professionals and wanted to learn from future leaders.

He first met my daughter Lindsay when she was just thirteen. He complimented her on the great job she did picking out her outfit and

---

* Eisenhower Fellowships is a mid-career leadership program that President Bush chaired for several years.

noted that she was the best dressed in the room. She beamed with pride, since she had, indeed, put significant thought into what would be appropriate to wear. It was a small encounter for the President, but it had a lasting impact on my daughter, boosting her confidence thanks to a world leader who likely didn't realize his quiet compliment would have value well beyond the encounter.

Early in 2013, President and Mrs. Obama hosted President Bush and Points of Light at the White House to recognize the 5,000th Daily Point of Light. The Obamas were gracious and generous, and the connection they had with President Bush was one of respect in living shared values, despite their political differences. Since then, I've often mused on the mutual regard that made this civil hospitality possible.

President Bush is deservedly well known for his lifelong accomplishments, but to those he interacted with on an individual basis, it was his genuine care and concern we remember. No matter your title, background, or political views, he made you feel valued. He related to people on a purely human level.

Little wonder, then, that his unique vision of "a thousand points of light spreading like stars throughout the nation" is emblematic of the person he was as President, family member, and friend. By seeing the worth of each person, he enabled everyone to shine brighter and inspired them to share their own warmth as a beacon to others.

Brad Meltzer, author:

I knew this would be my last visit with the President. I had gone to Kennebunkport to honor my friend Barbara Bush, who had died in April, at a literacy event. Before the event, I got the phone call, asking if I was free for some private time with President Bush. The staff had been bringing in authors and friends to read to him all summer.

"I'd be honored," I replied. My wife and I made our way over to Walker's Point, eager to see him, but also a bit nervous. President Bush was ninety-four years old. There's no joy in final goodbyes.

On the way in, they warned us that our visit would most likely be short—he'd probably fall asleep at some point during our stay. My wife made a joke about how I'm used to putting people to sleep. I laughed, pretending this was all normal.

We were playing with his service dog, Sully, as they wheeled him in. To my surprise, President Bush looked great. Alert. Big smile. Happy to see us. He wasn't talking much, but he'd nod to answer questions. What caught me more off-guard was what was on his desk: three or four books, including one that was dog-eared from being read and clearly reread. It was my new nonfiction book, *The First Conspiracy*, about a real-life plot to kill George Washington during the Revolutionary War.

The aide told me how much he enjoyed reading it and then left us alone, just me, my wife, Sully, and President Bush. He'd had offices in the CIA, Congress, and, of course, the White House. But here we were, the final stop, in a small office overlooking the ocean with nothing more than a desk, a few keepsakes, and a really nice rocking chair engraved with the presidential seal.

"You want me to read from this?" I asked the President, holding up my book. He nodded, so I read him some of my favorite passages, telling him the story about how George Washington fought back against those plotting against him. President Bush was listening, sometimes sleeping—or at least I thought. But this was the moment that got to me: When I got to the part where, for the very first time, the Declaration of Independence was read aloud to George Washington and his troops. Slowly, I started reading the words out loud: "We hold these truths to be self-evident, that all men are created equal..."

Right there, President Bush shot awake. He had been listening the entire time, but now his eyes were wide, soaking up every word, like it was part of his lifeblood. He couldn't get enough. As I read the Declaration, the tears swelled in my own eyes, as well as my wife's. For President Bush, it was like a transfusion. At the end of each chapter, I kept asking him if he wanted to hear another chapter. Yes. Yes again. We kept going, moving on to that part of the Revolutionary War where George Washington is pinned down in the Battle of Brooklyn.

It's a moment where Washington easily could've died. He was outgeneraled; our troops outmaneuvered. It would've been easy for Washington to beat his chest and go out in a blaze of glory, rushing in while trying to take out as many of the British as he could. Instead, Washington did what he always did best. He adapted.

That night, during a massive downpour, George Washington and his officers devised a secret plan—a daring escape. They arranged for all nearby watercraft to be commandeered and brought across the East River. One by one, regiment by regiment, the soldiers sneaked onto the boats. Most importantly, the troops witnessed something else. George Washington, their leader, made sure that every soldier was evacuated before he himself got on a boat. In other words, the soldiers saw Washington risk his own life to save the lives of his men.

It's one of my favorite stories about George Washington because it reveals his leadership, his sense of honor, and, most of all, his decency.

One of the great honors of my life was reading about the humility and decency of our first president to the man who then was our oldest living President. Putting the book back on his desk, I said my final goodbyes. President Bush shook my hand and didn't have to say a word. He'd given me lessons I'll carry with me forever.

When he died a few months later, there was one word that was mentioned over and over in nearly every tribute: decency.

In truth, it's because President Bush was a truly decent man. But it's also because our country is currently starving for decency. Our current political discourse—the way we talk to each other—we've lost that sense of decency. It's time to get it back.

### Bernard Milano, member of the Points of Light board of directors:

President Bush was born in 1924; my wife was born in 1956. While having lunch with President Bush as we were planning his eightieth birthday celebration, I mentioned that his birthday is the same as my wife's birthday. He looked at me and said:

**Why would you marry an eighty-year-old woman?**

I would love to know if any of our presidents since the beginning of time had a better sense of humor, or a sharper wit.

### Johnny Morris, founder and owner of Bass Pro Shops:

I admired and respected my father, John A. Morris, more than anyone I have ever met—my dad was and always will be my true hero in life! But President George H. W. Bush comes in a close second. These two extraordinary individuals were both decorated World War II veterans. Far more important, however, is the fact that they were both men of great moral character.

Thinking back on my treasured friendship with President Bush, I'm reminded of my all-time favorite quote about fishing from Ernest Hemingway. Hemingway wrote: "In a lifetime spent fishing, I've come to realize—it's not the big fish you catch, but the people you meet, the friends that you make along the way that matter the most."

It fills my heart with joy to remember my very special fishing buddy. What a true honor and blessing in my life, when "along the way" over thirty-five years ago, through our shared love of fishing and passion for conservation, I came to know this remarkably humble, kindhearted gentleman who was always led by his faith and love of his family and country.

I had the privilege to observe him interacting with people from all walks of life, at home with family members, engaging with heads of state, leaders of commerce and conservation.

But mostly he and I spent hours fishing together, and then sitting around a campfire with fellow anglers. There is no better way to really get to know the true character of a person than by spending one-on-one time with them, especially in the solitude of nature.

And not once did I ever see him waver from the three character traits that most defined him: humility, kindness, and passion.

- Humility

President Bush was, to me, the most humble, down-to-earth guy you could ever hope to meet—always putting others first before himself. He would constantly poke fun at himself for his shortcomings, even if they didn't exist.

- Kindness

President Bush was outwardly kind, thoughtful, and considerate of others. He always made it a priority to take the time to be engaging and to be a respectful listener to those around him. This trait helped make him a great unifier and to make well-informed decisions. He had a big, kind heart and would often go out of his way to personally express heartfelt thanks to everyone from all walks of life for good deeds or gestures.

- Passion

He had incredible passion for life, for loving his family, and for serving his country, and to be sure more than a little passion for his favorite pastimes of golf and...oh, yeah, fishing!

There can be no doubt that President Bush really, really, really loved to fish!

Like Theodore Roosevelt and James Audubon before him, it was through his love of the great outdoors and time spent fishing on rivers, lakes, streams, and the open sea that President Bush gained firsthand appreciation for the need for conservation and the stewardship of fish and wildlife and other precious natural resources.

President Bush was incredibly modest, and in my view, that is why he has not been more celebrated as one of the most extraordinary conservationists ever.

I would like to fix that oversight right now.

It makes me proud to join all fellow sportsmen and sportswomen and conservationists in remembering, thanking, and saluting President Bush for everything he has done to uphold our hunting and fishing traditions as well as for his work to restore and enhance wildlife and fisheries.

During his administration, President Bush was responsible for signing into law some of the most important legislation ever drafted to conserve our nation's abundant fish and wildlife, healthy landscapes, clean air, and rich soil.

Under his leadership and direction, the United States established an astonishing fifty-six new national wildlife refuges—more than any other president in our nation's history, including President Theodore Roosevelt.

He protected 17.8 million acres of public lands, including national parks, wildlife areas, and refuges.

He signed into law the expanded Clean Air Act in 1990, requiring cleaner burning fuels.

He also signed into law the North American Wetlands Conservation Act. This act has helped fund wetlands conservation projects (many in conjunction with Ducks Unlimited) on almost twenty-seven million acres in all fifty states, Canada, and Mexico. He personally spearheaded the first national policy goal of "no net loss of wetlands."

While serving as Vice President, he played a critical and essential role in assuring the passage of the 1984 amendments to the Sport Fish Restoration Act—an action second only to the original act's passage in 1950. Then, as President, he came to the act's rescue in 1991, making sure that the Office of Management and Budget did not divert any of the trust fund's monies from their intended purpose of supporting sport fisheries conservation and habitat restoration—ensuring recreational fishing's future.

President Bush relied upon all of his moral principles to become a well-informed and respected leader. His unselfish character helped unify people to make a profound positive impact on the natural world for generations to come.

Jim Nantz, CBS sportscaster:

The first time we paid a visit to Walker's Point was in the summer of 1994. The President took us on his boat down the coast for a casual ride and, on the spur of the moment, he docked his beloved *Fidelity III* in Ogunquit, Maine, for a midday treat. It was an unusually hot day and 41 wanted to visit his favorite ice cream parlor.

He wasn't the only one who had that idea. There was a long wait with the line dozens-deep. Everyone was yelling for him to move to the front of the line. But he just smiled, almost bashfully, and waved off their offer. President Bush graciously accommodated every request for autographs and photos. In his eyes, everyone was equal. There was no hierarchy of fame, power, or money. Cutting to the head of the line—or "pulling rank"—was discourteous and inconsiderate behavior. He would never be a party to that.

A few years later I was invited by the Bush family to a small reception in New York City. One of the guests was legendary jazz musician Lionel Hampton. When 41 walked into the room, Hampton was the first person he saw. Immediately the President knelt on one knee so that he could speak to the ailing, wheelchair-bound musician at eye level. The former President could have simply leaned over, as other guests of similar height did, but this instinctive gesture of dignity and respect was a perfect snapshot of the way George Herbert Walker Bush treated everyone he encountered. I brought up his remarkable act of kindness later that night over dinner. He said, "Jimmy, no one should ever be left to feel inferior by spending their entire time looking up toward everyone else. Treat all people equally and with respect. And talk to them at eye level."

Roxann Neumann, businesswoman and political activist:
The first time I met George H. W. Bush was also the first time he taught me a life lesson: The importance of taking time to show kindness when you see someone is being treated unfairly.

It was August 1984. He was Vice President of the United States. I was a twenty-five-year-old staffer working for the Republican Party of Texas. The Republican National Convention was being held in Dallas, and I was responsible for the distribution of all the very sought-after guest passes for the Texas delegation. It was impossible to have enough.

I was standing at the distribution table, relieved that I no longer had any left. They had all been given out. That good-feeling moment was fleeting. As I was gathering my stuff to close down, the future congressman Tom DeLay* stepped up to the table and asked for two guest passes. I politely informed him that all guest passes had been distributed. I quickly looked at my list to make sure his allocation had been picked up, and they had, by a staff member. He said he needed two additional passes and asked if I knew who he was. I said I did and was very sorry, but I had no more guest passes. He then asked me my name, asked who I worked for, and proceeded to let me know that my days in that position were likely coming to an end. He then walked off.

As I think back on it—I can still remember that sick feeling I felt at that moment. It appeared my being involved in anything political was over.

Then out of nowhere someone tapped me on the shoulder. I turned around to see Vice President Bush, who shook my hand, introduced himself, and told me things were going to be fine. After a brief chat, he said to me as he walked off:

**Just remember he puts his pants on one leg at a time just like everyone else.**

---

* In 1984, DeLay was a Texas state representative and was elected to Congress that November. A leader in the conservative movement, he eventually would serve as both House majority whip and House majority leader. He resigned from Congress in 2006 amid allegations of violating federal election laws. His conviction in 2011 was eventually overturned.

★  ★  ★

<u>Michelle Nunn, president and CEO of CARE USA:</u>

My first meeting with President Bush was at the Bayou Club in Houston for what I guess was a job interview to be head of Points of Light, which was about to merge with my organization, Hands On. It is highly intimidating to be interviewed for any job, much less to be interviewed by a former President. And in this case, as a lifelong Democrat, perhaps even more so.

He immediately put me at ease, and I knew that the typical interview expectation of singing my own praises was not required. He told me the now famous story of his mother admonishing him not to brag when he recounted his own soccer goals, asking him, "And how did the team do, George?"

I have never been with a more powerful person who emanated such deep humility. It was more than a personal virtue. It was a worldview that embraced transcendent purpose and the spiritual wisdom of our own relative smallness in the universe.

We all know of President Bush's courage as a nineteen-year-old flying combat missions, but I came to know the quiet courage of his last years when his body was failing him. Yet, he squeezed out life's gifts each and every day. (I confess that I love that he always ordered dessert with lunch.)

Even though his life was characterized by a vibrant athleticism, he defied the fear of appearing enfeebled, first walking with help, then a cane, and eventually, without hesitation, a wheelchair. He jumped out of airplanes to demonstrate the capacity for adventure even for those turning eighty, eighty-five, and finally ninety. Even when he struggled to walk unassisted, he would take out his speedboat and drive so fast that it would make your eyes water. (My children found it thrilling, while I confess to finding it a bit scary.) He demonstrated for all of us the capacity to live with joy and energy, even as our physical capacities fail us.

Over the years of knowing him, I experienced so many stories of his acts of empathy: standing up to a bully in his teenage years; bringing a Jewish friend to break the restrictions at a local country club; writing a letter to a distant friend in a time of need. There are literally thousands of acts of kindness that people around the world remember of President George H. W. Bush.

I well remember celebrating the anniversary of Points of Light with President Bush, hosted by President Obama in the White House. Hundreds of members of President Bush's family and friends joined together, including members of his administration. His former press secretary, Marlin Fitzwater, marveled that thirty years later one of the President's enduring and fundamental legacies would be Points of Light. With all of the legislative and diplomatic and military dimensions of his presidency, the more ethereal but deeply meaningful vision of a kinder and gentler nation had stood the test of time.

I believe President Bush's great light and wisdom was knowing that it is ultimately not power, wealth, or glory that defines a life well lived, but how we treat and lift up those around us.

We have no finer example. His life was, perhaps and after all, his greatest legacy.

### Nancy Pelosi, former Speaker of the House:

On October 17, 1989, the San Francisco Bay Area was shaken to its core by the most severe earthquake in generations. When the shaking stopped, we sadly mourned the more than sixty lives lost and more than 3,700 injured, while tens of thousands more families were left in despair, their lives upended by unimaginable destruction.

The Loma Prieta earthquake wrought a dark and difficult moment for the Bay Area. Yet in our hour of need, we found a champion in President George H. W. Bush.

Within days of the quake, the President boarded Air Force One for San Francisco. It was my privilege to brief him and join him in surveying the damage, touring the rubble from the hills to the highways and hearing from experts about the impact on our infrastructure. That included seeing the devastating collapse of the Bay Bridge, where most of the fatalities occurred.

When he returned to the White House, he followed through on his commitment to our recovery, ensuring that the Bay Area swiftly received the $3.45 billion in emergency assistance that I had worked with my colleagues in the Congress to secure.

It is important to remember that, at that time, "San Francisco Democrat" was among the nastiest epithets in the Republican Party. Our city was a constant target of attacks by those who disavowed our cherished values of compassion, liberty, equality, and justice for all.

Yet, President Bush had no hesitation in standing by our side. With his courage and graciousness, he defied heavy pressure from those within his own party who wanted to see San Francisco suffer—and those who have long opposed federal disaster relief. Strengthened by President Bush's commitment to our cause, our area was able to rise from the rubble stronger and more united than ever before.

Personally, it was my privilege to share a beautiful friendship with President Bush and his dear wife, Barbara. Their love and devotion to each other were a joy to behold.

God truly blessed America with the grace and goodness of President George H. W. Bush.

★  ★  ★

<u>Arnold Palmer, golf legend (from *41ON41*):</u>

I have said that you could learn more about a person in an eighteen-hole round of golf than if you spent many hours with them in an office. You learn the character of a person on the golf course... George Bush [is] honesty, integrity, and all the things that make you a good person that you would trust with your life.

<u>Richard Perry, President Bush's Maine physician:</u>

It was time for President Bush's appointment. The two SUVs arrived at noon sharp, and a member of his Secret Service detail opened the door. As usual, he was warmly greeted by two members of our nursing staff, and he enjoyed their attention.

I entered the exam room and, as I had done many times over the years, greeted the former President and asked how things were going, how he was feeling. In typical fashion, and despite his deteriorating health, George H. W. Bush replied:

**I'm fine. Go tend to the other patients who need you more than me.**

That was his way. It was the perfect example of who author Christopher Buckley later called "the most beautifully souled man," whose focus was on others rather than the "GREAT I AM."

<u>June Scobee Rodgers, widow of *Challenger* space shuttle commander Richard Scobee:</u>

First as Vice President and then as President of the United States, President Bush showed compassion for the families of the crew of the *Challenger* space shuttle, visiting with us the day of the 1986 accident and for years thereafter.

Having announced in 1985 that a teacher, Christa McAuliffe, would fly in space—becoming the first civilian to do so—he was familiar with the STS-51L crew led by my husband, Commander Dick Scobee. His words of sincere concern and counsel that day and many days afterward gave us the strength to meet the constant calls for interviews and information while struggling to overcome our own very public grief.

To help the families and Space City Houston overcome our loss, the other *Challenger* family members joined with me to create a space simulation experience as a tribute to the lost Teacher in Space Mission and for the students who were still waiting for their lessons from space.

Vice President Bush congratulated us for our idea and offered to help. When we stumbled in our outreach for financial support, he supported our efforts not only by writing letters on our behalf, but also by writing his own personal check. He taught us the importance of hard work, to roll up our sleeves, and boldly ask for support for a great cause.

After a few months working in our tiny Houston office, the Vice President suggested to me that we grow our organization nationally because the entire country was grieving the loss of *Challenger*. He encouraged us to move our office to Washington, DC, where we could gain additional support for our efforts. When I asked for advice on how I could involve national leaders, he suggested that we ask CEOs, university presidents, and a senator.

That was a scary proposition because I didn't know any people personally who represented his suggestions. My experience was that of a teacher. I told him we would be intimidated to work with such distinguished people. He then taught the teacher, saying:

**June, how do you work with a classroom full of students? Don't you prepare them to meet the objectives of the class? Encourage them, then test them to learn of their success?**

When I nodded, he said:

**You'll do the same thing as a chairman of a board of**

directors. **You provide the vision and an overview of goals, then challenge them to accomplish various objectives. After that we'll be able to evaluate the efforts of the board for success and accomplishments.**

With each new Challenger Learning Center created—even when he was the President—he would continue to congratulate our efforts. His support was not only in words but also in deeds.

I would suggest that the same qualities of character he used to guide us at the Challenger Center were also qualities among many others that he valued in his leadership as President. Yes, he was a great leader in my estimation, but he was also a person with a big heart, great wisdom, and tremendous experience that he shared, and humbly taught us how to establish an organization that is the living legacy of the seven *Challenger* astronauts.

I'll forever be grateful to him for showing me the way.

David Rubenstein, cofounder and cochairman of the Carlyle Group:

President Bush was traveling with my Carlyle partners and me in Italy. Two of my partners were very committed Catholics. They really wanted to see if President Bush could arrange a meeting with the pope the next day, the same day we were leaving Rome. I asked President Bush, and he said he thought he could do it. And sure enough, the next day we had a private session with Pope John Paul II.

In the meeting, President Bush introduced my partners and me this way:

**Your Holiness, this is Bill Conway, a committed Catholic. This is Dan D'Aniello, a committed Catholic. This is Kathy Super,\* a committed Catholic. And this is David Rubenstein.**

---

\* Kathy Super was one of his schedulers.

The pope looked up, recognizing that my name might not put me in the committed Catholic category. He looked surprised that I was there but was very pleasant despite my not being a committed Catholic. I was, of course, pleased to be blessed despite the religious difference. You never know when a papal blessing can come in handy.

I don't think I realized what a huge favor I had asked of President Bush to arrange this meeting. It wasn't until later that I learned how hard it is to arrange a private meeting with the pope, much less on short notice.

More importantly, I learned that President Bush would move mountains to help friends achieve a goal of theirs.

*Ron Sherr was one of America's most respected and sought-after portrait artists. His portrait of President Bush that hangs in the National Portrait Gallery in Washington, DC, was 41's favorite. After a brief illness, Ron died in December 2022. His widow, Lois, and his son, Alexander, worked together to retell one of Ron's favorite stories, when he was commissioned to paint the President of the United States, and the President's father, No. 41. It begins with his harrowing journey and entry into Camp David. They tell the story in Ron's voice:*

I left at 5:30 a.m. because I had no idea how long it would take. I had directions, but Camp David is literally unmarked. It doesn't say "Camp David" with big arrows pointing to it! I remember passing a guardhouse at the bottom of a big hill; the guy there checks my clearance and says go to the top and drive in.

At the top of the hill, I am met by a giant fence that you'd expect at Area 51 or somewhere like that. A sign reads "DANGER: BEYOND THIS POINT, TRESPASSERS WILL BE SHOT" or something like that. Quite a warning, right? There's nothing else around, literally nothing else there.

If I turn in, I risk being shot. I'm thinking, "I'm not doing this, no way, I am not doing this." So I drove all the way back down. I said to the guy at the bottom, "There's no place to go up there—it says you'll be shot if you go in!" He says, "No, no, no, that's it. You just have to go past that point. They're expecting you. Don't worry. Go ahead."

So back up I go and this time, the gate opens. I drive another stretch, and there's another gate, and then another gate. So finally, I get to a gate where there are actually some people. They're expecting me. That's where they start to do this huge security check, with mirrors under the car, the whole thing.

After the security check is done, and after a flurry of phone calls to confirm that two George Bushes really are expecting me, I am finally waved through and shown to the room where I am to meet with President Bush and President Bush.

After hearing they were going to breakfast and then to church I knew it was going to be a while, but I did not expect them to walk in at 11:30—three hours after I had arrived! The dad says, **Okay, we're ready**. So, off we go to find a place for them to pose; we finally settle on a spot. I get my camera gear out, get set up, and I can see George W. is already getting a little fidgety. Then I start taking pictures, and he's really getting fidgety. He's looking at his watch; he's looking around. I'm saying to them, "Mr. President, can you look over here? Sir, can you look over, uh, can you look that way?" They both look in the same direction. Meanwhile, George W. is getting more and more fidgety, and he starts making some noise about how long it's taking. So, I look at him and I say, "Sir, I'm not a photographer. I'm a portrait painter. This is going to take me a little while." I remind him I only have an hour sitting with them. George W. simmers down when he hears that and he's like, "Okay, okay, so how can we help?" So, I go back to it. "Sir, look over here." Both heads swivel. What am I going to do? "Mr. President, can you turn just a little bit that way?" Both heads end up going in exactly the same direction. They can see I'm getting frustrated.

So finally, the dad says: **Ron, just call us 41 and 43.**

I say to him, "Sir, I can't do that, sir. You know, you were the President and your son's the current president. I can't do that." So, I go back to "Sir, look over here." Boom, both heads, same direction. So this keeps going on for a little while. Finally, Bush Sr. pipes up again:

**Come on, Ron, you've got to call us 41 and 43.**

Then I look at my watch and realize I have only twenty minutes left! "Okay, 41, please look over there; 43, you look that way." And sure enough, they listened to me like obedient puppies.

When we finished the sitting, 41 wanted me to come over to their cabin, his and Barbara's cabin. He said, **Come on, come on, jump in the golf cart, let's go over. Barbara wants to say hello.** I was dumbfounded. I couldn't believe what I was hearing. As we're driving over, 41 got to talking about the president:

**I'm just kind of nervous. I have to watch out for him.**

He was very protective. This was three months after 9/11. He was talking to me as if I was a friend. A close friend. I didn't even know what to say. I kept trying to support him and say, oh, you know, he's doing a great job, and thinking up other things to say as I went along. All I could think was what a bizarre situation that he was the former President of the United States. His son is the President of the United States now. And he's talking to me like this. The thought that kept crossing my mind was, "What the heck did I do to deserve to be here?"

I learned a lot from this surreal experience on a mountaintop with two Presidents:

- Sometimes you just have to go with the flow and savor such wonderful moments.
- A true leader may ask you to do things that are out of your comfort zone but are key to the bigger picture.
- Sometimes you have to be strong, no matter who you are with, if it helps accomplish the goal.

R. C. Slocum, former head football coach for Texas A&M University:

I was privileged to do many fun things with President Bush. We came from different upbringings, which we discussed on many occasions. I was from a working-class family in southeast Texas where shipyard and refinery work were the norm. The President was from an affluent, educated family back east. To him, that was never a big deal. We both loved sports and people. We both loved Aggie football. We were a perfect match.

One of my favorite things about 41 was that he never, ever put himself above anyone. Here is one of my favorite examples:

President Bush invited me to play golf with him at Pine Valley Golf Club, which is in New Jersey just outside of Philadelphia. The course is consistently ranked as the top golf club in America, and he was excited to take me there. We arrived around noon and played the par three course that afternoon.

We stayed in a cottage on-site and had dinner at the club. We were joined at dinner by two of the President's friends, Tom Kelley and Spike Heminway. The next morning, we all gathered for breakfast. Shortly after we were seated, an older African American lady came to our table and said that she would be serving our breakfast. The President immediately turned to her and engaged her with:

**Good morning, how are you today?**

She had appeared somewhat nervous approaching our table to take the President's and his guests' orders. He immediately dispelled whatever anxiety she might have had. He asked her about her family and how they were doing. He made her feel special. Later, while our breakfast was being prepared, he asked someone if they would mind getting a couple of his golf balls from our cart, which was parked outside. When the lady came back to check on us, he asked if her husband or son would maybe like an autographed ball from the President. She immediately said that she had a grandson who loved golf and would really like one of the balls. The balls had the presidential seal on them, and the President added his autograph. By this time, the lady was beaming.

He had taken just a little of his time to make this nice lady feel like she was important to him. I thought to myself at that time, "This is so characteristic of how he treats people." Everyone was important to him regardless of background, status, or, for that matter, political party.

Michael W. Smith, singer, composer, and actor:

I first met the Bushes in 1989 at the annual televised *Christmas in Washington* event. I was pinching myself. There they sat—the President and First Lady of the United States of America—on the front row while I sang "Gloria" with an amazing high school choir. What a dream come true! And apparently my long mullet hair and stubbly beard didn't faze them.

After the show, my wife, Debbie, and I and the other performers were whisked away to the White House with a surprise invitation. Their warmth and kindness put us all at ease immediately. They even took us into their private quarters, showing us some of their treasured drawings by the grandkids. It was a little surreal to stand by the basket of toys in the President's den and talk about his recent meeting with Russian president Gorbachev. I probably pinched myself again.

The evening wrapped up in the East Room with President Bush's requested sing-along around the piano. I was the only piano player, so I played as we sang a few Christmas carols. Not a bad gig. And thus began a friendship that lasted almost three decades.

The Bushes graciously invited my wife and me to be a part of the last White House Christmas brunch in 1992. We had already witnessed the way the staff—from the maids to chefs to secretaries—seemed to genuinely love the First Couple. As the staff lined the walls of the East Room at the end of the brunch, many had tears running down their faces. The President knew their names and cared about them, and they were going to miss him.

And then there was the day in 2000 when I called him for help. The teen club I had started in my town of Franklin, Tennessee, to help troubled kids had lost its lease. The location we found in nearby Nashville, while a great deal, needed extensive renovation to build an indoor skate park, a music venue, and spaces for tutoring. He willingly agreed when I asked him to become my honorary campaign chairman. He played a significant role in the nearly $5 million we raised that led to the innovative faith-based safe environment that has blessed thousands of kids.

But perhaps this story summarizes the character of President Bush 41 best.

While at one of my Christmas concerts in Houston in the early

2000s, he and Barbara raised their hands when the Compassion International child sponsorship packets were held up for those willing to take them. They sponsored a child living in poverty that evening. Little did that child know that the letters that came on a regular basis from his sponsor (always with a picture of the dog, not the owner) was from the former President of the United States—and at that time, the father of the current one. Years later, after that young man had grown out of the program, he found out that the former Leader of the Free World had been his sponsor.

These random acts of kindness over the years have certainly left a mark on us. And Debbie and I are better for it.

### Nancy Sosa, Kennebunkport friend:

President Bush taught me to find fun in little things. We held an annual friends and family picnic in Kennebunkport that he named the BS Picnic, using the first initials of our last names. He knew there was nothing giggle-worthy about an SB Picnic. He assembled a BS Picnic planning committee and scheduled meetings for 1:58, 2:13, or 4:33 because he insisted those were perfectly good times that no one ever uses. He always had a sparkle in his eyes when we entered his office on the dot for those unusual meeting times.

He also taught me to always look forward, never look back. It didn't matter that a vacation came to an end or the summer was over, President Bush always looked forward to the next event. When I remember this advice, I am never sad. There's always something good ahead.

### Richard Sterban, member of the Oak Ridge Boys:

One of the favorite things the Oaks got to do almost every summer was for us and our wives to spend time with the Bushes in

Kennebunkport. President Bush especially loved if we were touring in the New England area, and we would show up on our very large tour bus, rolling through town and through the gate at Walker's Point.

Every summer we had this running game with him: Who was going to pay for lunch if we went out?

He, of course, wanted to pay.

We, of course, wanted to pay.

Finally, we figured out how to outsmart him.

I kept a bicycle on the bus, so what I would do is get the Oaks' credit card, ask President Bush where we were going for lunch, and as long as we weren't going by boat, I would get on my bike and make sure I beat the motorcade.

And the first thing I would do is prepay the bill.

He would pretend to be mad, but I think he loved it. He loved the game.

And, yes, it was expected that while we were there, we would sing a song or two. We spent many wonderful nights singing in their living room, standing in front of the fireplace, singing just for the family and some of their closest friends.

But one year President Bush had an idea: The Bushes had heard from some of his staff and a few others in town that there were a lot of new residents in Kennebunkport, and they were not being welcomed with open arms.

"Their ancestors didn't come off the *Mayflower*," someone explained to us.

So the Bushes invited all the newcomers to a cocktail party at Walker's Point, and invited just enough of the "oldcomers," so they could see that George and Barbara Bush had the welcome mat out. And it just so happened we were in town.

So we did a mini concert out on the driveway, with a sound system President Bush managed to find somewhere. Oh what a night.

Not too long before he passed away, he let it be known he wanted us to sing at his funeral. We of course told him, "You can count on us."

The night before his funeral in Houston, we were booked to do a Christmas show in Spokane, Washington. The minute the show was over, we headed to the airport, got on a plane donated by a friend, and flew all night, landing in Houston just in time to get to a hotel to freshen up and get to the church.

The Bush family could not thank us enough for making the effort to do this for their father and grandfather. We sang, "Amazing Grace," which was very emotional, but we got through it.

Then back to the airport we went, getting on the same plane and returning to the state of Washington, as we had a show that night in Kennewick.

We would have never canceled a show. President Bush would not have approved. He taught all of us to always do the right thing.

And from Richard's wife, Donna:

One thing that pops in my mind is the day a Coast Guard cutter was off Walker's Point repairing buoys. We were all in *Fidelity*, and 41 wanted to go by and say hi "to the guys." Someone on the cutter must have recognized the boat because as we got close we heard a whistle blow, and then as we came alongside, the entire crew was standing at attention.

President Bush yelled hello and thanked them for their service. Then he turned to us and said:

**They didn't have to do all that, I just wanted to say hi.**

This has stuck with me for years. His absolute humbleness.

★　★　★

<u>Carolyn Stettner, former CIA officer and widow of another:</u>

My deceased husband, Jim Pavitt, had a business colleague with whom we had become good friends. This gentleman and his wife had a wonderful young son, Brendan, who was enamored of Jim and his work with the CIA.

Brendan was doubly challenged in his life by having Down syndrome and also struggling with cancer from a young age. He wanted to be a spy when he grew up, and we showered him with appropriate tradecraft "gear" and books to study.

Brendan fought his cancer through many rounds of chemotherapy and several bone marrow transplants. During one of these times when he was hospitalized, Jim wrote to 41 telling him about this brave young patriot who wanted to become a spy and like Jim had once done, run the CIA's Clandestine Service. As we knew he would, the President wrote the most loving, kind, and encouraging note to Brendan, which was promptly framed and sat on the nightstand by his hospital bed, to be shown to every person who entered his room.

Young Brendan eventually succumbed to his cancer, but he never lost heart and never stopped believing he would be a spy. After all, his heroes were my husband and our forty-first President.

<u>Joe Straus III, former Speaker of the Texas House of Representatives:</u>

In early April 2023, I spent a few days as a Cameron Fellow at Texas A&M University's Bush School of Government and Public Service. Before my visit, I read over some of President Bush's most famous remarks and writings. Even as someone whose family has known the Bushes for decades and has long admired the forty-first President, I was struck by the graciousness of the tone he set for the country—a warmth that he was unafraid to show, because his strength as a leader spoke for itself.

He knew that grace was not a sign of weakness.

Standing on what he called the "front porch of democracy" to give his inaugural address on January 20, 1989, President Bush said:

**I take as my guide the hope of a saint: In crucial things, unity; in important things, diversity; in all things, generosity.**

In a present era when partisanship has risen and tribalism has spread, there is great impact in those three basic ideas: unity, diversity, and generosity.

Too often, the way to get ahead in politics is by appealing to someone's worst instincts rather than their better angels. We have been conditioned to think that the path to power is through dividing and conquering. In contrast, President Bush built bipartisan coalitions around lasting achievements, from the passage of the Americans with Disabilities Act to Operation Desert Storm.

When it comes to the issues that really matter, you need people with different experiences and perspectives working together. No party has a monopoly on good ideas—or bad ones.

I can think of no better remedy to the tribalism in our politics today than the words President Bush spoke and the approach he embodied. He knew how to tap into our common goodness rather than trying to exploit our differences.

Every day, people go to extraordinary lengths to extend a hand of help or compassion, whether in their vocation or their spare time. Why should our politics be so different? I understand—and certainly President Bush understood—that there are going to be differences, and that politics is a contact sport. Every campaign has a winner and a loser.

But we can be competitive without being caustic. The principles that President Bush promoted in his inaugural address and in so much of his life in and out of office are bigger than any one political party or ideology. Decency and goodness transcend any construct of conservative versus liberal or red versus blue.

The students I met at the Bush School seemed eager to embrace this approach. They were proud to be learning at a place named for such a gracious leader.

I believe the President would be proud of them as well.

Sally Struthers, actress:

My cell phone was ringing. This was August 23, 2018, a Thursday morning; a two-performance day at Ogunquit Playhouse. Sheesh! I am an actor! Who is calling me at this hour?! Don't they know I work nights?!

When I looked at my phone, I saw that it was none other than my friend Jean Becker, President Bush's chief of staff. She was calling to see if I could drive up the road to Kennebunkport for a private visit with 41. When I explained my two-performance day, we decided the next day would be better.

I arrived at Walker's Point midmorning on Friday, August 24, the last day he and I would spend time together.

I entered the room grinning. President Bush was grinning too. He asked me what musical I was in down at the playhouse. He and Barbara attended so many of the productions I did there over the years, and they always came backstage at intermission, coming all the way down the narrow hallway to my dressing room for a little visit. And then, remarkably, they would segue to the main stage and take photos with the entire cast. This is unique to the Bush family.

The thoughtfulness of knowing how exciting it would be for the actors to have a photo of themselves with the President and First Lady.

When I told my buddy that we were doing the premiere of the new musical *Grumpy Old Men*, he lit up. I sang a couple of songs from the show, humorous with some ribald lyrics. His laughter filled the office.

His new dog, Sully, sat at his feet. Being an unabashed admirer of all things canine, I was thrilled to meet this darling young yellow Lab. Not wanting to take up too much of his day, I stood up and started my goodbyes. Seemingly out of nowhere, Jean asked if I would like a photo with the President. I happily have many photos with the Bushes, either backstage or at their home. But this would be my first (and last) with just the President. As Jean took the photo, I leaned in close to give this great man a squeeze.

Three months later the nation said goodbye. It dawned on me this is why Jean Becker called me that Thursday morning. How fortunate was I to have that quiet moment in time with him, sitting in his wheelchair; the ocean breeze cooling his simple office this August morning.

A new pup by his side. A great joker with his hundreds of pairs of colorful and sometimes bizarre socks. An optimist. A war hero. My friend.

A man always finding joy in life.


Tom Tiernan, Army marketing specialist:

The night before President Reagan's funeral and a few days before President Bush's eightieth birthday celebration, he hosted a dinner for the Golden Knights team who traveled to College Station to support one of his parachute jumps at his library.

He and my team were among the last to get in line for the buffet. After he got his food, we figured an aide had saved him a place to sit. We went on to find a place to sit. The only table available was at the end of the hallway. As we took our seats, we looked up to see President Bush headed our way, a plate of food in hand. He insisted on taking the worst seat at the table.

He was the most gracious host for a group of soldiers and Army civilian employees. He insisted that we, his table companions, were taken care of before himself. He asked each of us about our life stories. And he made sure we all got a dish of his favorite Blue Bell ice cream.

Mark Updegrove, president and CEO of the LBJ Foundation:

Never let your ambition exceed your grace. Don't crow when you win, nor cower when you lose. Share credit. Always think of others. Let people know you care.

Those are some of the lessons in character I learned from President Bush's towering example, among the many things I took from our friendship for which I will always be deeply grateful. But here's what I'll remember most about George Herbert Walker Bush: He was just so fun to be around. Barbara too. They were utterly delightful, never taking themselves too seriously, always ready to laugh.

There were the times when 41 tried to circumvent the strict dietary instructions of his wife, "the Enforcer," who kept a close watch on his intake of salt, sugar, and alcohol. Her insistence that he restrict the amount of bread and butter he consumed resulted in a small bucket of biscuits that he had secretly ordered being surreptitiously placed by the server at the leg of his chair. Or at another dinner when he asked for half of a vodka martini after drinking down a first one that had been generously poured to the rim. "What self-respecting waiter is going to give a former President half a martini?" I asked him, and we both laughed. Sure enough, when the drink arrived the half was a whole. (Meanwhile, I had somewhat self-consciously ordered a Cosmopolitan, distinctly pink and, well, a little girly. **Shirley Temple?** he asked with mock disdain when it arrived.)

Then there was the time when Barbara, who shared my wife Amy's love for jigsaw puzzling, told us that she often got to the very end of a puzzle only to discover that the last piece was missing. The mystery was solved when she realized that her husband was secretly pocketing them just **to keep things interesting.**

And then there was the time 41 recounted to Jean Becker and me a 1970 meeting he had with Lyndon Johnson at the LBJ Ranch, where he sought the ex-President's counsel on whether to give up a safe seat in the House of Representatives for a chancy run at the Senate.

"George, the difference between the House and the Senate is the difference between chicken shit and chicken salad," LBJ colorfully advised. Bush recalled the extensive tour of the ranch LBJ gave him that included a visit to his closet—**a sea of slacks**, Bush observed—as LBJ barked to houseguest Jake Pickle, Bush's fellow member of Congress, "Get George a drink!"

As icing on the cake, there was often something thoughtful that came from 41 after our visits, characteristic small gestures that had outsized impact: an invitation to bring our children to his office for a family visit with him and Barbara; a surprise letter of recommendation after I told him offhandedly that I was pursuing a promising job change; one of his trademark handwritten notes.

The last time Amy and I saw 41 was in the final months of his life. Ailing but ever gracious, he invited us to a mid-summer lunch at Walker's Point so that I could read him portions of my recently published book, *The Last Republicans: Inside the Extraordinary Relationship Between George H. W. Bush and George W. Bush.* I chose the penultimate chapter in which I offer my take on his legacy, or "the L-word" as 41 always called it. As the sun-dappled Atlantic Ocean churned off the shore and waves crashed into the craggy Maine coastline beneath us, I read aloud to him on the back patio of the house:

"Time would be a friend to George H. W. Bush. Two decades after leaving office, Bush would begin to be recognized for his sheer competence as President during a seminal time, credited for his incisive foreign-policy mind, diplomatic facility, and steady, prudent hand as commander-in-chief...Moreover, in a barbed, self-aggrandizing age when passion all too often overcame reason, America came to value 41's character...In the unexpected warmth of his winter years, the public servant who called for a 'kinder, gentler' nation got a little of it back."

When I finished the chapter, 41's eyes were closed. We thought he might have drifted off to sleep. Then, after what seemed a long pause, he deadpanned:

**That's a lot about me.**

Tyson Voelkel, president of the Texas A&M Foundation:

Our friendship began while I was a graduate student in the Bush School's international affairs program and ended with me as one of the military members of his funeral planning team. It was an honor yet a knee-shaking responsibility.

The world was better with President George Herbert Walker Bush in it. Now more than ever I am reminded of the impact he and Mrs. Bush had on our country and on my family. Our paths intersected in unique ways, and President Bush always provided humor, perspective, and authenticity with each engagement.

His life was lived in a way that encouraged, inspired, and influenced millions. Humility and authenticity oozed from his personality, and all who he embraced felt the warmth of his smile and the genuineness of his heart anytime we were around him. Most evident was his desire to help others, to lift others up, and to share in joy and pain.

Here are two key lessons I learned from him. Each has shaped me and helped me understand that I can be more.

1.  We say what we mean and mean what we say. Our word is our bond. We may not be the smartest person in the room, but most of the time we should be the hardest working. We have an edge, a hunger, a desire to do more, to be more, to serve more. That's what should drive those in public service.

2.  How we live our lives and how we choose to be a light to others is our choice. We should choose to be a light in someone else's life when we can.

I once asked him what his life lessons were from public service. His answer: civility, compromise, and courage.

President Bush insisted on the idea that elected officials must fight for their constituents but also must remember to be civil and not vilify their opponents. He said we can't go into our corners and just talk to the people that are like us.

He went on to discuss the need for compromise in government, the need to often "meet in the middle" on difficult topics, as he believed democracy demanded incremental changes more often than sea changes.

Lastly, he talked about courage. To do the right thing for

America, even if it meant losing an election or looking like a "flip-flopper" when it came to decisions.

Civility. Compromise. Courage. Interesting lessons from a man who spent his life in service of others.

Our meetings would always start with the President asking about my wife, Christi, and about our family. The conversations would then turn to leadership, life, and service.

When our daughter Lily passed away, our family was gathered in the kitchen and getting ready to head to her visitation. It was tense. We were shells of our normal selves. The phone rang, and I reluctantly picked up the phone and was told "hold for the President."

It was President Bush.

He and Barbara wanted us to know they were sorry for our loss; that we would always have a hole in our hearts, as they did when they lost their daughter Robin. He encouraged us to fill that hole by doing for others whenever we could; that service mattered and that he was proud of us.

That call was like a spark for us, a catalyst. He lifted us up when we needed it the most. He did it by humbling himself, by being vulnerable, and by challenging us to do for others rather than feel sorry for ourselves.

We left for the visitation with a different perspective. We viewed Lily's passing as an opportunity to share her light.

So when the inevitable day arrived for their funerals—first Mrs. Bush and just a few months later President Bush—their deaths took on special significance for us.

For a few days, the world watched as we laid to rest President Bush. It was a unifying moment for our country.

Most poignant for me that week, after years of planning, was the sight of the Union Pacific train 4141 inching down the tracks.

That final horn sounding; the rain; the thousands of people lining the tracks for miles to pay respects; and then seeing the flag-draped casket masterfully carried by the honor guard.

As the train came into College Station, and as I stood in the drizzling rain, my mind replayed his life story, and rather than sadness my emotions turned to gratitude. I realized in that moment, even in his final wishes for his funeral, he wanted to thank America and to embrace every citizen, all symbolized by the role of the train, the flag-draped casket, the students and A&M Cadets, and the active-duty military honor guards. It was his final "do what's right" moment. Even in death, he was more concerned about others than himself, and in doing so remind us that we can all "be more."

I will always try to "be more," Mr. President.

Andy von Eschenbach, former head of the Food and Drug Administration:

Humility is one of the most admired, treasured, and perhaps most elusive of character traits in a person of great accomplishments and abilities.

Two stories portray the richness of this character in President Bush.

There was a problem with the swimming pool at Walker's Point that could not be resolved with the pumps removing the water. The water had to be siphoned out. The former President readily joined in by crawling on the pool deck to make it happen. Not usual decorum for the former Leader of the Free World.

When he and Mrs. Bush became the founders and chairs of the National Dialogue on Cancer,* President Bush insisted on sharing

---

* Eventually called C-Change, the organization was designed to bring together for the first time under one tent doctors, scientists, heads of nonprofits, governors, and other leaders to work together on cancer.

that role with a leading Democrat. When the invitation was declined by President and Mrs. Carter, the President was sufficiently humble "to go hat in hand" to extend the invitation on behalf of the dialogue to Senator Dianne Feinstein. She said yes.

No arrogance or pride in this man but only the greatness of humility.

Wait, did I mention he insisted on standing in line at the checkout in stores?!

Armin Weinberg, member of C-Change board of directors:

Of all the lessons and experiences I shared with President Bush, the one I chose to write about is the Americans with Disabilities Act (ADA).

I recall sharing with President Bush my father's vision that when he designed a medical office building in Solon, Ohio, in the early '60s, he was concerned that his patients (my dad was an ophthalmologist) in wheelchairs would not be able to have access to the two levels of the new office building. So he had a concrete ramp built. What a concept! Obviously, I was tickled that I could proudly share with President Bush that this preceded the ADA. However, his signing ADA into law made accommodations like this infinitely more meaningful to millions not only here but throughout the world who learned from our attention to those with disabilities. (My dad couldn't believe that I actually shared the ramp story with the former President!)

I did a fair bit of traveling to professional meetings in my career, not to mention many wonderful vacations with family and friends. Thus, airplanes and airports have been and will always be a part of my life.

Did you ever feel a great sense of anticipation as your plane taxied to the gate and then relief as you exited the airplane and headed to the nearest restroom? Well, each time I do I thank #41. Why? This is where the ADA comes in! Prior to the ADA I would typically encounter a row of urinals installed by people who were probably Texans and at least six foot six. Since I was five foot five, this put most urinals at my eye level. However, after the ADA there is at least one in the row set lower to accommodate those in wheelchairs and—probably unbeknownst to the policy folks—people like me who are short! An unintended but greatly appreciated benefit.

My dad used to say, "My mind knows what I want to do but my body is no longer able to do it!" Both men used all their remaining strength and commitment to do as much as they could, adapting to the limits of their bodies that now more than ever reflected their amazing spirit and desire to help others. Thanks to the ADA, they really could still stay engaged and active albeit at a level appropriately adjusted for their respective conditions until their passing.

President Bush, through his welcoming my voice representing minority and underserved communities into the National Dialogue on Cancer (later called C-Change), allowed my role as a leader of the Intercultural Cancer Council to extend opportunities to speak openly and honestly with business, government, and nonprofit leaders and help them realize that none of their well-intentioned goals and objectives to address cancer's toll would ever be achieved if we didn't include the voice of the minority and underserved communities and address and remove the barriers that stood in their way.

I'll forever be grateful to President Bush for that opportunity and for teaching all of us the importance of inclusivity.

But honestly, I will also remember his leadership every time I access a public restroom! After all, height does matter.

Mark Welsh, dean of the Bush School of Government and Public Service:

The Bush School produces public servants who leave here determined to reflect the personal ethics and professional competence of our namesake.

I don't believe George H. W. Bush ever formally committed to a life of service. Helping others came as naturally to him as breathing; it was just part of who he was. I don't think he was capable of passing anyone, anywhere, without trying to connect with them in some way—not as a politician, but as a person. He was so eminently qualified to sit in the Oval Office, but the foundation of that success was that he was first and foremost a good human being and a man of honor. Any assessment of his life should start there.

Bush School graduates head out into the world confident they are ready to serve their fellow citizens. They carry with them a truly remarkable sense of pride. They know they carry the legacy of our forty-first President with them, and they treasure it, just as he treasured them. These students, already making a difference in our world, are proving to be his greatest legacy. They are putting the life lessons they learned from him to work for all of us.

Daisy White, consultant to the George & Barbara Bush Foundation:

On December 12, 2012, Texas A&M staged a celebration ceremony on campus for our football quarterback Johnny Manziel, the recent winner of the Heisman Trophy. There was to be a reception afterward where, we were told, Johnny would sign autographs.

As a true fan, I bought seven footballs for him to sign—five for our grandchildren; one for my husband, John, and me; and one for President Bush. The President had been admitted to Houston Methodist Hospital for upper respiratory issues. Knowing how much he enjoyed all sports—particularly A&M football—I thought an autographed football would be therapeutic.

Because the crowd and speeches were so enthusiastic, the celebration went too long. Sadly, we were told Johnny could not sign any autographs. I was not to be deterred, so I managed to get a few private minutes with him, explaining that the only autograph I really wanted was for President Bush. Johnny said: "I heard he was in the hospital. I hope he is doing better." Then he said with sincere humility: "He would really want a football signed by me?" I explained that President Bush was a huge fan and would truly appreciate the autographed football. The ONLY autograph Johnny gave that day was: "To President Bush 41, I hope you feel better, #2 Johnny Manziel."

Driving back to Houston from College Station, I called Jean Becker to tell her we would drop off an autographed football at the office. She encouraged us to go see him at the hospital and deliver the football ourselves.

So off we went the next morning and were happy to see him reading the paper and drinking coffee and looking much improved. I said, "Mr. President, we don't have flowers or food, we have something starting with an F that we believe you will enjoy more—a football signed by Johnny Manziel." His response:

**Johnny would sign a football for me?**

The reaction was as humble and sincere as Johnny's question to us.

Up very early the next morning putting up Christmas decorations, I was watching news anchor Greta Van Susteren on national news. She announced: "President George H. W. Bush is feeling better this morning. One of the reasons he is feeling better is that he received an autographed football from Heisman Trophy winner Johnny Manziel," then showed a picture of the autographed football! I'm not sure how she found out, but I could not have been more thrilled.

*A P.S. to this story: When Daisy sent me this story, I wasn't sure Johnny Manziel belonged in this book, as he always seemed to be embroiled in controversy. So I asked former Aggie football coach R. C. Slocum what he thought: "When he was inducted into the A&M Athletic Hall of Fame, a very contrite Johnny gave a great acceptance speech, apologizing to the fans for some of his life choices and thanking them for their support. He got a standing ovation. He deserves to be in this book."*

*What would President Bush say? I'm proud of you, Johnny.*

Blake Winchell, a friend from the Bohemian Grove:*

In 2015 I shot and directed a show about President Bush entitled *41*. Jim Baker was the host. President Bush and I went out to lunch after our morning video session, and he looked up at me with a Cheshire cat grin and asked:

**Wanna have a cocktail?** Which was followed immediately by:
**But you can't tell Barbara.**

That moment taught me that, despite age and infirmity, you should relish all of the small moments in life.

---

* The elite summer camp in Northern California owned by the Bohemian Club of San Francisco.

★  ★  ★

*I will end this chapter with how Prime Minister Brian Mulroney ended his eulogy of President Bush at his state funeral at the National Cathedral in Washington, quoting an Irish proverb:*

> *There are wooden ships,*
> *There are sailing ships,*
> *There are ships that sail the sea,*
> *But the best ships are friendships*
> *And may they always be.*

# CHAPTER SIX

# HERE IS MY ADVICE...

## *Wisdom*

From now on in America, any definition of a successful life
must include serving others.

—*George H. W. Bush*

*U*p *until now, this book has been about "lessons learned from George H. W.
Bush," almost always through the examples he set by the way he lived his life
and by the way he led.*

*The word "advice" has come up rarely.*

*That's because he rarely gave it.*

*As I began work on this book, President Bush's post–White House
speechwriter, Jim McGrath, reminded me that one of the boss's favorite quotes
was, "Preach the gospel. Use words when necessary."\**

*But when asked to do so—either through a speech or through the written
word—President Bush was actually pretty good at it. A great example would
be the commencement address he gave at Prairie View A&M University, May
9, 1998:*

---

\* The quote is attributed to Saint Francis of Assisi.

. . . Let me encourage you that, in whatever path you choose to follow, don't waste time. Start right away. After all, commencement days are for commencing.

So start something. Start a business. Start a family. Start getting involved in our community.

Most importantly, start dreaming—and never stop. It's been said that "man never gets old until regrets take the place of his dream." Never let that be you.

And when you dream, dream big. Don't be daunted or limited. Be bold.

To dream big dreams, you can't be afraid of failure. You can't be afraid to extend yourself, to take qualified risks, to do something new.

One of my heroes, Teddy Roosevelt, once said: "The only person who never makes mistakes is the person who never does anything."

Roosevelt knew that, just as nobody can dream your dream for you, it takes a sustained effort to make your dreams come true.

It also takes values—simple, basic values such as always do your best.

If you accept responsibility, honor it.

If you are a leader, lead by example.

Be accountable for your actions. Remember that actions are more important than words because they give your words truer meaning.

*Here are some excerpts from his own speeches and writings, in chronological order:*

★ ★ ★

Inaugural Address, January 20, 1989:

...I come before you and assume the presidency at a moment rich with promise. We live in a peaceful, prosperous time, but we can make it better. For a new breeze is blowing, and a world refreshed by freedom seems reborn. For in man's heart, if not in fact, the day of the dictator is over. The totalitarian era is passing, its old ideas blown away like leaves from an ancient, lifeless tree. A new breeze is blowing, and a nation refreshed by freedom stands ready to push on. There is new ground to be broken and new action to be taken. There are times when the future seems thick as a fog; you sit and wait, hoping the mists will lift and reveal the right path. But this is a time when the future seems like a door you can walk right through into a room called tomorrow.

... We know what works: Freedom works. We know what's right: Freedom is right. We know how to secure a more just and prosperous life for man on Earth: through free markets, free speech, free elections, and the exercise of free will unhampered by the state.

For the first time in this century, for the first time in perhaps all history, man does not have to invent a system by which to live. We don't have to talk late into the night about which form of government is better. We don't have to wrest justice from the kings. We only have to summon it from within ourselves. We must act on what we know. I take as my guide the hope of a saint: In crucial things, unity; in important things, diversity; in all things, generosity.

... My friends, we are not the sum of our possessions. They are not the measure of our lives. In our hearts we know what matters. We cannot hope only to leave our children a bigger car, a bigger bank account. We must hope to give them a sense of what it means to be a loyal friend; a loving parent; a citizen who leaves his home, his neighborhood, and town better than he found it. And what do we want the men and women who work with us to say when we're no longer there? That we were more driven to succeed than anyone around us? Or that we stopped to ask if a sick child had gotten better and stayed a moment there to trade a word of friendship?

No president, no government can teach us to remember what is best in what we are. But if the man you have chosen to lead this government can help make a difference; if he can celebrate the quieter, deeper successes that are made not of gold and silk but of better hearts and finer souls; if he can do these things, then he must.

America is never wholly herself unless she is engaged in high moral principle. We as a people have such a purpose today. It is to make kinder the face of the Nation and gentler the face of the world. My friends, we have work to do. There are the homeless, lost and roaming. There are the children who have nothing, no love and no normalcy. There are those who cannot free themselves of enslavement to whatever addiction—drugs, welfare, the demoralization that rules the slums. There is crime to be conquered, the rough crime of the streets. There are young women to be helped who are about to become mothers of children they can't care for and might not love. They need our care, our guidance, and our education, though we bless them for choosing life.

The old solution, the old way, was to think that public money alone could end these problems. But we have learned that that is not so. And in any case, our funds are low. We have a deficit to bring down. We have more will than wallet but will is what we need. We will make the hard choices, looking at what we have and perhaps allocating it differently, making our decisions based on honest need and prudent safety. And then we will do the wisest thing of all. We will turn to the only resource we have that in times of need always grows: the goodness and the courage of the American people.

And I am speaking of a new engagement in the lives of others, a new activism, hands-on and involved, that gets the job done. We must bring in the generations, harnessing the unused talent of the elderly and the unfocused energy of the young. For not only leadership is passed from generation to generation but so is stewardship. And the generation born after the Second World War has come of age.

I have spoken of a Thousand Points of Light, of all the community organizations that are spread like stars throughout the nation, doing good. We will work hand in hand, encouraging, sometimes leading, sometimes being led, rewarding. We will work on this in the White House, in the Cabinet agencies. I will go to the people and the programs that are the brighter points of light, and I'll ask every member of my government to become involved. The old ideas are new again because they're not old, they are timeless: duty, sacrifice, commitment, and a patriotism that finds its expression in taking part and pitching in.

We need a new engagement, too, between the Executive and the Congress. The challenges before us will be thrashed out with the House and the Senate. And we must bring the federal budget into balance. And we must ensure that America stands before the world united, strong, at peace, and fiscally sound. But of course things may be difficult. We need to compromise; we've had dissension. We need harmony; we've had a chorus of discordant voices.

. . . Let us negotiate soon and hard. But in the end, let us produce. The American people await action. They didn't send us here to bicker. They ask us to rise above the merely partisan. "In crucial things, unity"—and this, my friends, is crucial.

Great nations like great men must keep their word. When America says something, America means it, whether a treaty or an agreement or a vow made on marble steps. We will always try to speak clearly, for candor is a compliment; but subtlety, too, is good and has its place. While keeping our alliances and friendships around the world strong, ever strong, we will continue the new closeness with the Soviet Union, consistent both with our security and with progress. One might say that our new relationship in part reflects the triumph of hope and strength over experience. But hope is good, and so is strength and vigilance.

. . . Our children are watching in schools throughout our great land. And to them I say thank you for watching democracy's big day. For democracy belongs to us all, and freedom is like a beautiful kite that can go higher and higher with the breeze. And to all I say, no matter what your circumstances or where you are, you are part of this day, you are part of the life of our great nation.

Presenting the Presidential Medal of Freedom to Polish hero Lech Walesa, November 13, 1989:

The story of our times is the story of brave men and women who seized a moment, who took a stand. Lech Walesa showed how one individual could inspire others—in them a faith so powerful that it vindicated itself and changed the course of a nation. History may make men, but Lech Walesa has made history. And I believe history continues to be made every day by small daily acts of courage, by people who strive to make a difference. Such people, says Lech, "are everywhere, in every factory, steel mill, mine, and shipyard—everywhere." And we've certainly seen them in the American labor movement, where from the leadership of Lane Kirkland★ to the rank and file across the country, they have struggled in the vanguard of the free labor movement around the world.

Our own humble electrician, Ben Franklin, declared that "Our cause is the cause of all mankind, for we are fighting for their liberty in defending our own." And like Franklin, who seized lightning from the skies and brought it to Earth, Lech Walesa seized an idea, a powerful idea, and with it electrified the world. The idea is freedom. And the time is now.

Lighting the National Christmas Tree, December 14, 1989:

We've worked hard this year, all of us, all of you, to help build a better America, help someone else, help make this a kinder and gentler nation. But there remains a world of need all around us. In this holiday season, reach out to someone right where you live. Because from now on in America, "There's no room at the inn"—that's simply not an acceptable answer. From now on in America, any definition of a successful life must include serving others. For Christmas is measured not by what's beneath your tree but by what's inside your

---

★ President of the AFL-CIO from 1979 to 1995.

heart. And so, this year, the spirit of the holidays is at long last matched by the spirit of the time. And it's the beginning of a new decade at the ending of an old century. And whatever your dream, whatever star you're following, the future is bright with possibility.

Speaking to the National Leadership Coalition on AIDS, March 29, 1990:

. . . This virus is our challenge—not a challenge we sought; not a challenge we chose. But today our responsibility is clear: We must meet this challenge. We must beat this virus. For whether talking about a nation or an individual, character is measured not by our tragedies but by our response to those tragedies.

And for those who are living with HIV and AIDS, our response is clear: They deserve our compassion, they deserve our care, and they deserve more than a chance—they deserve a cure. America will accept nothing less. We're slashing red tape, accelerating schedules, boosting research. And somewhere out there, there is a Nobel Prize and the gratitude of planet Earth waiting for the man or woman who discovers the answer that's eluded everyone else.

. . . And every American must learn what AIDS is and what AIDS is not, and they must learn now. You in this room are leaders. You already know. The HIV virus is not spread by handshakes or hugs. You can't get it from food or drink, coughing or sneezing, or by sharing bathrooms or towels or conversation . . . it is our duty to make certain that every American has the essential information needed to prevent the spread of HIV and AIDS, because while the ignorant may discriminate against AIDS, AIDS won't discriminate among the ignorant.

...In this nation, in this decade, there is only one way to deal with an individual who is sick: with dignity, with compassion, care, and confidentiality—and without discrimination. Once disease strikes, we don't blame those who are suffering. We don't spurn the accident victim who didn't wear a seatbelt. We don't reject the cancer patient who didn't quit smoking. We try to love them and care for them and comfort them. We don't fire them; we don't evict them; we don't cancel their insurance.

Today I call on the House of Representatives to get on with the job of passing a law, as embodied in the Americans with Disabilities Act, that prohibits discrimination against those with HIV and AIDS. We're in a fight against a disease, not a fight against people. And we will not, and we must not, in America tolerate discrimination.

Addressing the nation from the Oval Office, following the "not guilty" verdict in the Rodney King police brutality case in Los Angeles, which sparked days of violent rioting across the nation, May 1, 1992:

What we saw last night and the night before in Los Angeles is not about civil rights. It's not about the great cause of equality that all Americans must uphold. It's not a message of protest. It's been the brutality of a mob, pure and simple. And let me assure you: I will use whatever force is necessary to restore order. What is going on in L.A. must and will stop. As your President I guarantee you this violence will end.

Now let's talk about the beating of Rodney King, because beyond the urgent need to restore order is the second issue, the question of justice: Whether Rodney King's Federal civil rights were violated, what you saw and what I saw on the TV video was revolting. I felt anger. I felt pain. I thought: How can I explain this to my grandchildren?

...[But] in a civilized society, there can be no excuse, no excuse for the murder, arson, theft, and vandalism that have terrorized the law-abiding citizens of Los Angeles. Mayor Bradley, just a few minutes ago, mentioned to me his particular concern, among others, regarding the safety of the Korean community. My heart goes out to them and all others who have suffered losses.

The wanton destruction of life and property is not a legitimate expression of outrage with injustice. It is itself injustice. And no rationalization, no matter how heartfelt, no matter how eloquent, can make it otherwise.

Television has become a medium that often brings us together. But its vivid display of Rodney King's beating shocked us. The America it has shown us on our screens these last 48 hours has appalled us. None of this is what we wish to think of as American. It's as if we were looking in a mirror that distorted our better selves and turned us ugly. We cannot let that happen. We cannot do that to ourselves.

...We must understand that no one in Los Angeles or any other city has rendered a verdict on America. If we are to remain the most vibrant and hopeful nation on earth, we must allow our diversity to bring us together, not drive us apart. This must be the rallying cry of good and decent people.

...We must build a future where, in every city across this country, empty rage gives way to hope, where poverty and despair give way to opportunity. After peace is restored to Los Angeles, we must then turn again to the underlying causes of such tragic events. We must keep on working to create a climate of understanding and tolerance, a climate that refuses to accept racism, bigotry, anti-Semitism, and hate of any kind, anytime, anywhere.

Tonight, I ask all Americans to lend their hearts, their voices, and their prayers to the healing of hatred.

Radio address to the nation on the results of the 1992 presidential election, November 7, 1992. This speech is less about advice and more about character:

Way back in 1945, Winston Churchill was defeated at the polls. He said, "I have been given the Order of the Boot." That is the exact same position in which I find myself today.

I admit, this is not the position I would have preferred, but it is a judgment I honor. Having known the sweet taste of popular favor, I can more readily accept the sour taste of defeat, because it is seasoned for me by my deep devotion to the political system under which this Nation has thrived for two centuries.

. . . Ours is a nation that has shed the blood of war and cried the tears of depression. We have stretched the limits of human imagination and seen the technologically miraculous become almost mundane. Always, always, our advantage has been our spirit, a constant confidence, a sense that in America the only things not yet accomplished are the things that have not yet been tried. President-elect Clinton needs all Americans to unite behind him so he can move our nation forward. But more than that, he will need to draw upon this unique American spirit.

There are no magic outside solutions to our problems. The

real answers lie within us. We need more than a philosophy of entitlement. We need to all pitch in, lend a hand, and do our part to help forge a brighter future for this country.

On January 20th, Barbara and I will head back to Texas. For us there will be no more elections, no more politics. But we will rededicate ourselves to serving others because, after all, that is the secret of this unique American spirit. With this spirit, we can realize the golden opportunities before us and make sure that our new day, like every American day, is filled with hope and promise.

Addressing Daily Points of Light winners in the East Room of the White House, January 14, 1993:

I've always believed that in each individual, there's a Point of Light waiting to be revealed; in each community, a thousand miracles waiting to happen. And when I assumed this great office, I pledged to do all I could to honor, encourage, and increase volunteer efforts until their light filled every dark corner of our country.

... You see, it's not just Points of Light that are important. It's the idea that every community in America could be filled with light.

... Regardless of what we believe Government should do, all of us agree that no serious social problem in this country is going to be solved without the active engagement of millions of citizens in tens of thousands of institutions, schools and businesses, churches and clubs, armies of ordinary people doing extraordinary things.

Government has a critical role in helping people and so does solid, sustainable economic growth. But people, people, not programs, solve problems. And somewhere in America, every serious social problem is being solved through voluntary service, for therein lies the greatest national resource of all. It doesn't matter who you are. Everybody's got something to give: a job skill, a free hour, a pair of strong arms. And that's what I mean when I say that from now on, any definition of a successful life must include serving others.

...Barbara and I will soon be making our way back to Texas, and I'd like to leave you with one thought: If I could leave but one legacy to this country, it would not be found in policy papers or even in treaties signed or even wars won; it would be return to the moral compass that must guide America through the next century, the changeless values that can and must guide change. And I'm talking about a respect for the goodness that made this country great, a rekindling of that light lit from within to reveal America as it truly is, a country with strong families, a country of millions of Points of Light.

*President Bush truly had a servant's heart and never felt any task was too big or too small. I found this note from him on my desk one Monday morning (I should note that I tried to convince him many times not to answer the phones when he was in the office by himself on weekends. It was a losing battle):*

April 16, 1995

Jean:

It's Easter, and I am doing case work; for I answered the phone here in the office.

A Mr. Jesse Kirk, unemployed welder, called in. He wanted Barbara for he has a reading problem.

When queried, I told him "It is I."

He then told me his problem. A good welder, he cannot find work because of his dyslexia and bad reading over all.

He is in construction and makes, sometimes, $15 per hour. Because of his reading failure he can't get work now.

He hates welfare. He doesn't want a handout.

I gave him the usual disclaimer "out of office, unemployed myself, call the Congressman."

Can someone call him?★

Maybe BPB knows of an adult reading program. Just any call back might encourage the guy. Even if we said, "We've checked, and have no suggestions."

Can we help Jesse?—GB

*We did help Jesse. We helped get him enrolled in a Houston adult literacy program, and he learned to read.*

*President Bush did give some advice to his sons George W. and Jeb, one of whom was running for reelection as governor of Texas and one of whom was running for governor of Florida, both races they would win:*

August 1, 1998

Dear George and Jeb,

... Your Mother tells me that both of you have mentioned to her your concerns about some of the political stories—the ones that seem to put me down and make me seem irrelevant—that contrast you

---

★ I deleted Mr. Kirk's phone number.

favorably to a father who had no vision and who was but a place holder in the broader scheme of things.

I have been reluctant to pass along advice. Both of you are charting your own course, spelling out what direction you want to take your State, in George's case running on a record of accomplishment.

But the advice is this. Do not worry when you see the stories that compare you favorably to a Dad for whom English was a second language and for whom the word destiny meant nothing.

First, I am content with how historians will judge my administration—even on the economy. I hope and think they will say we helped change the world in a positive sense...

It is inevitable that the new breed journalists will have to find a hook in stories, will have to write not only on your plans and your dreams but will have to compare those with what, in their view, I failed to accomplish.

That can be hurtful to a family that loves each other. That can hurt you boys who have been wonderful to me, you two of whom I am so very proud. But the advice is don't worry about it. At some point both of you may want to say "Well, I don't agree with my Dad on that point" or "Frankly I think Dad was wrong on that." Do it. Chart your own course, not just on the issues but on defining yourselves. No one will ever question your love of family—your devotion to your parents. We have all lived long enough and lived in a way that demonstrates our closeness; so do not worry when the comparisons might be hurtful to your Dad for nothing can ever be written that will drive a wedge between us—nothing at all . . .

. . . So read my lips—no more worrying. Go on out there and, as they say in the oil fields, "Show 'em a clean one."

> This from your
> very proud and
> devoted,
> Dad

*President Bush's former speechwriter and good friend author Christopher Buckley—or Christo, as 41 called him—occasionally asked President Bush to write an essay for his* FYI *magazine, a publication of Forbes. As Bill Clinton prepared to leave office after the 2000 election, President Bush wrote this essay for Chris, entitled "10 Rules for a Former President":*

1. **Get out of Dodge—fast. You're history on that cold January day. So be pleasant about it all. Smile a lot. Try not to wave to the huge inaugural crowd too much. They're there to see the new guy . . .**

2. **As you fly back home on Air Force One look around. Take a shower . . . Grab a few napkins and some notepads and Lifesavers with the Presidential seal on them . . . Lie down on the bed in the President's cabin because 34E on the commercial airlines is quite different . . .**

3. **When you get off Air Force One wave from the top of the steps. A TV camera from the local station will probably be there. "How does it feel to be home?" [the**

reporter] will ask. "Great to be back!" And you look ahead and you try not to think what it used to be like just four or five hours before. You'll hurt a little but that will go away—sooner than you might think.

4. ...Don't try to shape history by writing op-ed pieces all the time or by criticizing your successor. If you really want to make news and get back on TV you'll find the best way to do that is to criticize your successor...Don't!...If you really feel strongly about something, drop your successor a line but don't leak it to the press. The important thing is to quit worrying about your legacy. It's up to others to decide that.

5. When you're out walking your dog, try not to argue when you see the guy down the street who always insists on giving you his views on every issue. Oh, you've got to listen, but it is better to nod silently and not disagree when he says, "You should've invaded Cuba and gotten the CIA to knock off Saddam Hussein"...smile pleasantly and try to keep moving.

6. Play some golf but resist telling everyone what it was like to play with Jack [Nicklaus] or Arnie [Palmer] at the course near Camp David...And no one wants to know how many times you had the legends of sports to the White House. (They didn't really love you. They just wanted to see the White House.)

7. Be nice to all autograph seekers and tourists and people who interrupt your dinner. After all, some of them probably voted for you, and those who didn't will swear they now wish they did.

8.  Remember the five "stay" rules:
    a)  Stay out of the way, out of Washington, out of the news, away from press conferences, off TV.
    b)  Stay away from bashing the national press, even those that knocked your socks off when you were President.
    c)  Stay away from most of those yellow pad think tank events—the ones where the conference proceedings are carefully written then printed, never to be read by anyone ever again. You might want to consider the occasional world peace seminar in Bermuda but be sure the organizers get you a tee time.
    d)  Stay away from saying "here's the way I did it." You had your chance...
    e)  Stay well. And when you get older, resist telling everyone about which body part hurts. Drink bulk stuff, exercise, stretch, keep younger people around you. Smile a lot. Feel young at heart.

9.  Always count your blessings. Quietly remember the wonders of the White House. Never forget the many people that helped you get there or those that worked in your administration or the dedicated civil servants who treat the White House with such respect and dignity while making those who live there feel "at home." Remember the majesty of the Oval Office. And as the years go by, give thanks to God for your family, your true friends, and for having given you the chance to be President of the greatest country on the face of the earth.

10. **Hug your grandkids. If you don't have any, get some. And if by chance you have a son or daughter who has a chance to be President of the USA ask yourself, "Might this really come true? Only in America!"**

<u>Remarks to the Arab American Cultural & Community Center Seventh Annual Unity and Friendship Gala in Houston on November 2, 2002:</u>

**Since leaving the Presidency, and especially since our son was elected President, I have tried to stay out of the public eye. I don't do op-ed pieces or press conferences; and I darn sure stay out of the shouting matches that we see so often on TV these days.**

**... Every once in a while, I will speak out, but only when I feel something deep in my heart ... I wanted to speak here to condemn intolerance, to condemn the stereotyping that has hurt so many American families, adults and children alike.**

**I reject the tendency to condemn Arabs in general or an entire religion in particular because of the extreme views of some extremists who smear the good name "Muslim."**

**I am not here to single out one or two misguided critics of Islam but rather to say how offensive I find the relentless attacks on Arabs.**

**Some evangelical Christians in this country have made inflammatory statements about Islam. I am very glad that Jerry Falwell corrected the record and apologized for his remarks that caused so much grief, so much hurt in many Arab countries.**

**But to be fair here, I have seen terrible inflammatory statements made by some Mullahs about our country and about other religions.**

**I would say that it would be grossly unfair to judge Islam**

by the extreme rantings of some radical Mullahs, just as it would be grossly unfair to judge Christianity by some of its intolerant practitioners here and abroad.

The 9/11 attacks should not be used by any American to condemn all Muslims and certainly not to teach hatred towards Arabs.

Arab Americans condemn terrorism and yet often they get stereotyped right here in Houston, right here in America. This must not be.

Al Qaida extremists are evil. I hope we can all agree on that. They are our enemy. They have brought death and destruction to our society, killing the innocent to achieve their dishonorable goals.

What bothers me today is that, because all the 9/11 terrorists had Arab surnames, many Americans seem quick to condemn Arabs in general...

The 9/11 attacks should not be used by believers of any faith to condemn the prophet Muhammad or the peace-loving leaders of Islam today.

The President spoke to the nation about the need for tolerance yet his administration is attacked like this, thus proving that intolerance often begets intolerance; hatred begets hatred.

And insidious lies often go unchallenged.

...When Oklahoma City's Federal building was blown up, many Americans hastened to the conclusion that this must have been the evil work of an "Arab terrorist."

When the recent sniper attacks were going on,* I literally

---

\* A shooter had killed ten and wounded three others over three weeks in October in the Washington, DC, area.

prayed, "Please do not have these killers be of Arab descent, be Muslim extremists." When John Muhammad's name surfaced, some were quick to again condemn Arabs and Islam. This alleged killer probably knows less about Islam than my dog Sadie, but his actions bring prejudice down on the heads of many innocents because of the propensity out there to stereotype.

Listen to these words from a friend of mine,* a dedicated Catholic seminarian: "What those terrorists did on September 11th a year ago had nothing to do with serving God. They may have called themselves Muslims but they have nothing in common with my Muslim friends, just as I have nothing in common with neo-Nazis who call themselves Christians and try to use the Bible to justify their violence and racism."

My appeal is for tolerance and understanding, for avoiding polarizing rhetoric, for working as best we can for your goals of "peace and justice."

I came here to say thanks for all you do for our community; to say I empathize with each and every one of you who may have felt the sting of prejudice right here in this land of the free and the brave.

... I can assure you that this President, like his Dad before him, certainly abhors war and the horrors it can bring to innocents ... we must continue to fight against stereotyping as we fight and win the war against terror. No freedom-loving, patriotic American should ever be subjected to prejudice because of his looks or his religious preference.

We must be tolerant, and as the rallying cry of this organization says, we must stand for "Peace and Justice."

---

* His adviser in this case was actually my little brother, a Catholic priest.

★ ★ ★

*In 2003, President Bush's friend Henry O. Dormann, chairman and editor in chief of LEADERS magazine, asked him to write a piece answering this question: "What is the greatest challenge you have had to overcome in your life?"*

*Instead of talking about his greatest challenge, President Bush decided to give the readers some of his rare advice. His answer was classic George H. W. Bush—simple yet profound:*

1. **Don't get down when your life takes a bad turn. Out of adversity comes challenge and often success.**
2. **Don't blame others for your setbacks.**
3. **When things go well, always give credit to others.**
4. **Don't talk all the time. Listen to your friends and mentors and learn from them.**
5. **Don't brag about yourself. Let others point out your virtues, your strong points.**
6. **Give someone else a hand. When a friend is hurting, show that friend you care.**
7. **Nobody likes an overbearing big shot.**
8. **As you succeed, be kind to people. Thank those who help you along the way.**
9. **Don't be afraid to shed a tear when your heart is broken because a friend is hurting.**
10. **Say your prayers!!**

Commencement address, with President Bill Clinton, at Tulane University in New Orleans on May 13, 2006, nine months after Hurricane Katrina devastated the city:

**...It is each of you assembled here today that has inspired me, our nation, and indeed the world.**

...Each of you here has your own story to tell of the day the waters came, and the days of profound hardship that followed. Hurricane Katrina left in its wake a path of devastation biblical in proportion, and we struggled at first to come to terms with an unimaginable reality. How can you repair a shattered home if you cannot find the pieces? Where can you go when the sea swallows the land?

...The floodwaters may have breached the levees that surrounded this city; they may have destroyed home-after-home, on block-after-block; but today we also know they could not break the spirit of the people who call this remarkable, improbable city home.

...Everywhere President Clinton and I have gone, we hear stories just like that. It's been said that adversity doesn't test your character—it reveals it. If so, then here in the aftermath of Katrina, the world has seen the essence of the American spirit: courage, compassion, resourcefulness, determination.

...Billy Graham once said, "Time is the capital we've been given by God to invest wisely, so the question is, where do we invest it? God calls us to invest our time capital in the very lives of people—not in projects, not in possessions."

So even as I stand here to congratulate you for reaching this proud moment of achievement in your lives, let me also encourage you to continue investing your time in your fellowman.

That means getting off the sidelines and staking a personal claim in your country, your state, your community. It doesn't have to be running for office. It doesn't have to involve politics in any way. But find a way to be of service to others.

I got more of a kick out of being one of the founders of the

YMCA in Midland, Texas back in 1952 than almost anything I've done. We did something positive. We didn't change the world—just a small corner of it. But we helped a lot of great kids by doing it.

A lot of people out there like to talk about the cynical times in which we live, but as I look around this room, make no mistake: I still believe there are people out there who care, who are willing to open their hearts to the pain and the need around them, and do the hard work that makes a positive difference in our world.

I still believe there are people out there who seek a higher purpose to serve with their lives during our time together on this earth. No, when I look at what happened all along the Gulf Coast, I still believe in heroes. When I look at our world, the good I see far outweighs the bad—which maybe explains why I am optimistic about our future, about your future.

Let me put it this way: Back during World War II, Navy pilots had a saying to describe a cloudless, perfect day for flying. That saying was "Ceiling and Visibility Unlimited," or CAVU. That's what you wanted to hear when you were climbing into your plane and preparing for the mission ahead—that the skies were clear.

Such is my wish for each of you. As you prepare to leave Tulane—to tackle the challenges of life ahead—I wish all your days will be blessed with "ceiling and visibility unlimited." Lord knows, I'll be pulling for you—so get out there and make us all proud.

Memorial Day speech in Kennebunkport, May 26, 2008:

As we gather in the heart of this wonderful community, and call to mind the countless sacrifices that a long line of

American patriots have so selflessly made that we might live in freedom, my message to each of you today relates not to the fallen—to those who have given our Nation their last full measure of devotion.

As President Lincoln rightly observed at Gettysburg, there is little that those of us who remain can say to add to the glory and honor that the valor of the fallen has rightly earned them.

Rather, I have come here today to encourage the rest of us—the living, the able-bodied—to do everything we can to be worthy of such courage and sacrifice. To give Memorial Day the significance it deserves, it seems to me that this day should involve more than the act of remembering—as vitally important as that surely is.

If we were to encounter the patriots of Bunker Hill or the Battle of New Orleans, what could we tell them we do to help sustain the grand experiment in self-governance they sacrificed so much to set in motion? Could each of us say, for example, that we take the time to vote?

If we were to encounter the dead from Antietam—the bloodiest battle not only of the Civil War, but in all of American history—could we say that we have fully endeavored to treat every American born under our Declaration with equality and fairness?

If we were to talk today to those who served in World Wars I and II, or Korea, or Vietnam—or anywhere before or since—could we say that we have tried to give back to our own community as active citizens, as volunteers?

Ladies and gentlemen, the men and women we honor today—those who have served, those who have fallen—have done their part. And yet there is so much that each of us can do in our own way, in our own lives, to keep our Nation free, and strong.

So I join you today in honoring all who wear our Nation's uniform, particularly at this time of war. I join you in honoring our military families, who bear a burden every bit as heavy as the soldier's pack.

Most of all, I join you in asking the continued blessings, and mercy, of a loving God for our Nation, and all who take her noble cause upon their shoulders—be they on the front lines, or here on the home front...

God Bless America.

*I would like to end this chapter by sharing some advice President Bush gave... well, himself. He wrote this in his diary the night he lost the election to Bill Clinton:*

It's 12:15 in the morning, November 4th. The election is over—it's come and gone. It's hard to describe the emotions of something like this...the job is not finished and that kills me...

Now into bed, prepared to face tomorrow:

Be strong, be kind, be generous of spirit, be understanding and let people know how grateful you are. Don't get even. Comfort the ones I've hurt and let down. Say your prayers and ask for God's understanding and strength. Finish with a smile and some gusto and do what's right and finish strong.

# CHAPTER SEVEN

# A NEW BEGINNING
## *Faith*

If we listen closely enough, we can hear that heartbeat even now, for it's the heartbeat of a lion—a lion who not only led us, but who loved us.

—*Jon Meacham*

*That might be an odd title for a chapter that focuses on the final days of George Herbert Walker Bush.*

*Except that is exactly how 41 felt about dying: Maybe life as he knew it was coming to an end, but only because it was time to move on to the next big adventure.*

*That is what you call "faith."*

*His good friend Susan Baker, wife of Secretary James Baker, said about President Bush's faith in 41ON41:*

Prayer was an indispensable part of his life, and I think that's one of the reasons he had such wisdom . . . that he had the inspiration that he did. He often said that he could not possibly do the job of being President without prayer and without spending time on his knees and getting truth through prayer. I think the whole world has benefited from his faith.

★  ★  ★

*And because of his deep faith, our forty-first President was not afraid of dying.*

*He was never in a hurry to get there—he had hoped to make it to age one hundred but fell short by six years. His determination on that goal maybe weakened a bit when his wife of seventy-three years died in April 2018. I told him a few days before she died that I hoped he would "stick around for a while." He told me he absolutely would—his children would need him.*

*In general, he was fascinated by the subject. He liked to talk about his funeral. Getting out the funeral files and making adjustments was one of his favorite lunchtime activities.*

*Once he challenged me to help him count the number of times he almost died. We got up to nine.*

*We talked about heaven and hell—he was curious about who I thought was in hell. (My answer: Saddam Hussein and Adolf Hitler for sure.) We talked about what would happen when we got to heaven—**if I get there**, the ever-modest 41 would always say. He was especially excited to see their daughter Robin, who had died from leukemia at age three in 1953. He wondered if the dogs would be there.*

*His friend Daisy White remembers sitting next to President Bush when out of the blue he asked her: **Are you afraid to die?** The question caught her off guard, but she answered truthfully. "No, President Bush, I am not afraid, but I am just not quite ready."*

*Squeezing her hand, the forty-first President said, **I am not either**.*

*I learned a lot watching George Herbert Walker Bush die.*

*How to die with dignity. How to die with courage. How to die while making everyone around you feel it was okay.*

*Some of the people who had a front-row seat to his final years agreed to share their stories. President Bush would approve that we are going to start with some mostly humorous observations from one of his doctors.*

★ ★ ★

<u>Clinton Doerr:</u>

As all doctors know, you learn a lot about someone watching them die. Just to be President Bush's doctor was an honor. To be with him until the end was so much more. Here are my random observations I'd like to share with you.

- President Bush rarely complained about his medical conditions or drew attention to himself.

Nearly every one of my house calls to the Bush residence in Houston were initiated by either Mrs. Bush or his medical or personal aide notifying me something was wrong.

Never once did President Bush complain about his symptoms unless in response to a specific query. Nor would he himself request a visit. True to form, there was rarely any reference to the "I." Not to imply that he was stoic or minimalizing his symptoms, but he just simply would state the facts and not dwell on them. In fact, he'd often throw out the occasional, "It's not the cough that carries you off; it's the coffin that they carry you off in."

- Politics pervades everything.

Early one morning during President Bush's January 2017 hospitalization, I was updating him on his recovery from another flare-up of his chronic bronchitis. During our conversation, he switched course and asked me about his bowels. I replied that although my focus was primarily on his lungs, I was informed by the nurses that his bowels were functioning normally overnight, and then I smiled and jokingly said, "Nobody's going to claim that you're FOS,★ Mr. President."

---

★ For the innocent among you, FOS means full of shit.

Without missing a beat, he replied, **Oh, they will anyway, Doc**. To which I fired back, "Well, that's politics, sir." He chuckled in acknowledgment.

- Grey Goose* among friends is medicinal.

Another evening while President Bush was undergoing another hospitalization for a flare-up of his chronic bronchitis, I was finishing rounds and wanted to check in with him before leaving for home.

His room was dark except for a solitary lamp dimly silhouetting two figures. One was President Bush reclined in an easy chair. The other, a distinguished-looking gentleman who was sitting on a couch nearby. I apologized for interrupting and President Bush immediately responded: **Hey Doc, meet my friend Jim.**

As I greeted Secretary James Baker and shook his hand, I immediately took note of the Grey Goose bottle on the coffee table but did not make mention. Nor did I divulge details to Mrs. Bush the following day when she was at her husband's bedside. Patient-doctor confidentiality was preserved, AND he was clinically better. I was not entirely certain if the improvement was due to the Grey Goose, the social company, or the official medical care that was being rendered—but who am I to argue? Furthermore, once an Army officer, always an Army officer, so I was not about to question my commander in chief!

- The spoken word is therapeutic.

There were many times during President Bush's hospitalizations that I found his son Neil reading to him, his eyes closed but attentive to the book content (history seemed to be a favorite theme). I

---

* President Bush's favorite brand of vodka.

was always impressed that even when ill, usually with a distracting cough or shortness of breath, he would still prefer to listen to the sound of someone's voice, constantly learning and taking in new information. I realize in the past few years, compared to the interval that I was involved in his care from 2012 through 2018, that the world has become so much more saturated with cell-phone-derived information, be it via texting or social media platforms, but it seems that nothing can replace the connectivity and therapeutic benefit of verbalization. Listening and hearing. Both being a skill and an art.

• Thinking of others, outside of oneself.

This story is actually about Barbara Bush but could be about her husband as well.

The Secret Service contacted me one weekend to tell me that President Bush had an abrupt onset of shortness of breath and low oxygen and they were en route by ambulance to Houston Methodist Hospital. My wife was on duty at the county hospital, so I grabbed our then six-year-old son Jakob and took him with me. Having no choice at the spur of the moment, I dropped Jakob off in the secure Physician's Library, which was right next to the ER, and went to evaluate President Bush.

Fortunately, he had been stabilized by the ER staff. I spoke with Mrs. Bush, coordinating care with the ER personnel and Dr. Amy Mynderse,* who had also arrived. Dr. Mynderse pointed out to Mrs. Bush that it was my weekend off and my wife was out of pocket, so I had my son in tow. Mrs. Bush immediately insisted on meeting Jakob. I was shocked. Her husband had just experienced a serious flare of his chronic breathing issues and we were still sorting

---

* Another of President Bush's physicians.

through the triggering event, yet she wanted to take the time to greet my son.

Accordingly, I escorted Jakob from the library and prepared him that he was about to meet these important people. I told him that President Bush would be on a stretcher with some oxygen tubing and monitors and that it would be okay but a bit "busy." He took it all in stride. We entered the room, and he was immediately greeted by Mrs. Bush. He was wearing a T-shirt imprinted with German shepherds (we had a German shepherd at the time), and she took notice, prompting a discussion of dogs and pets. He mentioned that he and his sister also had a guinea pig, and Mrs. Bush commented that she wasn't too fond of rodents.

I was blessed to be at this great man's side when he died on November 30, 2018.

*Dr. Doerr mentioned seeing Neil Bush reading to his dad. Neil lived right across the street from his parents and saw them almost every day during those final years.*
<u>Neil Bush:</u>

My father has always been my hero. The guy that treated everyone with respect, that enjoyed life "its own self," a guy who lifted others in so many ways.

While Mom was the disciplinarian, Dad didn't need to use words. His leadership in government, business, and family was largely through the example he set. And that was true to the very end of his life.

I've observed with both my mother and father that as we age, the filters drop and one's true character shines through. In Mom's case, she became a bit more direct in expressing opinions, her sometimes biting humor popping out from time to time, and her deep love and mama bear commitment to family intensified.

As for Dad, no matter how challenging the health issue of the moment might have been, his natural tendency to lean into daily interactions with love became more evident. In his healthier stages of aging, he would write handwritten notes to console friends or celebrate successes. These notes are treasured by the recipients. As a wheelchair-bound former President, he was always thoughtful to linger in restaurants or public events with people who were dying to have a photo. He knew that simple gestures would fill hearts with happiness.

As Dad aged and was nearing the end, he became less verbal. As I was bending down to kiss him and to say, "I love you," he would inevitably utter, **love you more**. When asked how he was feeling or how he was doing, he'd give a thumbs-up. When sharing good news, he'd smile; when sharing news of concern to the family, he would give an empathetic frown. It was a blessing to be around a man so loving.

It was a blessing to live across the street from my parents during the latter years of their lives. Maria and I were able to spend a lot of time reading to them, doing puzzles with Mom, sharing news of the day, gossiping about family and friends, and watching *Law & Order*.

On November 30, 2018, the day of Dad's passing, we witnessed the soul of a beautiful human transition. In that last day, as he did all his life, my father set a great example for leaving this earthly life with dignity, embracing the core values that were truly important: faith, family, and friends.

Houston family members gathered that day and most of the extended family was reached by phone to have a last word. The strength he received from his loving family was palpable.

Dad's closest friend, Jim Baker, and his wife, Susan, were present throughout the day. They had visited with Dad often over the days and months leading to his passing. To see the Bakers at Dad's bedside on that final day drove home the importance of friendships in living a fuller life.

Also there was Jean Becker and Evan Sisley, loyal staff members who fell deeply into the friend category and whose presence in Dad's life brought him comfort and joy.

Dad's faith certainly was evident that day, a faith reinforced by the Reverend Russ Levenson, who visited Mom and Dad frequently, prayed with and for them, and was such a reassuring messenger of their faith. Russ's prayers and peaceful presence during the last moments were perfect for a guy whose quiet faith was deeply inculcated into his being.

What lessons did we learn from the example that my father set? From his life we learned to show gratitude, sing the praises of others, count your blessings, put yourself in the other guy's shoes, spread goodwill and joy through authentic interactions, be kind and gracious, live a life of dignity, honor, and patriotism, and leave the world a better place.

And on the last day we could see the importance of cultivating a loving family and close friends while living your faith. George H. W. Bush's life was a blessing to me and to many, many others who were influenced by the example he set.

Earlier that day, Dad had a visit from a great friend, the amazing Irish tenor Ronan Tynan, who sat by his bedside holding Dad's hand while singing several songs, including "Silent Night."

The words were perfect: "All is calm, all is bright...sleep in heavenly peace."

The Reverend Dr. Russell Levenson, the Bushes' pastor:

Without question, in my now over three decades of ordained ministry, among the greatest honors and privileges was to serve and pastor to George H. W. Bush—and out of that service came a friendship I would have never imagined.

Over the nearly twelve years that I came to know him, from my observation, our forty-first President did all he could to help anyone who needed him—for he, like his beloved Barbara, was a loving man.

He loved his friends and his family, and I think that was the fruit of his sincere faith. In the Episcopal room of the greater house of the Christian faith, we often sing Peter Raymond Scholtes' hymn that mirrors Jesus' words from John 13:35—others will know who we are . . . "by our love."

I often use the word "generous" when I reflect on both President and Mrs. Bush's love of others because there seemed to be no circle too large for them to draw in order to take others into the love they knew and the love they wanted to share. They had friends from every walk of life and every nation, language, race, gender, sexual orientation, and political persuasion.

I witnessed this visibly in the faces of the more than twelve thousand people who waited hours in line to pay their respects at the visitation before his final funeral service, at his home church, St. Martin's in Houston. He was—he is—deeply loved, but it is because so many witnessed his love lived so fully.

The imperative to love others is the basis for every major faith tradition on planet Earth, and I think out of his devotion to his own faith, the President practiced that imperative.

In the last hours of his life, I sat nearby and watched the steady stream of friends and family come to bid their loved one farewell as he prepared to leave this life for the next. The last words of this remarkable man were, unremarkably, "I love you," because love dwelt fully in his spiritual DNA.

And because he did live in this way, what better way to slip out of this room we call planet Earth and take that next step into the place we call the kingdom of God?

In my book *Witness to Dignity: The Life and Faith of George H. W. and Barbara Bush,*⋆ I offered an invitation—and it is the same invitation that I offer to you, the reader of this book, as well. As you reflect on this remarkable collection of memories about this man who rightly deserves the accolades and admiration spilled so liberally in these pages, may they inspire you to deal with the ache about the way things are in our world and our desire to turn that tide, that we cannot just long for better days, but see them return.

George H. W. Bush raised the bar of human service, and in doing so he changed our nation, changed our world, and changed all of our lives for the better.

He was a living point of light, and he showed us what it meant to lead, to live, and to love with a servant's heart.

By God's grace, may we find our way there again . . . and again . . . and again.

Evan Sisley, personal aide to President Bush (2015–2018):

I had the honor of being President Bush's last personal aide. The job, much like the men who held it, changed considerably over time. While early aides had busy schedules with frequent trips abroad, my time with President Bush slowly transitioned toward a gentler pace with frequent stays in the hospital. Several of my immediate predecessors grew up in southern Maine and had started working for the President from a young age, when they started as "summer lads," doing yard work and running errands at Walker's Point.

---

⋆ Published by Hachette in 2022.

I came from a different background. I was part of a small group of reserve Navy corpsmen who were hired to work as medics for President and Mrs. Bush. Many of us had been deployed to Afghanistan or Iraq, and we volunteered to care for our former commander in chief with the same dignity and respect that we would the flag that we fought under.

Though he lived a remarkable life, the most remarkable part of President Bush's aging process—and eventual death—was that it was no different than most Americans'. The man who oversaw our country's peaceful transition to become the world's sole superpower was unable to command his own body from failing. Legs accustomed to running the trails of Camp David or chasing tennis balls on the court at Walker's Point stiffened from Parkinson's disease. A heart and lungs that fueled his aerobic metabolism through the endless slog of the campaign trail struggled to survive flu season. Where some might have resented the loss of autonomy, he set the example for aging with grace and dignity.

He was always kind and considerate of those who cared for him. The hardest part of having President Bush as my patient was treating the pain of a man who wouldn't complain.

By now you all know that President Bush was a prolific letter writer. I cannot imagine an aide who left the job without learning the importance of a handwritten note. As the last aide, my only regret is not having the ability to write him a thank-you note. Undoubtedly, working for him changed the course of my life. I wouldn't be where I am now if it wasn't for the opportunities that his employment afforded me.

When Jean asked me to write something for this book, I decided maybe it was time to finally write that letter.

Dear President Bush,

In a couple of days, I will load up the Penske★ and move back to Maine. It feels both familiar and new, moving there for the first time without you and Mrs. Bush. Your love of Maine was infectious, and I am thankful for the ability to return. You used to say that Walker's Point was your "anchor towards windward" during trying times. I am hoping I can channel that same comfort in Portland as I push through graduate school.

I never had the chance to properly thank you for all that you have done for me. Your dedication to public service inspired me to aim higher and dream bigger than I would have ever imagined. Your words of encouragement to pursue medicine have motivated me when I have questioned my capabilities as a student or lost sight of my goals. And your loving devotion to Mrs. Bush set the example for me to follow in my own marriage.

Most importantly, you taught me the things that I could never learn in a classroom: How to recognize discomfort in a patient's face, or how to broach the most difficult topics like the end of life or the death of a spouse. These were lessons that will affect the way I treat patients for the rest of my life. I also am sorry for the mistakes that I made—the times that you maybe were frustrated with my inability to understand the care that you needed.

I am forever grateful for the patience, kindness, and compassion you showed me while teaching me how to

---

★ One of the personal aides' many responsibilities was helping the Bushes and the staff move between Texas and Maine every summer. They always rented a Penske.

become a better healthcare provider. My future patients thank you, too.

Best,

Evan

*When I asked President Bush's biographer, Jon Meacham, if he would contribute something to this book, his reaction was honest: "Of course. But I think I've said everything there is to say about him." After pondering for a few weeks, he came back and suggested I share with you the eulogy he gave at President Bush's state funeral. I knew it was right. His eulogy had been an exclamation point on the life of 41. We'll share the eulogy after Jon's introduction:*

He was, to put it mildly, skeptical. It was September 1998, and George H. W. Bush had agreed to an interview with the presidential historian Michael Beschloss to launch *A World Transformed*, the foreign policy book the forty-first President had written with Brent Scowcroft. At the time, Michael was a contributor to *Newsweek*, the weekly newsmagazine where I was the national-affairs editor. Michael kindly let me tag along for the interview, which the former President scheduled for 7:00 a.m. in order to be done with it early. This strategy was not a reflection on Michael, whom Bush admired, but on the magazine, which had long had a tense relationship with Bush, one that stretched back to his vice presidential days under Ronald Reagan.*

Michael and I ended up spending much of the day at Walker's Point—and there began a long journey with George Herbert Walker Bush. I became his biographer, publishing *Destiny and Power* in 2015. Below is the eulogy I delivered at Washington National Cathedral in December 2018. It was the honor of a lifetime.

---

* Think Wimp cover.

In the summer of 2018, on the same first floor of the house where we had first met with Michael and General Scowcroft twenty years before, I read these remarks to an ailing President Bush.

When the reading was done, the president paused, then said:

**Beautiful. But that's an awful lot about *me*.**

In character to the very end—that was George Herbert Walker Bush.

My eulogy as prepared for delivery:

The story was almost over even before it had fully begun. Shortly after dawn on Saturday, September 2, 1944, Lt. j.g. George Herbert Walker Bush, joined by two crewmates, took off from the USS *San Jacinto* to attack a radio tower on Chichijima. As they approached the target, the air was heavy with flak. The plane was hit. Smoke filled the cockpit. Flames raced along the wings. My God, Lt. Bush thought, this thing's gonna go down.

Yet he kept the plane in its 35-degree dive, dropped his bombs, and then roared off, out to sea, telling his crewmates to "Hit the silk!" Following protocol, Lt. Bush turned the plane so they could bail out. Only then did Bush parachute from the cockpit. The wind propelled him backward, and he gashed his head on the tail as he flew through the sky.

Lt. Bush plunged deep into the ocean, bobbed to the surface, and flopped onto a tiny raft. His head bleeding, his eyes burning, his mouth and throat raw from salt water, the future 41st President was alone. Sensing that his men had not made it, he was overcome. He felt the weight of responsibility as a nearly physical burden, and he wept. Then, at four minutes shy of noon, a submarine emerged to rescue the downed pilot. George Herbert Walker Bush was safe.

The story—his story, and ours—would go on, by God's grace.

Through the decades President Bush would ask himself: **Why me? Why was I spared?** In a sense, the rest of his life was a perennial effort to prove himself worthy of his salvation on that distant morning. To him, his life was no longer wholly his own. There were always more missions to undertake, more lives to touch, more love to give.

And what a headlong race he made of it all. He *never* slowed down. On the primary campaign trail he once shook the hand of a department-store mannequin in New Hampshire, seeking votes. When he realized his mistake, he said: **Never know. Always gotta ask.** You can hear the voice, can't you? As Dana Carvey said, the key to a Bush 41 impression was "Mr. Rogers trying to be John Wayne."

George Herbert Walker Bush was America's last great soldier-statesman, a 20th-century Founding Father. He governed with virtues that most closely resemble those of Washington and of Adams, of TR and of FDR, of Truman and of Eisenhower—of men who believed in causes larger than themselves.

Six-foot-two, handsome, dominant in person, President Bush spoke with his big, strong hands, making fists to underscore his points. A master of what Franklin Roosevelt called "the science of human relationships," George H. W. Bush believed that to whom much is given, much is expected.

And because life gave him much, he gave back. He stood in the breach in the Cold War against totalitarianism. He stood in the breach in Washington against unthinking partisanship. He stood in the breach against tyranny and discrimination, and on his watch a wall fell in Berlin, a dictator's aggression did not stand, and doors across America opened to those with disabilities. And he stood in the breach against heartbreak and hurt, always, always offering an outstretched hand, a warm word, a sympathetic tear. If your heart were troubled, he would rush to mend it; if your life were soaring, he would make haste to celebrate your success. Strong and gracious, comforting and charming, loving and loyal, he was our shield in danger's hour.

Of course, there was ambition, too: loads of that. To serve he had to succeed; to preside he had to prevail. Politics, he once admitted, **isn't a pure undertaking—not if you want to win, it's not.** An imperfect man, he left us a more perfect union.

And it must be said that for a keenly intelligent statesman of stirring private eloquence, public speaking wasn't exactly his strongest suit. **Fluency in English**, President Bush once remarked, **is something that I'm often not accused of.** Looking ahead to the 1988 election, he observed that **it's no exaggeration to say the undecideds could go one way or another.** Late in his presidency, he said: **We're enjoying sluggish times, and we're not enjoying them very much.**

His tongue may have run amok at times, but his heart was steadfast. His life code, as he said, was: **Tell the truth. Don't blame people. Be strong. Do your Best. Try hard. Forgive. Stay the course.**

It was—and is—the most American of creeds. Abraham Lincoln's "better angels of our nature" and George H. W. Bush's "thousand points of light" are companion verses in America's national hymn, for Lincoln and Bush both called on us to choose the right over the convenient, to hope rather than to fear, to heed not our worst impulses but our best instincts.

In this work he had the most wonderful of allies in Barbara Pierce Bush, his wife of 73 years. He was the only boy she ever kissed. Her children, she liked to say, always wanted to throw up when they heard that. In a letter to Barbara during the war, young George

H. W. Bush had written: **I love you, precious, with all my heart and to know that you love me means my life. How lucky our children will be to have a mother like you.** And, as they will tell you, they surely were.

As Vice President, Bush once visited a children's leukemia ward in Krakow. Thirty-five years before, he and Barbara had lost a daughter, Robin, to the disease. In Krakow, a small boy wanted to greet the American Vice President. Learning that the child was sick with the cancer that had taken Robin, Bush began to cry.

To his diary, the vice president later recalled: **My eyes flooded with tears, and behind me was a bank of television cameras. I thought, 'I can't turn around. I can't dissolve because of personal tragedy in the face of the nurses that give of themselves every day.' So I stood there looking at this little guy, tears running down my cheek, hoping he wouldn't see, but, if he did, hoping he'd feel that I loved him.**

*That* was the real George H. W. Bush—a loving man with a big, vibrant, all-enveloping heart.

And so, as we commend his soul to God, we ask, as he so often did: *Why him? Why was he spared?* The workings of Providence are mysterious, but this much is clear: the George Herbert Walker Bush who survived that fiery fall into the waters of the Pacific made our lives, and the lives of nations, freer, better, warmer, *nobler.*

That was his mission. That was his heartbeat. And if we listen closely enough, we can hear that heartbeat even now, for it's the heartbeat of a lion—a lion who not only led us, but who loved us.

*That's* why him. *That's* why he was spared.

# EPILOGUE

---

*It's more important than ever that we remember who he was,
so that we can be inspired by his example.*

—*Dan Quayle*

Jean Becker, President Bush's longtime and loyal assistant, has done an excellent job assembling thoughts, from those who knew him best, on the character of America's forty-first President. What you've just read is a remarkable testament to a man we all loved and respected for the grace and honor with which he served America.

Throughout history, societies have revered those leaders who demonstrate a strong sense of character. In today's world, where instability and dysfunction seem everywhere the norm, it is even more crucial that we recognize and appreciate the principled virtues of George H. W. Bush.

President Bush—always putting the needs of the country before his own—embodied the values of integrity, loyalty, and selflessness. I remember our discussion, back in 1990, about the politics involved in his agreeing to the tax increase Democrats were demanding before they would pass a budget. He said to me in the Oval Office: **Dan, I have to put politics aside and do what's in the best interest of the country.**

Love of country always came first. He was a man who believed in the power of service, whether as a young pilot during World War II or as the head of a giant global alliance thwarting tyranny in the Persian Gulf. In the White House he fostered an environment of trust, respect, and humility, which not only inspired those around him but also paved the way toward a more cooperative political landscape at home and an extraordinary degree of unity across much of the globe.

In stark contrast, today's political world is rife with self-interest and disregard for the common good. The discord and chaos that we see today stem from a deficiency of character in our leaders, an erosion of the values that once held our democracy together. Duty, Honor, Country—words boldly displayed at the Bush Library in College Station, Texas—were the words George H. W. Bush lived by. How many of our current politicians can say they live by them too?

To reflect on the life and legacy of President Bush is to remember that true leadership is rooted in character, in the strength of one's convictions, and in the courage to make difficult decisions for the betterment of all. I hope this book will serve as a reminder that character does indeed matter, and that it will inspire future generations of leaders to practice the kind of moral fortitude that President Bush exemplified.

He was a buoyant, optimistic man, but much tougher than his charming, casual manner made him appear. He was an excellent listener, and during meetings with foreign leaders he tended to say less than they did. Those sitting across the table from him may have thought they were in charge of the discussion, but George Bush knew what his objectives were and never let himself be pushed beyond where he wanted to go. When traveling abroad as his vice president, I came to appreciate the reputation he had built over many years. Heads of government, even if they didn't know the President personally, knew they were dealing with a serious man with serious purposes. A man they could trust. That is certainly missing in our political culture, both domestic and international, today.

If you have a chance to visit the White House and you get to see President Bush's portrait, you'll notice that he's standing near a large globe, the kind one finds in an old-fashioned gentleman's library. There's no doubt that the artist wanted to convey the enormous global changes—the explosion of freedom—that took place during President Bush's administration, and also to symbolize the extent to which George H. W. Bush was quietly responsible for so many of them. Every modern president is called the "Leader of the Free World," but for most of them it's a courtesy title. One can make a good argument that "41" was the last American President who actually performed that role, day after day and year after year. However low-key his manner may have been, he *led*.

It was my privilege to work in close partnership with George H. W. Bush between 1989 and 1993. In my memoir of that time, *Standing Firm*, I wrote of him: "He went into and out of the office as absolutely the *same* man, and I think that says it all about the solidity of his character. He knew who he was. He didn't need power to tell him that."

It's more important than ever that we remember who he was, so that we can be inspired by his example.

*Dan Quayle*
*Vice President of*
*the United States*
*1989–1993*

# GLOSSARY OF
# CONTRIBUTORS

*To help you keep track of who said what, below are brief biographies of the people who sent me a contribution for this book. Sadly, we would have to kill a lot of trees to list everyone's complete résumé, their awards, the boards on which they serve, or their volunteer work. Just know this is a black-belt, award-winning active group.*

**41:** That would be President Bush. When George W. Bush became President of the United States on January 20, 2001, there was mass confusion when people spoke or wrote about President Bush. Which President Bush? The current one? The former one? It was especially complicated when they were in the same room. To the rescue came Michigan congressman John Dingell, who at the annual Alfalfa Club dinner in Washington, DC, announced his solution to this problem: George H. W. Bush was the forty-first President of the United States, so therefore and henceforth would be called "41." President George W. Bush was the forty-third President and would be "43."

**Allen, Duane:** Lead singer for the Oak Ridge Boys, he was a college student when he first campaigned for President Bush in the 1960s. The Oaks traveled with President Bush during all of his campaigns, and at his request, sang "Amazing Grace" at his funeral service in

Houston. He and his wife, Norah Lee, live in Nashville, Tennessee, and have two children and four grandchildren.

**Anderson, David:** Served as a lead advance representative during President Bush's term and the reelection campaign. He also served as a senior staff member for the President's Commission on Base Closures and the President's Commission on the Assignment of Women in the Armed Forces. Today David is an entrepreneur who has started several companies, serving as CEO for two of them and working as an executive coach. David and his wife, Debbie, live in Gilbert, Arizona, and have two sons.

**Andrews, Elizabeth (Lizzie):** Daughter of Neil and Maria Bush, Lizzie is a dermatology resident at Icahn School of Medicine at Mount Sinai. She and her husband, Kevin Joseph, live in New York City.

**Baker, James:** He served as the sixty-first secretary of state from 1989 to 1992; sixty-seventh secretary of the Treasury from 1985 to 1988; and White House chief of staff for Presidents George H. W. Bush and Ronald Reagan. He is the only person to run five presidential campaigns for three different candidates. The author of numerous books and chairman of various boards and committees, he is honorary chairman of the James A. Baker III Institute of Public Policy at Rice University. He and his wife, Susan, live in Houston. Between them, they have eight children and nineteen grandchildren.

**Bates, David:** President Bush's personal aide from 1978 to 1980, David served Vice President Bush as his deputy chief of staff, and during the presidency as assistant to the President and secretary to the cabinet. From 1994 to 2009, he was managing director and then senior adviser for Public Strategies Inc., a strategic consulting firm. He now is CEO of his own consulting company. He and his wife, Anne, live in San Antonio and have three children and four grandchildren.

**Beach, Becky Brady:** Aide to Barbara Bush from 1978 to 1982, Becky is CEO of the Puppy Jake Foundation. She and her husband, Charlie, have two children and six grandchildren and live in Rio Verde, Arizona.

**Beamish, Rita:** A former Associated Press reporter in Los Angeles and then Washington, DC, Rita covered George H. W. Bush's campaigns and presidency. She also has worked for California newspapers, most recently as an editor at the *San Francisco Chronicle*. She and her husband, Paul Costello, have two daughters and live in San Mateo, California.

**Becker, Edward:** He practiced law for nearly ten years before entering seminary to become a Catholic priest. Ordained just before his fortieth birthday, Father Ed currently serves at Holy Trinity Church in Ladera Ranch, California. His sisters call him Eddie; his parishioners call him Father Ed; President and Mrs. Bush called him Father Eddie and were very supportive of his second calling as a Catholic priest.

**Behrendt, Theresa "Tee" Elmore:** Tee began her fund-raising career working for President Bush at the RNC in 1973 and then served in national roles for both his 1980 and 1988 presidential campaigns. Her current fund-raising initiatives include Newport

Preservation and the White House Historical Association's "1700" project. Tee and her husband, John, divide their time between Boca Grande, Florida; Saratoga Springs, New York; and the Argentine pampas.

**Benedi, Antonio:** Tony worked in a variety of roles during President Bush's vice presidency, including as an advance lead and events coordinator, and was deputy director of the Office of Presidential Appointments and Scheduling during his presidency. He is a member of the board and past chairman of the Washington Regional Transplant Community. He and his wife, Maria, live in Springfield, Virginia, and have two sons and one grandchild.

**Benson, Jeff W.:** A captain in the Navy and a 2003 graduate of the Bush School of Government and Public Service, Jeff commanded the destroyer USS *Stethem* (DDG 63) while deployed in Japan. He is the first commanding officer of the USS *Louis H. Wilson Jr.* (DDG 126), currently being built in Bath, Maine. Jeff and his wife, Elizabeth, live in Cumberland, Maine, with their three boys and a golden retriever.

**Biddle, Susan:** Susan was a photojournalist before working for President Bush as one of his White House photographers. She then returned to journalism, working for the *Washington Post* until she retired. She and her husband, Robert Barkin, live in Silver Spring, Maryland, and have one daughter.

**Blanton, Taylor:** Taylor worked as a volunteer in President Bush's first two campaigns in 1964 and 1966. He is retired from the US Department of State and runs an event business in the Rio Grande Valley of Texas with his wife, Martha.

**Brady, Phil:** During President Bush's administration, Phil served as general counsel in the Department of Transportation and then as assistant to the President and staff secretary in the White House. Later positions included president of the National Automobile Dealers Association and senior vice president of Government Affairs for Phillips 66. He and his wife, Katie, live in Washington, DC, and have three sons and four grandchildren.

**Branch, Catherine:** Aide to Barbara Bush from 2014 to 2017, Catherine currently serves as chief of staff to the CEO of Texas Capital Bank, as well as a volunteer for various organizations. She lives in Dallas.

**Bringle, Donald:** Aide to Vice President Bush from 1983 to 1984, Don graduated from the US Naval Academy in 1976 and spent his Navy career as an F-14 carrier aviator. He retired from the Navy in 1998 and then flew for United Airlines until 2019. He and his wife, Emily, live in New York and have two children.

**Brock, Ann:** Director of scheduling for First Lady Barbara Bush, after leaving the White House Ann served as the assistant director of the George H. W. Bush Presidential Library Foundation and director of the library's dedication ceremonies. After teaching middle school art in her hometown of Jackson, Mississippi, she is now retired and living in Oxford, Mississippi, with her dog Houston.

**Brokaw, Tom:** Coanchor of *The Today Show* from 1976 to 1982, he then anchored the *NBC Nightly News* for twenty-two years. He was known as one of the Big Three, along with ABC's Peter Jennings and CBS's Dan Rather. He is the author of several books, including *The Greatest Generation*. He and his wife, Meredith, have three children and spend a great deal of their time at their ranch in Montana.

**Buckley, Christopher:** A best-selling author and political satirist, Christopher (or Christo, as President Bush called him) was Vice President George Bush's speechwriter from 1981 until 1983. He and his wife, Katy, live in South Carolina and Connecticut.

**Bush, Barbara:** First Lady of the United States from 1989 to 1993. She married George Herbert Walker Bush on January 6, 1945. They had six children—George W., Robin, Jeb, Neil, Marvin, and Doro. Robin died of leukemia at age three in 1953. Besides her family and friends, her main passion in life was making America more literate. She founded the Barbara Bush Foundation for Family Literacy in 1989. She wrote four books: *C. Fred's Story*; *Millie's Book*; *Barbara Bush: A Memoir;* and *Reflections*: *Life After the White House.* She died April 17, 2018, at her home in Houston, Texas, with her husband of seventy-three years holding her hand.

**Bush, Billy:** Billy is the second son of President Bush's brother Jonathan and Jody Bush. He is a TV journalist and broadcaster who currently hosts the television program *Extra*. He lives in Los Angeles with his three daughters.

**Bush, Jamie:** Son of President Bush's oldest brother, Prescott, and Elizabeth Kauffman Bush, Jamie is a partner in the firm of Bush & Company, which helps families and businesses with family governance issues and succession planning. He also is developing a ministry to help the faith community in Boston engage more meaningfully with people coming out of prison. He and his wife, Sue, live in Boston and have two children and six grandchildren.

**Bush, Jody:** Jody Bush is the widow of President Bush's brother Jonathan. They have two sons and ten grandchildren. She splits her time between Hobe Sound, Florida, and North Haven, Maine. Jody is the last surviving member of President Bush's siblings and their spouses.

**Bush, Neil:** The third son of George and Barbara Bush, Neil is engaged in international business development while serving to promote family legacies as chairman of Points of Light, the George H. W. Bush US China Relations Foundation, the Barbara Bush Houston Literacy Foundation, and the advisory board of the Bush School of Government and Public Service. He and his wife, Maria, live in Houston and together are the parents of six and grandparents of four.

**Bush, Noelle:** The daughter of Jeb and Columba Bush, she lives in Orlando, Florida, where she is an operations assistant at the law firm Nelson Mullins. She loves to paint.

**Bush, Pierce:** Son of Neil and Sharon Bush, Pierce is CEO of Big Brothers Big Sisters Lone Star, the largest Big Brothers Big Sisters affiliate agency in the country and the single largest one-to-one youth mentoring organization in the world. He and his wife, Sarahbeth, and their daughter live in Houston.

**Card, Andy:** Andy was deputy White House chief of staff under President Bush before being named secretary of transportation in 1992. He was White House chief of staff under President George W. Bush from 2001 to 2006. He got his start in politics serving in the Massachusetts

House of Representatives from 1975 to 1983. His post–White House career has included serving as acting dean of the Bush School of Government and Public Service; as president of Franklin Pierce University in Rindge, New Hampshire; and as chairman of the National Endowment for Democracy from 2018 to 2022. He and his wife, Kathleene, live in Jaffrey, New Hampshire, and have three children and six grandchildren.

**Carvey, Dana:** A stand-up comedian, Dana is probably best known for his seven seasons as a cast member on NBC's *Saturday Night Live* from 1986 to 1993, which earned him five Emmy Award nominations. Among his many characters was impersonating President Bush. He's also a screenwriter, producer, and actor, having starred in numerous movies. He and his wife, Paula, live in Mill Valley, California, and have two sons.

**Cary, Mary Kate:** A White House speechwriter for President Bush, Mary Kate currently teaches political speechwriting at the University of Virginia. She serves as chair of the advisory board of the George & Barbara Bush Foundation. She and her husband, Rob, live in Charlottesville, Virginia, and have two daughters.

**Caughman, Bruce:** Retired from the Air Force, Bruce was President Bush's personal aide from 1990 to 1991, after serving as his Air Force military aide from 1989 to 1990, and as his military aide during Vice President Bush's last year in office. He currently is a co-owner/chief operating officer of GAME Beverage Group, LLC. He and his wife, Deborah, have three children and three grandchildren and live in Fort Mill, South Carolina.

**Chambers, Ray:** A philanthropist and humanitarian, Ray was the founding chairman of Points of Light and cofounded America's

Promise-Alliance for Youth with Colin Powell. He also was the cofounder of National Mentoring Partnership and of Malaria No More. He was the UN secretary general's first special envoy for malaria. Currently he serves as ambassador to the World Health Organization for Technology and Health Financing and is chairman of Wesray Social Investments. He and his wife, Patti, live in New Jersey and have three children and six grandchildren.

**Cheney, Richard:** He served as the forty-sixth vice president of the United States from 2001 to 2009 under President George W. Bush, secretary of defense from 1989 to 1993 under President George H. W. Bush, and represented Wyoming in the U.S. House of Representatives from 1979 to 1989. Cheney also served as White House chief of staff to President Gerald Ford, making him the youngest person in U.S. history to hold that position. He has authored numerous books, held positions on several boards and committees, and served as chairman and CEO of Halliburton. He and his wife, Lynne, live in the Washington, D.C., area. They have two daughters and seven grandchildren.

**Cicconi, Jim:** Policy assistant to James Baker when he was chief of staff to President Reagan, Jim was deputy chief of staff for President Bush and also served as a senior issues adviser to his presidential campaigns. Jim was a partner at Akin Gump Strauss Hauer & Feld law firm, and then general counsel and senior executive vice president at AT&T for eighteen years. Now retired, he and his wife, Trisha, have three daughters and nine grandchildren, all close to them in northern Virginia.

**Clinton, William Jefferson:** Forty-second President of the United States and a former governor of Arkansas, he also is the founder and board chair of the Clinton Foundation. President Clinton joined forces with former President George H. W. Bush three times to raise money for disaster victims: after the 2004 tsunami in South Asia, Hurricane Katrina in 2005, and Hurricane Ike in 2008; and with President George W. Bush in Haiti in the aftermath of the 2010 earthquake. He and his wife, Secretary Hillary Rodham Clinton, have one daughter, Chelsea, and three grandchildren.

**Compton, Ann:** Assigned to cover the White House for ABC News in 1974, Ann traveled the globe with seven presidents, from Gerald Ford to Barack Obama, during a dramatic forty-year span of American history. She also covered ten presidential campaigns and was elected president of the White House Correspondents' Association. Ann and her husband, Dr. William Hughes, live in Washington, DC, and have four children and ten grandchildren.

**Cooke, Julie:** An assistant to Barbara Bush during her husband's vice presidency, Julie was director of projects for the First Lady from 1989 to 1992. Retired from Washington National Cathedral where she was director for the Cathedral Centennial Celebration, Visitor Programs and Volunteer Services, Julie and her husband, Tom, live in Washington, DC, and have two sons and two granddaughters.

**Crawford, Quincy Hicks:** Starting as a receptionist in the Office of George Bush, Quincy served as Barbara Bush's personal aide from 1994 to 1998. She was director of Scheduling and Advance to First Lady Laura Bush from 2001 to 2002. She is currently an executive recruiter for Tangent West. She and her husband, J.T., live in New Orleans with their two sons.

**Csorba, Les:** Les served in the White House as special assistant to the President in Presidential Personnel (National Security Affairs) and served on the President's Commission on White House Fellowships during President George W. Bush's administration. He is the partner in charge (Houston office) of Heidrick & Struggles, where he is an executive coach and advises clients in the energy industry on CEO and board of director succession. He and his wife, Anne, live in Houston and have four children and four grandchildren.

**Cutler, Kim Brady:** Starting as a volunteer for George Bush for President in 1979, Kim worked for Vice President Bush in his scheduling and advance offices before serving as personal aide to Barbara Bush from 1981 to 1985. She served in a variety of roles for the Bushes over the years, including as director of advance for the First Lady from 1989 to 1991. Now a full-time volunteer, Kim and her husband, Nick, live in Wenham, Massachusetts, and have two children.

**DeLorenzo, Dante:** Dante started working for the Bush family as a summer lad at Walker's Point in 2017 and kept that job until he graduated from college. He currently is the personal aide to President George W. Bush and lives in Dallas.

**Demarest, David:** Currently a lecturer at Stanford University School of Business, David served as communications director of President Bush's 1988 presidential campaign, then was White House communications director during his presidency. He is married to the former Dianne Burch, enduring the joy of six daughters in their blended family and splitting their time between Sausalito, California, and Houston, Texas.

**Dill, Tony:** A former Green Beret colonel and the commander of the Army's Golden Knights during several of President Bush's parachute jumps, Tony retired from the military after thirty-one years of service. He is now a senior management consultant for the defense industry and forensic security services. He and his wife, Josephine, live in Dawsonville, Georgia, and have three children.

**Doerr, Clinton:** Dr. Doerr, who specializes in pulmonary, critical care, and sleep medicine, coordinated and cared for President and Mrs. Bush both at their home and when hospitalized. He remains in private practice in Houston, where he lives with his wife, Dr. Allison Pritchett, and their two children.

**Doublet, Elizabeth Wise:** Aide to Mrs. Bush from 1985 to 1987, Elizabeth spent some time living overseas as a foreign correspondent. She now divides her time between France and Washington, DC, with her husband, Jean-Louis, and their two sons.

**Dowd, Maureen:** Winner of the 1999 Pulitzer Prize for distinguished commentary and author of three *New York Times* bestsellers, Maureen became an op-ed columnist in 1995 for the *Times*. She lives in Washington, DC.

**Dvorsky, George:** George has starred on Broadway, Off-Broadway, and in regional theaters and in concerts for more than forty years. He is the voice of George H. W. Bush in the audio book of *The Man I Knew.* He lives in New York City.

**Eckstein, John:** Dr. Eckstein was President Bush's primary internist at the Mayo Clinic Arizona from 1994 until 2008. He spent most of his medical career at Mayo but worked in the United States Public Health Service at the Centers for Disease Control in Atlanta, Georgia, from 1972 to 1974. He and his wife, Diane, live in Phoenix, Arizona, and have two daughters and one granddaughter.

**Elliott, Mike:** "Big Mike" is a combat veteran who served in the Army for more than twenty-six years. He served his final eleven years as a member of the Army Parachute Team, the Golden Knights, completing more than sixteen thousand free-fall jumps. After retiring from the military, he founded the All Veteran Group jump team in 2011. He is proud to have completed three tandem jumps with President Bush. Mike has one son and lives in Raeford, North Carolina.

**Ellis, Alexander "Hap":** The eldest son of Nancy Bush Ellis, President Bush's only sister, Hap serves as chairman of the board of directors for the George & Barbara Bush Foundation. He is a cofounding partner in a venture capital firm, RockPort Capital Partners, that focuses on innovative, sustainable energy technologies. Hap and his wife, Robin Rand Ellis, have three sons and nine grandchildren, and they split their time between Boston and Kennebunkport.

**Fitzwater, Marlin:** Marlin was press secretary to George H. W. Bush when he was Vice President and President, also serving as press secretary to Ronald Reagan. Since leaving the White House, Marlin has written numerous books on various subjects. He and his wife, Melinda, live on the banks of the Chesapeake Bay in Maryland.

**Franklin, Barbara Hackman:** The twenty-ninth US secretary of commerce, she is CEO of Barbara Franklin Enterprises. Named by *TIME* as one of "50 Women Who Made Political History,"

Barbara led the first White House effort to advance women in the federal government and was an original commissioner of the US Consumer Product Safety Commission. She lives in Washington, DC, and thanks to her late husband, Wallace Barnes, has eighteen step-great-grandchildren.

**Frechette, Tom:** Tom began working for President Bush while in high school as a summer lad on Walker's Point and then an office intern before serving as his personal aide from 2000 to 2006. He currently is a managing director at Avenue Capital and a member of the George & Barbara Bush Foundation Advisory Council. He lives in New York City with his wife, Jennifer, and their three children.

**Gangel, Jamie:** Jamie covered President Bush first as national correspondent for NBC's *Today* show and then in her present job as special correspondent for CNN. She interviewed President and Mrs. Bush more than a dozen times over the years. She is married to the *New York Times* best-selling author Daniel Silva. They split their time between Florida and Washington, with their twins, Lily and Nicholas Silva.

**Gates, Robert M.:** Served as the twenty-second secretary of defense from 2006 to 2011 and is the only secretary of defense in US history to be asked to remain in that office by a newly elected president. Previously Bob was the president of Texas A&M University and before that served as interim dean of the Bush School of Government and Public Service. He served President Bush as deputy national security adviser until he became director of Central Intelligence in 1991. The author of numerous books, he and his wife, Becky, live in Sedro Woolley, Washington, and have two children.

**Gelb, Bruce:** The retired president of Clairol and former vice-chairman of Bristol-Myers Squibb, Bruce headed up the United States Information Agency before President Bush appointed him ambassador to Belgium. A philanthropist, he's been especially active in the Madison Square Boys and Girls Club. He and his late wife, Lueza, have four children and five grandchildren. He lives in Naples, Florida.

**Gibbons, Gene:** Former chief White House correspondent for Reuters news agency, Gene covered Presidents Carter through Clinton and was a panelist in one of the presidential debates during the 1992 campaign. Now retired and an avid photographer, Gene and his wife, Becky, have seven children and fourteen grandchildren between them and live in Alexandria, Virginia.

**Gillespie, Edward:** Ed is the senior executive vice president for External and Legislative Affairs at AT&T. He was chairman of the Republican National Committee in the 2004 election cycle and served as counselor to the President for President George W. Bush in his second term. Ed and his wife, Cathy, have three children and live near George Washington's historic Mount Vernon in Fairfax County, Virginia.

**Gray, C. Boyden:** Boyden clerked for Chief Justice Earl Warren before joining the law firm of Wilmer Cutler & Pickering. He served as counsel to George H. W. Bush for twelve years during both the vice presidential and presidential years. President George W. Bush appointed Boyden ambassador to the European Union, after which he continued the work with his law firm, Gray and Associates. Boyden died in 2023. He is survived by one daughter, Eliza, and two grandchildren.

**Guerin, Dava:** Author of numerous books about wounded warriors, veterans, and first responders, Dava is the former communications director for the US Association of Former Members of Congress. She first met President Bush in Philadelphia when she worked with his advance team on his many visits there. She has been an active participant in the Barbara Bush Foundation for Family Literacy, including helping to relaunch Mrs. Bush's *Story Time.* She lives with her two rescue dogs in Sarasota, Florida.

**Hagin, Joe:** Joe served as White House deputy chief of staff from January 2001 to July 2008 for President George W. Bush and held the same position from January 2017 to August 2018. For President Bush, his jobs included: deputy assistant to the President from 1989 to 1991; assistant to the Vice President for Legislative Affairs from 1983 to 1985; and as personal aide from 1981 to 1983. He currently is executive vice president of corporate affairs for LG Group, a South Korean multinational corporation. Joe lives in Washington, DC.

**Haley, Sondra:** From 1983 to 1993, Sondra served in various communications roles in Vice President Bush's office and the Office of the First Lady, including deputy press secretary to Barbara Bush. Starting in 1993, her career focused on strategic communications, including roles with the Walt Disney Company and the National Basketball Association. Currently she is a principal with the Red Bee Group, living in Southern California.

**Hermann, Charles:** Chuck was the founding director of the Bush School of Government and Public Service at Texas A&M University, and then transitioned to chairing the International Affairs Department for fourteen years while holding the Brent Scowcroft Chair in International Policy Studies. He and his wife, Dr. Lorraine Eden Hermann—both retired—have three children and three grandchildren and still call College Station, Texas, home.

**Higgins, Hutton Hinson:** Aide to Barbara Bush from 2010 to 2014, Hutton currently serves as the director of communications and external relations for the George & Barbara Bush Foundation. She and her husband, Taylor, live in Houston with their three daughters.

**Hoffman, Jeff:** Working at the Walt Disney Company for more than thirty years, Jeff most recently served as vice president of Disney Worldwide Outreach. In this role, he had global responsibility for Disney's philanthropy, community relations, and cause marketing activities, including its award-winning employee volunteer program, Disney VoluntEARS. He currently has a consulting business, Jeff Hoffman & Associates, and lives with his husband, Bob Lane, in Long Beach, California.

**Holiday, Ede:** Served as general counsel to President Bush's 1988 presidential campaign; as general counsel of the Department of Treasury; and as assistant to the President and secretary of the cabinet. She currently serves on several corporate boards. She and her husband, Terry Adamson, live in Florida and North Carolina and have three children—including two girls born during her White House years—and three grandchildren.

**James, Gordon:** Gordon officially worked in the White House Office of Advance from 1989 to 1990 but spent years doing volunteer advance work for both Presidents Bush. He now owns Gordon C. James Public

Relations. The father of eight children and grandfather of eight grandchildren, he and his wife, Lisa, live in Scottsdale, Arizona.

**Johnson, Cynthia:** After early careers in social work and advertising, Cynthia became the official photographer for Vice President Bush from the 1980 inauguration to 1984. She then moved to *TIME* magazine, where, among other things, she covered the White House. Retiring in 2000, she now lives on a farm in rural Virginia.

**Kaufman, Ron:** Ron started working and campaigning for the Bushes in 1977. At the White House, he was first deputy assistant to the President for personnel and then White House political director. Ron helped build and then sell the government affairs firm Dutko Worldwide. He recently retired from Dentons Worldwide Law, where he served as the senior strategic adviser; and as the treasurer of the Republican National Committee. He has two daughters and five grandchildren and lives in Washington, DC.

**Kennedy, Annie:** In 2010, Barbara Bush asked Annie to care for the many existing gardens at Walker's Point and to design new ones. She was known as "Annie the Gardener" until she retired in 2021. She and her husband, Michael Phelps, spend their summers in Kennebunk, Maine, and the winter months in Rome, Italy.

**Kilberg, Bobbie Greene:** Served as deputy assistant to the President for Public Liaison and as deputy assistant to the President and director of the Office of Intergovernmental Affairs. After twenty-two years, Bobbie recently retired as CEO of the Northern Virginia Technology Council. She and her husband, Bill—both former

White House fellows—have five children and sixteen grandchildren and live in McLean, Virginia.

**Killblane, Casey Healey:** Aide to Barbara Bush from 1987 to 1989, she left Barbara Bush only to marry her husband, Hugh. They live in Davis, Oklahoma, where they have an oil and gas investment company and a property management company, in addition to helping manage the family ranch, Flying L Ranch. They have two sons.

**Knight, Barbara:** Currently working in communications and marketing for McDermott International, Barbara was deputy White House press secretary for First Lady Laura Bush. From 2004 to 2008, she worked for President and Barbara Bush in Houston. She is married to Jim Knight and lives in Dubai, United Arab Emirates, with their three children.

**Koch, Doro Bush:** Youngest child of George and Barbara Bush, Doro is the cofounder of BB&R Wellness Consulting; the honorary chairman and a member of the board of the Barbara Bush Foundation for Family Literacy; and a member of the board of the George & Barbara Bush Foundation. She is the author of *My Father, My President*. She and her husband, Bobby, live in Bethesda, Maryland, and have four children and two grandchildren.

**Koch, Gigi:** Daughter of Doro and Bobby Koch, Gigi lives in New York, where she works for NBCUniversal. She loves being outdoors and spending time with her family in Maine, and especially loves her sweet nieces, Dottie and Loulie.

**Lamb, Lucy:** Just out of college, Lucy joined President Bush's administration in the White House Advance Office, serving first as a trip coordinator and then as executive assistant to the director of press advance. She finished the term as executive secretary to the US ambassador to Iceland. She currently works for Fairfax County Public Schools. She and her husband, Faron, live in Alexandria, Virginia, and have five daughters and one grandson.

**Lamoreaux, Melinda:** Melinda began working as a volunteer for both President and Mrs. Bush in 1994. In 2000, she joined President Bush's staff with administrative and special projects responsibilities. Today Melinda works for the George & Barbara Bush Foundation as the legacy liaison for the Bush Legacy Groups. She and her husband, Scott, have one daughter and live in Houston.

**Lapointe, Coleman:** After working for President Bush in 2004 as a summer lad and then as an office intern, Coleman was President Bush's personal aide from 2012 to 2015. He joined Governor Jeb Bush on the campaign trail during his 2016 presidential bid, serving as his personal aide. From 2017 to 2020, Coleman worked at the Pentagon, where he was the director of travel operations for the secretary and deputy secretary of defense. He now works for General Dynamics Bath Iron Works in Bath, Maine. He and his wife, Sarah, and their son live in Kennebunk, Maine.

**Lauren, Lauren Bush:** Daughter of Neil Bush and Sharon Bush, she is the founder and CEO of FEED, a social business with a mission to create good products that help feed the world. Since 2007, FEED has been able to provide more than 126 million meals to kids around the world. Lauren lives in New York City with her husband, David, and their three children.

**LeFevre, Ashley Bush:** The daughter of Neil and Sharon Bush, Ashley lives in Los Angeles with her husband, Julian, where they work in film and TV. She is currently producing a documentary series for Netflix about Twitter. Also a film director, Ashley recently won an Audience Award at the Dallas International Film Festival for *The Queen's New Clothes*.

**Levenson, Russell J., Jr.:** The Reverend Dr. Levenson is the rector of St. Martin's Episcopal Church, the Bushes' longtime home parish. He officiated at both President and Mrs. Bush's funeral services in Houston and at President Bush's state funeral at the National Cathedral. He is the author of *Witness to Dignity: The Life and Faith of George H. W. and Barbara Bush*. He and his wife, Laura, live in Houston and have three children and two grandchildren.

**Lisenby, Nancy:** Nancy started volunteering in the Office of George Bush in 1997, becoming a part-time receptionist the next year. In 2000, she became my assistant and among her many jobs was to listen to me vent and help me decipher my own handwriting. She and her husband, John, live in Houston and have three children and ten grandchildren.

**Lorelle, Linda:** An Emmy- and Gracie Award–winning broadcast journalist, Linda reported on President Bush's post-presidency as the evening anchor at KPRC-TV in Houston. One of those hair-raising assignments included a tandem skydive with the same Golden

Knight who guided President Bush to a safe landing on his eightieth birthday. Linda is CEO and executive producer of Linda Lorelle Media and host of the *Our Voices Matter* podcast. She and her husband, Lou Gregory, live in Houston with their daughter Lindsey and grand-puppy, Layla.

**Maer, Peter:** A retired CBS News White House correspondent, Peter covered Presidents Carter through Obama. A winner of numerous awards, he is a visiting fellow on the Presidency & the Press at the Marlin Fitzwater Center for Communication at Franklin Pierce University. He and his wife, Elizabeth, live in Fairfax, Virginia.

**Magaw, John:** John began his career as a public servant in 1959 as an Ohio state trooper. He joined the Secret Service in 1967, and was head of President Bush's Secret Service detail until the President named John director of the Secret Service in 1992. He was head of the Bureau of Alcohol, Tobacco, and Firearms from 1993 to 1999 under President Clinton

**Major, John:** Prime Minister of the United Kingdom from 1990 until 1997, Sir John previously served as foreign secretary and chancellor of the Exchequer in Margaret Thatcher's cabinet. He retired from the British Parliament in 2001. In 2005, Queen Elizabeth II appointed him a Knight Companion of the Most Noble Order of the Garter—England's highest award for chivalry, which is in the personal gift of the Sovereign. He and his wife, Dame Norma, have two children and three grandchildren.

**McBride, Tim:** Serving President Bush in a variety of roles, Tim was his personal aide from 1985 to 1990. In 1990, the US Senate confirmed

Tim as assistant secretary of commerce for trade development. He later returned to the White House as assistant to the President for management and administration. Tim currently is president of ST Engineering North America, following a long career of leading global government relationships teams for Fortune 500 companies. Tim and his wife, Anita, live in Washington, DC, and have two children.

**McClure, Fred:** Fred was President Bush's assistant for legislative affairs. He has served as CEO of the Bush Presidential Library Foundation and is a member of the board of directors of the George & Barbara Bush Foundation. Currently, Fred is associate vice president of Leadership & Engagement at Texas A&M University. He and his wife, Harriet, live in College Station, Texas, and have two children and three grandchildren.

**McCullough, David:** One of America's most beloved and respected historians, David won a Pulitzer Prize for his biographies of John Adams and Harry Truman. He started his writing career as an intern at *Sports Illustrated*, eventually becoming an editor and writer for the United States Information Agency. His breakout book was *The Johnstown Flood*, published in 1968. He died in 2022 at age eighty-nine. He and his wife, Rosalee, had four children.

**McEntire, Reba:** A country music superstar, Reba has sold more than fifty-eight million albums worldwide and has had thirty-five singles hit number one on the music charts. She was named a Kennedy Honors recipient in 2018; is a member of the Country Music Hall of Fame; and has won dozens of music awards, including two Grammys and seven Country Music awards. Also an accomplished actress, she was the star and executive producer of her own television series, *Reba*, and starred on Broadway in *Annie Get Your Gun*. She currently is a coach on NBC's *The Voice*. Reba lives in Nashville and has one son and several stepchildren and step-grandchildren.

**McGrath, Jim:** Jim started at the White House in 1991 in the correspondence office. He came to Houston to serve as President Bush's post–White House press secretary and speechwriter; during the Bushes' funerals in 2018, he oversaw all press operations. The author of several books, Jim currently is co-owner of Begala-McGrath public relations firm. Jim and his wife, Paulina, live in Houston and have three children.

**McLane, Drayton:** Former owner and CEO of the Houston Astros baseball club, Drayton serves as chairman of the McLane Group. He propelled the McLane Company into a $19 billion enterprise, which merged with Walmart in 1990. He then served as vice-chairman of Walmart until 1994. He and his wife, Elizabeth, live in Temple, Texas, and have two sons and five grandsons.

**Meacham, Jon:** A presidential historian and professor at Vanderbilt University, Jon is the author of *Destiny and Power: The American Odyssey of George Herbert Walker Bush*. In 2009, he won the Pulitzer Prize for *American Lion: Andrew Jackson in the White House*. He and his wife, Keith, live in Nashville, Tennessee, with their three children.

**Melley, Diane:** Diane, formerly a decades-long IBM senior executive, is a global business leader and pioneering female technologist committed to designing and delivering technology solutions to complex social issues at scale worldwide. In 2001, she was awarded an

Eisenhower Fellowship to the European Union and Ireland. Diane and her husband, Brian, live in the Philadelphia suburbs and have two daughters.

**Meltzer, Brad:** The author of more than fifty books, Brad is a number one *New York Times* best-selling writer of thrillers such as *The Lightning Rod* and nonfiction books such as *The Nazi Conspiracy*. He also is the author of the Ordinary People Change the World kids book series, which inspired the TV show on PBS KIDS, *Xavier Riddle and the Secret Museum*. He is the host of *Brad Meltzer's Decoded* on the History Channel. He and his wife, Cori Flam, live in Hollywood, Florida, and have three children.

**Milano, Bernard:** A member of the Points of Light board of directors for twenty years, Bernie recently retired as president of the KPMG Foundation after fifty-eight years with the firm. He has six children and six grandchildren, including two children with his wife, Dr. Sharon Pierson. They live in Allendale, New Jersey.

**Mitchell, Brad:** A member of the Office of Policy Development for President Bush, Brad was the founding president and CEO of ChainDrugStore.net. Based on his extensive experience working with C-Level and executive groups within major companies, he currently focuses on coaching successful leaders and executive teams. He and his wife, Julia, live in Romulus, New York, and have two children and one granddaughter.

**Mohr, Larry:** Dr. Mohr was a White House physician to Presidents Reagan and Bush. After his White House service, he joined the faculty of the Medical University of South Carolina where he is a Distinguished University Professor. He and his wife, Linda, live in Charleston, South Carolina, and have one daughter.

**Morris, Johnny:** Johnny got his start in business selling fishing tackle out of the back of his father's store before becoming the founder, majority owner, and CEO of Bass Pro Shops. He often is referred to as a modern-day Theodore Roosevelt for his leadership, personal commitment, and dedication to the careful management and use of our natural resources. He and his wife, Jeannie, have four children and seven grandchildren and split their time between Springfield and Branson, Missouri.

**Mulberger, Ginny Lampley:** Ginny served as special assistant to the President and senior director for Legislative Affairs for the National Security Council from 1989 to 1993. Prior to joining the White House staff, she served as an Air Force officer, retiring as a lieutenant colonel. She cofounded the Scowcroft Group in 1995 with Brent Scowcroft, retiring as the managing partner in 2017. She and her husband, Robb, live in Alexandria, Virginia, and have two children.

**Mulroney, Brian:** Elected in 1984 and reelected in 1988, Mr. Mulroney was Canada's eighteenth prime minister. From the Canada-US Acid Rain Treaty, to NAFTA, to the first Gulf War, to the end of the Cold War and the reunification of Germany, there were very few issues of importance upon which he and President Bush did not work closely. Mr. Mulroney is a successful lawyer and a best-selling author. He and his wife, Mila, live in Montreal and have four children and sixteen grandchildren.

**Nantz, Jim:** A commentator for CBS Sports, Jim has been the voice of some of America's biggest sporting events since 1985. The multi–Emmy Award winner and National Sportscaster of the Year is an author of the *New York Times* bestseller *Always by My Side*, for which President Bush wrote the foreword. Jim founded the Nantz National Alzheimer Center, in honor of his dad, at Houston Methodist Hospital, to provide hope and treatment for those suffering from Alzheimer's disease. The father of three children, he lives in Nashville.

**Newman, Bonnie J.:** Chancellor emeritus of the community college system of New Hampshire, Bonnie previously served as the interim president of the University of New Hampshire; executive dean at Harvard University's Kennedy School of Government; and as assistant to the President for management and administration for President Bush. She and her West Highland terrier, Figgy, split their time between New Castle, New Hampshire, and Palm Coast, Florida.

**Neumann, Roxann:** Roxann began working in Texas Republican politics in the early 1980s. She was executive director of the host committee for the 1990 G7 Economic Summit and has worked on many projects and events with the Office of George Bush over the years. She currently works with Silver Eagle Beverages and John Nau. She and her husband, Tim, live in Houston and have one daughter.

**Nunn, Michelle:** Michelle is president and CEO of CARE USA, a leading humanitarian organization that fights global poverty and provides lifesaving assistance in emergencies. Prior to CARE, she ran for the US Senate and served as Points of Light CEO from 2007 to 2013. Michelle and her husband, Ron Martin, have two children and live in Atlanta.

**Palmer, Arnold:** Considered one of the best and most popular golfers to play the game, "the King" won sixty-two PGA tournaments—fifth on the all-time win list—including seven major championships. He was considered a trailblazer, one of the first superstars of sports' television era. He died in 2016 at age eighty-seven. He and his wife, Winifred, had two children.

**Pears, Laura:** After working for the 1990 G7 Economic Summit and the 1992 Republican National Convention—both held in Houston—Laura joined President Bush's staff in 1993 when he returned to Houston. Initially a volunteer, she joined the full-time staff in 1995, working on special events and later serving as director of scheduling. She lives in Houston with her husband, Dan.

**Pelosi, Nancy:** A Democratic congresswoman from California, she made history in 2007 when she was elected the first woman to serve as Speaker of the House, and again in 2019 when she became the first in more than six decades to regain the post. She and her husband, Paul, live in San Francisco and have five children and nine grandchildren.

**Peressutti, Gian-Carlo:** Aide to President Bush from 1996 to 2000, Gian-Carlo left in 2001 to join the White House staff of George W. Bush as associate director of the Office of Public Liaison. He currently is director of Public Affairs at IFM Investors and serves on the advisory board of the Bush School of Government and Public Service. He lives in Ridgefield, Connecticut, with his wife, Amanda (whom he met on the job in Kennebunkport), and their two daughters.

**Perry, Richard:** Dr. Perry served as President Bush's personal physician in Kennebunkport. Now retired, he was on the clinical faculty at Tufts, Brown, and the University of New England and served as medical director for Harvard Pilgrim Health Care. He and his wife, Elaine Carlson, live in Cape Porpoise, Maine, and have two daughters and one grandchild.

**Petersmeyer, Gregg:** A member of President Bush's senior White House staff, Gregg helped him make Points of Light a hallmark of his presidency. He has contributed to creating and building organizations in the public, private, and nonprofit sectors; is on the Points of Light board; and is chair of America's Promise Alliance. He and his wife, Julie, live in Bethesda, Maryland, and have four children and six grandchildren.

**Pierce, Jim:** The son of Barbara Bush's brother James, Jim is a retired insurance executive, serving the energy industry for forty-five years. He recently penned a book entitled *Treachery*, a story about Abraham Lincoln's first eighteen months in office. He and his wife, Dabney, have four children and two grandchildren and live in Houston.

**Poepsel, Linda Casey:** Linda worked for President Bush for thirty-seven years, first serving in the Vice President's office in a variety of positions. In the White House, she worked in the chief of staff's office, and in early 1992, joined newly appointed secretary Andy Card at the Department of Transportation. Post–White House, she was President Bush's director of correspondence. She and her husband, Jim, live in Houston with their three dogs, including Mrs. Bush's dogs, Mini-Me and Bibi.

**Porter, Roger:** The IBM professor of business and government at Harvard University, Roger joined the Harvard faculty in 1977. He served for more than a decade in senior economic policy positions in the White House, including as assistant to the President for economic and domestic policy for President Bush. He and his late wife, Ann, are the parents of four children and ten grandchildren. He lives in Belmont, Massachusetts.

**Portman, Rob:** Rob served twelve years in the US House, held two cabinet-level jobs in the President George W. Bush administration, and then served two terms in the US Senate from Ohio, choosing not to run again in 2022. He got his start in public service doing volunteer advance work for Vice President Bush, then as associate counsel and deputy assistant and director of the Office of Legislative Affairs for President Bush. He and his wife, Jane, now live full-time in Cincinnati, Ohio, where he is founder and Chair of the Portman Center for Policy Solutions at the University of Cincinnati and is a Fellow at the American Enterprise Institute. They are the parents of three children.

**Powell, Colin:** Born to Jamaican immigrants, General Powell was in the Army for thirty-five years, including serving in Vietnam. After being President Reagan's national security adviser from 1987 to 1989, he was chairman of the Joint Chiefs of Staff under President Bush from 1989 to 1993. Under President George W. Bush, he served as the sixty-fifth secretary of state from 2001 to 2005, becoming the first African American in that post. In 1997 he was the founding chairman of America's Promise Alliance, which focused on America's youth. He died in 2021. He and his wife, Alma, have three children.

**Powers, Carol:** Having worked as a staff photographer on several major newspapers, including the *Palm Beach Post*, the *Miami Herald*, the *Washington Times*, and the *Dallas Morning News*, Carol's career highlight was to be an official White House photographer for President and Mrs. Bush. She and her husband, Don Coyer, live in Vero Beach, Florida, and have one daughter.

**Quayle, Dan:** He became the forty-fourth vice president of the United States on January 20, 1989. He was elected to the House in 1976 and the Senate in 1980, representing Indiana. Since 2001 he has been chairman of Cerberus Global Investments with more than $60 billion under management. He has written three books and serves on many corporate and charitable boards. He and his wife, Marilyn, live in Paradise Valley, Arizona, and have three children and nine grandchildren.

**Raether, Mary Matthews:** Starting as the manager of Congressman George Bush's Houston office, Mary went to Washington in the fall of 1967 to be his legislative assistant. She also worked for the Ways and Means Committee and Congressman Barber B. Conable Jr. before retiring to raise her children and to become a Bush campaign volunteer. President Bush nominated her twice and she was confirmed by the Senate to serve on the National Council on Disability. She and her husband, Carl, have two children and live in McLean, Virginia.

**Rice, Condoleezza:** She was the national security adviser to President George W. Bush before serving as the sixty-sixth secretary of state from 2005 to 2009, becoming the first African American woman in that role. In the first Bush administration, she was the Soviet specialist on the National Security Council. An accomplished concert pianist, she currently is the director of the

Hoover Institution at Stanford University and lives in Stanford, California.

**Rodgers, June Scobee:** The widow of *Challenger* space shuttle commander Richard Scobee, June worked with the lost crew's families to continue the "Teacher in Space" educational mission. An author, June wrote *Silver Linings: My Life Before and After Challenger 7.* She recently received the Apollo 50th Education Award, saluting her pioneering work and dedication to motivating our future science, technology, engineering, and mathematics (STEM) workforce.

**Rogich, Sig:** Former US ambassador to Iceland, senior assistant to President Bush, and director of advertising for Bush for President in 1988, Sig is a founder of the Rogich Communications Group. He was one of three former directors of the Tuesday Team that created the Ronald Reagan and George Bush "Morning in America" campaign in 1984. He has five children, including three with his wife, Lori. They live in Las Vegas.

**Rubenstein, David:** Cofounder and cochairman of the Carlyle Group, David is a leader in patriotic philanthropy and is the host of the *David Rubenstein Show: Peer-to-Peer Conversations*; *Bloomberg Wealth with David Rubenstein*; and *Iconic America: Our Symbols and Stories*. He is the author of several books, including *The American Story: Conversations with Master Historians*. A resident of Maryland, he has three children and two grandchildren.

**Ruebling, Diane:** Diane met George Bush in 1978 at a Republican Leadership Conference in Indianapolis, the beginning of decades of campaigning and support for the Bush family. Her career encompassed many leadership roles in financial services companies, and over the last decade she has worked as an executive business coach. She served on the Defense Advisory Committee on Women in the Services and on the Overseas Private Investment Corporation Board. She and her late husband, Charles, have two children and one grandchild. She lives in Scottsdale, Arizona.

**Sage, Mary:** After volunteering for the 1990 G7 Economic Summit and the 1992 Republican National Convention, both held in Houston, Mary was a full-time volunteer on President Bush's 1992 campaign. She joined his post–White House staff as a volunteer in 1993, then became the part-time receptionist and office administrator in 1995, overseeing technology issues and serving as liaison between the office and the General Services Administration. Mary has one son and lives in Houston.

**Sanders, Kara Babers:** Aide to Barbara Bush from 1998 to 2000, Kara lives in Houston with her husband, Dax, where she loves being a stay-at-home mom to their two daughters and dog Pippa.

**Schuler, Rob:** Rob worked for all of President Bush's campaigns beginning in 1980. While continuing to work as a volunteer advance man during the administration, he was special assistant to the general counsel at the Department of Energy. He and his wife, Stephanie, live in St. Petersburg, Florida, and have two children.

**Scowcroft, Brent:** Served as national security adviser to President Bush and President Ford—the only person to have held this position twice. A 1947 graduate of West Point, his Air Force service included postings at West Point; Belgrade, Yugoslavia; US Air Force Academy; Office of the Secretary of Defense; and Joint Chiefs of Staff. He died in 2020 and is survived by his daughter, Karen, and granddaughter, Meghan.

**Sheldon, Brooke:** Aide to Barbara Bush from 2000 to 2003, Brooke's career began as a legislative assistant on Capitol Hill and then transitioned to coordinating political and social events while working at one of Washington's top fund-raising, event, and public relations firms. Today she is an events coordinator and consultant and lives on the East Coast.

**Sherr, Ron:** Ron won his first of many national awards for his artwork at age five for a likeness of Abraham Lincoln. In 1995, his portrait of President Bush was unveiled at the National Portrait Gallery in Washington, DC. He later painted a historic father-son portrait of the two President Bushes. Ron died after a short illness in 2022. He is survived by his wife of thirty-six years, Lois, who resides in Hong Kong, where she owns a luggage design consulting firm. Their son, Alex, lives and works in Shenzhen, China. They compiled and edited Ron's story for this book.

**Sherzer, Amanda Aulds:** Aide to Barbara Bush from 2008 to 2010, Amanda is a graduate of Dallas Theological Seminary and writes for faith-based nonprofit organizations. She and her husband, David, live in Colleyville, Texas, with their three children.

**Simpson, Alan:** Served from 1979 to 1997 as a US senator from Wyoming. He was elected the assistant majority leader in 1984 and served in that capacity for ten years. He wrote *Right in the Old Gazoo: A Lifetime of Scrapping with the Press*, which chronicles his personal experiences and views of the Fourth Estate; and a biography, *Shooting from the Lip*. When asked, "Have you lived in Wyoming all your life?" he replied, "Not yet!" He and his wife, Ann, live in Cody, Wyoming, and have three children, six grandchildren, and two great-grandchildren.

**Sisley, Evan:** Evan was President Bush's final personal aide and senior medic. Previously he worked as a paramedic and served as a Navy corpsman with the Marine Corps, including a deployment to Afghanistan. He is currently enrolled at the University of New England and is pursuing a master's of science in physician assistant. He and his husband, Ian, live in Washington DC.

**Siv, Sichan:** Sichan escaped from Cambodia's killing fields in 1976 after missing the US evacuation helicopters the year before. He served as a deputy assistant to President Bush at the White House and as an ambassador to the United Nations under President George W. Bush. The author of several books, Sichan lives in San Antonio and was married to Martha Pattillo Siv from Pampa, Texas, for thirty-three years until her liftoff to heaven in 2016.

**Slocum, R. C.:** Former head football coach at Texas A&M University, R.C. is the winningest coach in A&M history and is in the College Football Hall of Fame. He and his wife, Nel, live in College Station, Texas, where he is a special adviser to the president of Texas A&M.

**Smith, Dorrance:** Dorrance served in the Bush White House as assistant to the President for Media Affairs. Post-presidency, he produced numerous legacy events for the George & Barbara Bush Foundation and helped coordinate the media for both Bush funerals. Dorrance was an Emmy Award–winning producer for ABC News and Sports, as executive producer of *This Week with David Brinkley*, *Nightline*, and five Olympic Games. He and his wife, Tamara, live in Arlington, Virginia, with their two teenage children.

**Smith, Michael W.:** During his forty years in the music industry, Michael has written and recorded thirty-six number one songs and has won three Grammy Awards, forty-five Dove Awards, and one American Music Award. He was inducted into the Gospel Music Hall of Fame and has sold more than fifteen million albums. He has raised funds to battle AIDS in Africa; started Rocketown, a safe haven for young people in Tennessee to meet and find hope; and has helped more than seventy thousand children through Compassion International. Michael and his wife, Deborah, live in Franklin, Tennessee, and have five children and seventeen grandchildren.

**Sosa, Ellie LeBlond:** The daughter of Doro Koch and Billy LeBlond, Ellie lives in the Washington, DC, area with her husband, Nick, and their two daughters, Dottie and Loulie. She is the coauthor of *George and Barbara Bush: A Great American Love Story*.

**Sosa, Nancy:** A Kennebunk Beach friend of President and Mrs. Bush, Nancy volunteers for the nonprofit Operation Shower, providing baby showers for expectant moms whose loved ones are deployed on the USS *George H. W. Bush*. She cowrote a children's book with Judi Marchand, based on real-life stories of President Bush, *POPPY! A Tale of Leading with Love*, with proceeds going to the George &

Barbara Bush Foundation. Nancy and her husband, Ignacio, live in Arlington, Virginia, and have two children and two grandchildren.

**Sterban, Richard:** Previously a backup singer for Elvis Presley, Richard joined the Oak Ridge Boys in 1972. He's likely most famous for his "oom-pa-pa-oom-pa-pa-mow-mow" bass solo in the 1981 hit single "Elvira." He and his wife, Donna, live in Hendersonville, Tennessee, and have two daughters. Along with Richard's three sons from his first marriage, their children have given them seven grandchildren and two great-grandchildren.

**Stettner, Carolyn:** A career intelligence officer, Carolyn specialized in chemical and biological weapons, arms control, and counterterrorism. Her favorite career opportunity was serving on President Bush's National Security staff with her late husband, James Pavitt, who served as NSC's special assistant to the President for intelligence. Jim later became the CIA deputy director for operations, or as President Bush called him: Head Spook. Carolyn lives in Santa Fe, New Mexico.

**Straus III, Joe:** Speaker of the Texas House of Representatives from 2009 to 2019, Joe is chairman of the Texas Forever Forward PAC. He served in the Commerce Department during President Bush's tenure. He and his wife, Julie, live in San Antonio, Texas, and have two daughters.

**Struthers, Sally:** Film, television, and theater actress, Sally is known by the older generation as Archie Bunker's daughter, Gloria, in *All in the Family,* while younger generations know her as Babette in *Gilmore Girls*. For thirty-five years she traveled the world for Christian Children's Fund and then Save the Children on behalf of hungry and disenfranchised children. Sally continues to perform in plays and musicals throughout the country.

**Sununu, John H.:** Former three-term governor of New Hampshire and White House chief of staff to President Bush, Governor Sununu is the author of *The Quiet Man: The Indispensable Presidency of George H. W. Bush*. He and his wife, Nancy, live in Hampton Falls, New Hampshire, and have eight children and sixteen grandchildren.

**Taylor, Kristin Clark:** An award-winning author, journalist, and communications strategist, Kristin was special assistant to Vice President Bush for press relations and director of media relations for President Bush. The mother of two children, Kristin lives in suburban Washington, DC.

**Teeley, Peter:** Peter served as press secretary to Vice President George Bush from 1979 to 1985, and press secretary for the 1980 and 1988 presidential campaigns. He was appointed by President Bush as US representative to UNICEF (1990) and ambassador to Canada (1992). He is the founder of the Children's Charities Foundation in Washington, DC, which has raised millions of dollars to support more than one hundred charities and provide 55,000 at-risk children with new winter coats. He and his wife, Dr. Victoria Casey, live in Bethesda, Maryland, and have one daughter.

**Tiernan, Tom:** As a marketing specialist for the US Army, Tom assisted with several of President Bush's parachute jumps and other events including 41's eightieth birthday. He retired in 2023 after fifty years of service and lives in Vine Grove, Kentucky. He and his wife, Kay, have two children, six grandchildren, and two great-grandchildren.

**Trivette, Paula:** A retired lieutenant colonel in the US Army, Paula served as a nurse in the White House Medical Unit for the last year of the Reagan administration and during all of President Bush's White House years. She and her husband, Bill—also a retired lieutenant colonel—live in Greensboro, North Carolina. They have two active-duty sons and one active-duty daughter-in-law, all lieutenant colonels. They also have five grandchildren, none of whom have yet joined the military.

**Untermeyer, Chase:** Chase worked for the Bush for Congress campaign in Houston in 1966 and was an intern for Congressman Bush the next two summers. In later life he was a Texas state representative, executive assistant to Vice President Bush, and an assistant secretary of the Navy. During the first Bush administration, he was director of presidential personnel and director of the Voice of America. The second President Bush appointed him US ambassador to Qatar. He and his wife, Diana, who met in the West Wing of the White House, have one daughter and live in Houston.

**Updegrove, Mark:** Mark is the president and CEO of the LBJ Foundation. He serves as the presidential historian for ABC News and is the author of five books on the presidency, including *The Last Republicans: Inside the Extraordinary Relationship Between George H. W. Bush and George W. Bush*. He and his wife, Amy, live in Austin, Texas, and have four children.

**Voelkel, Margaret:** A volunteer for President Bush for nearly forty years, Margaret was an anchor in the volunteer room at the Office of George Bush. She and her late husband, Stan, have seven children, thirteen grandchildren, and one great-grandchild. She lives in Katy, Texas.

**Voelkel, Tyson:** A decorated combat veteran and a successful business leader, Tyson currently is president of the Texas A&M Foundation. He and his wife, Christi, have three daughters and live in College Station, Texas.

**von Eschenbach, Andrew:** After twenty-six years as a urologic oncologist serving in various roles at the University of Texas MD Anderson Cancer Center, Dr. von Eschenbach was appointed by President George W. Bush first to be the director of the National Cancer Institute and then commissioner of the Food and Drug Administration. He also served as a lieutenant commander in the Navy Medical Corps. Today he is president of Samaritan Health Initiatives. He and his wife, Madelyn, live in Houston and have four children and seven grandchildren.

**Walker, Diana:** A contract photographer for *TIME* for many years, Diana has produced three books of her photographs: *Public & Private: Twenty Years Photographing the Presidency*; *The Bigger Picture*; and *Hillary: The Photographs of Diana Walker*. Among her many prizes, she was awarded the Henry Luce Life Achievement Award from TIME, Inc., in 2012. She and her husband, Mallory, live in Washington, DC, and have two sons and five grandchildren.

**Walker, Ned:** A lifetime professional communicator, Ned most recently served as senior vice president and chief communications officer of Delta Air Lines before his retirement. Prior to his thirty-five-year airline career, he was a television reporter and held several newsroom management positions for KWGN-TV in Denver, Colorado. He and his wife, Jeanne, live in Aspen, Colorado, and have three children.

**Webster, William and Lynda:** A retired lawyer and federal judge, William H. was director of the Federal Bureau of Investigation and director of Central Intelligence. Lynda spent fifteen years as a senior manager in the luxury hotel business; in 1996 she founded the Webster Group, a global event design and production firm. The Websters split their time between Washington, Virginia, and Sun Valley, Idaho.

**Weinberg, Armin:** Armin was a professor at Baylor College of Medicine, cofounder of the Intercultural Cancer Council, and a founding board member of C-Change. He focused on translating discoveries in cancer prevention, screening, treatment, and control activities to state and national initiatives. He is now an adjunct professor at Rice University, where he mentors students in the medical humanities program. Armin and his wife, Karen, have one daughter and two granddaughters and live in Houston.

**Welsh, Mark:** Mark is the dean of the Bush School of Government and Public Service at Texas A&M University. He spent forty years in the Air Force, the last four as the service's twentieth chief of staff. He and his wife, Betty, live in College Station, Texas, and have four children and eight grandchildren.

**White, Daisy:** A special events consultant and coordinator, Daisy was part of the team that organized President Bush's eightieth birthday party—known as 41@80—as well as many other events celebrating landmark anniversaries. A senior adviser for the George & Barbara Bush Foundation, she and her husband, John, live in College Station, Texas, and have two daughters and five grandchildren.

**White, Peggy Swift:** Aide to Barbara Bush from 1989 to 1993, Peggy now dedicates her time as a civic volunteer after a career in public relations, corporate communications, and project management. She lives with her husband, Brian, and their puppy Shecky in Chicago and Charleston, South Carolina.

**Winchell, Blake:** A former campmate of President Bush in the HillBillies Camp at Bohemian Grove, Blake is a director, author, and erstwhile venture capitalist. He and his wife, Lou Ann, live in Park City, Utah, and have three children.

**Zanca, Bruce:** Now retired, Bruce was a longtime press aide to Vice President and President Bush. Later in life he had a very successful career as a C-suite corporate business executive. He and his wife, Michele, split their time between Bluffton, South Carolina, and Ludlow, Vermont.

# ACKNOWLEDGMENTS

I will end where I began: thanking my editor, Sean Desmond, who you know from the Author's Note suggested I write this book. I am most grateful to him for not only his vision, but his support, encouragement, and patience—especially when I got lost a time or two. He always knew the path forward. I cannot imagine doing a book with another editor.

And then of course there are my fellow authors—the people who took the time to share their stories about President Bush. I am simply the book's narrator; they really wrote the book. I would list them all but at last count there were 154 contributors. What a gift to me and to all of us that they were willing to tell us what they learned—and what we can learn—from President Bush. Dinner on me the next time I see you.

Organizing and editing 154 different authors is not easy. So I would like to go back to thanking the people at Twelve, who at times had to help me wrestle this book to the ground—and then out of my clutches. They include Sean's assistant Zohal Karimy, who was very good at sending me gentle deadline reminders; Jim Datz, the art director who designed the cover—a cover that George H. W. Bush would absolutely love; and the best publicity team in publishing, Megan Perritt-Jacobson, director of publicity, and Estefania Acquaviva, associate publicist.

A special shoutout to Carolyn Kurek, the production editor. It is our third book together and my guess is—I drive her nuts. As a former journalist, I will forever have the Associated Press Stylebook etched into my brain, which is very different from the Chicago Manual of Style, used in the world of book publishing. In addition to style differences, she also found mistakes I should have caught in the first place—like having people out of alphabetical order. I am most grateful for her patience and for never giving up on me. (Note to Carolyn: One day I will remember to spell out all the numbers, I promise.)

It's not possible to write a book about George and Barbara Bush without the help of the team of archivists at the George H. W. Bush Library. Led by the boss, Acting Library Director Bob Holzweiss, the incredible team who helped on this book were: head archivist Chis Pembleton; archivists Doug Campbell, Zachary Roberts, John Blair, and Buffie Hollis; and as always, audiovisual archivist Mary Finch. They were always ready to dig deep to confirm that what I had written—or someone else had written—was actually true or to find a speech or letter for me. Simply put, they are miracle workers.

To put together chapter 6, I leaned on the advice of three of President Bush's speechwriters—Ed McNally, Mary Kate Cary, and Jim McGrath—to guide me in what speeches were among his best and should be included in this book. I probably would still be researching chapter 6 if it were not for their wonderful advice.

Mary Kate gets a second shout-out, for sending me the transcript of her excellent documentary, *41ON41*. Rights to the documentary are owned by the George & Barbara Bush Foundation, so I also appreciate the foundation's president and CEO, Max Angerholzer, allowing me to use the material.

I am grateful to my little brother, the Reverend Ed Becker, who volunteered to proofread the galley when all my other proofreaders stopped taking my calls. He caught things no one else did!

Speaking of which, there are no words to properly thank my blackbelt volunteer proofreaders. They read every single word at least twice and prevented me from all sorts of things like putting the wrong people in the wrong place at the wrong time. (For the record, that only happened once. I swear.) Drinks will be on me for the rest of their lives. They are Governor Jeb Bush; my sisters, Millie Aulbur and Jo Ann Heppermann; former White House staffers Tom Collamore, Kristin Clark Taylor, and Chase Untermeyer; post–White House staffers Melinda Lamoreaux, Nancy Lisenby, and Laura Pears; and my great friend and fellow author Dava Guerin. They are my heroes.

As is, of course, George Herbert Walker Bush. There would be no book if he had not been the person he was. We need his voice more than ever, a kinder and gentler reminder that yes, character really does matter. Let's get out there and make him proud.

# ABOUT THE AUTHOR

**Jean Becker** was President George H. W. Bush's chief of staff for nearly twenty-five years. She's the editor of *Pearls of Wisdom* by Barbara Bush and the *New York Times* best-selling author of *The Man I Knew*.